# RESEARCH
# METHODS for
# COMMUNITY
# CHANGE

# RESEARCH METHODS for COMMUNITY CHANGE

## A Project-Based Approach

# Randy Stoecker

*University of Toledo*

**SAGE Publications**
Thousand Oaks ▪ London ▪ New Delhi

*For information:*

Sage Publications, Inc.
2455 Teller Road
Thousand Oaks, California 91320
E-mail: order@sagepub.com

Sage Publications Ltd.
1 Oliver's Yard
55 City Road
London EC1Y 1SP
United Kingdom

Sage Publications India Pvt. Ltd.
B-42, Panchsheel Enclave
Post Box 4109
New Delhi 110 017  India

Printed in the United States of America

*Library of Congress Cataloging-in-Publication Data*

Stoecker, Randy, 1959-
Research methods for community change: A project-based approach / Randy Stoecker.
    p. cm.
Includes bibliographical references and index.
ISBN 0-7619-2888-X (cloth)—ISBN 0-7619-2889-8 (pbk.)
    1. Community development—Research. I.  Title.
HN49.C6S76 2005
307.1'4'072—dc22

                                    2004022906

This book is printed on acid-free paper.

05   06   07   08   10   9   8   7   6   5   4   3   2   1

| | |
|---|---|
| *Acquisitions Editor:* | Lisa Cuevas Shaw |
| *Editorial Assistant:* | Margo Beth Crouppen |
| *Production Editor:* | Melanie Birdsall |
| *Copy Editor:* | Bill Bowers, Interactive Composition Corporation |
| *Typesetter:* | C&M Digitals (P) Ltd. |
| *Proofreader:* | Mary Meagher |
| *Indexer:* | Teri Greenberg |
| *Cover Designer:* | Michelle Kenny |

# Contents

# Acknowledgments

L ittle did I know nearly 20 years ago that my career would become focused on finding ways for community organizations to do and use research. I thought I was training to be a regular professor at a regular university, learning the techniques of traditional sociological research, classroom lecturing, and institutional committee work. To the extent that I am able to survive in a traditional university environment, I must credit my university-based mentors in giving me the tough skin and intellectual self-defense skills needed for the task. But the most important mentors who have guided me down the path that led to this book were not from the academy but from various communities. Many of them, such as Tim Mungavan and Dave Beckwith, you will meet in the pages of this book. They didn't just *ask* me to contribute to the important work of community organizing and development they were doing, they *expected* me to contribute. It was Tim and Dave who first got me thinking seriously about what a new model of research, which served the goals and practices of community organizations, might look like.

But there were also those in the academy who helped me figure out how to be an academic outside of the ivory towers of the university. When I was just a young assistant professor, Barry Checkoway, the former director of the Edward Ginsberg Center for Community Service and Learning at the University of Michigan, graciously invited me to participate in a faculty seminar on participatory action research, where I could learn from those who had gone before me. I am forever grateful to him and his colleagues for allowing me to hang out with them and learn that there were in fact models for academics working with communities. Not long after I began participating in that seminar, I was asked to share a room at a sociology conference with John Gaventa, who at that time directed the Highlander Research and Education Center, which you will also read about in these pages. I felt like a Little Leaguer invited into the dugout with a World Series pitcher. John was the role model for

ix

many of us—someone who had risked his career by using his skills to further community-based social change and had been able to work both inside and outside of the academy. And then there was Phil Nyden, the director of the Project Research Action Group, who gave me my first opportunity to look at university-community collaboration from the outside when he invited me to facilitate PRAG's evaluation process.

But the most recent impetus for this book has come from the privilege I had working on a project led by Bobby Hackett, the Vice-President of the Corella and Bertram F. Bonner Foundation. The Bonner Foundation, at the time, had embarked on a project supporting higher education institutions to develop community-based research programs. And he found me money to follow the progress of those institutions over the five years the program continued. It gave me the opportunity to take a step back from my immersion in my own work to see how others did it. It was through this program that I met so many important role models—Marie Cirillo, Frankie Patton Rutherford, Steve Fisher, Tal Stanley, George Loveland, Susan Ambler, Larry Osborne, Tom Plaut, Kerry Strand, Sam Marullo, Nick Cutforth, Pat Donohue, Barbara Ferman, Dan Dougherty. There are many others whom I encountered less frequently through the project but whose work has remained an important influence.

One thing I noticed as I spent more and more time among academics working with communities, and among community-based activists, is what wonderful people they are. Absent is the petty political bickering that occurs far too frequently in higher education and also far too frequently among progressive political activists not rooted in communities. These are the most genuine, caring people I have ever encountered, and I continue to aspire to the standards of human dignity that they set.

All of these people and the many other communities I have worked with are the reason for this book. I have written a great deal with many of them about the process of how academics and communities collaborate—the challenges and benefits of combining talents. But I increasingly noticed that what was lacking was writing on the actual research being done in those community settings. So much of the writing is about the partnership rather than the process. And much of it is also written for the academic side of the aisle. There was no work between two covers that talked about how to integrate research into a wide range of community change projects. So I set out to fill that gap.

As I put the idea together, and started talking with publishers, I was helped along by Stan Wakefield. His is an interesting position—helping authors find publishers and helping publishers find authors. He helped me find C. Deborah Laughton, the Senior Editor at Sage. I have learned from my past successes and failures at writing books how important the editor is to the process. And for me personally, the most important thing is not how much they know but how excited they get about the ideas. C. Deborah got excited, and it kept me excited. As she left Sage halfway through this project to pursue other endeavors, Lisa Cuevas Shaw took her place and thankfully maintained that excitement. Her exuberance about the project maintained me through the awful process of dotting Is, crossing Ts, formatting references, and all the other detail stuff that is so difficult for me. She also found me a solid set of reviewers— Christina von Mayrhauser, Elisia Cohen, and Robert Silverman— who understood what I was trying to do and were engaged in helping me to do it. Sage's Margo Beth Crouppen and Melanie Birdsall should not go without mention for motivating me through the final copy preparation and guiding me through the bureaucratic maze of permission gathering toward a clean and legal final copy. And Bill Bowers was not only eagle-eyed but was perhaps the most gentle copyeditor I have ever encountered. Thanks also to Kelly Spivey, who brought her real-life experiences in the nonprofit world to a careful critique of an early version of this book and the wonderful graphic in Chapter 8.

Of course, projects like this don't happen in a vacuum—they must be juggled and keyholed in among life's many tasks, not the least of which is family. At various times during this project both Tammy Raduege, my life partner and wife, and Haley, my daughter, have had to endure me sequestering myself away while I ignored everything but the writing. My thanks to them are for much more than their simply putting up with me through this. During those dark early days of writer's block, Tammy would lean over my shoulder and ever so gently ask me how it was going— knowing full well how badly it was going but never offering advice on what to do or reminding me of the time I was wasting that could have been better spent on things like laundry and dishes. Her wisdom and gentle encouragement were the only things that got me through those hours of staring at a blank computer screen. Haley, who was writing her own research papers during the time I was working on this book, was an important source of commiseration as we traded stories on what a pain in the butt this work can be. And silly as it might seem to some of you, I must also recognize Lady the Wonder Dog, our 50-pound standard poodle, in these pages. Lady has been my constant writing companion. As I would fight writer's block by giving up on the desktop computer and shifting to a laptop in another room, she would get up and follow me. It didn't matter—upstairs, on the porch, in the office—she was there with me. There is barely a word in this book that she has not been party to.

The more I work with these things called communities, the more I also realize I only recognize them because of the place where I grew up. Mukwonago, Wisconsin didn't get its first stoplight until I left. You could ride your bicycle from one end of the town to the other in ten minutes. Of course, small doesn't make the community, the people do. It is ultimately because of the example my parents, Rex and Joan Stoecker, and their neighbors set that I know a community when I encounter it. All those neighborhood block parties, birthday parties, cookouts, late-night card parties, and bartered labor as neighbors collaborated to repair broken pipes, install basketball hoops, and all manner of other do-it-yourself activities set the example.

Finally, this book is only possible because of the many community organizers and leaders I have had the privilege of working with these many years. They have trusted me in ways I could not have imagined and hit me upside the head when I screwed up. People like Terry Glazer, Rose Newton, Larry Stillman, Ramon Perez, WilliAnn Moore, Madeline Talbott, Tim and Dave mentioned above, and many others have taught me more about how to do research in community settings than I could have ever imagined. A number of the research approaches and techniques you will find in the coming pages were developed with them in their communities. So as you read the pages that follow, please remember that this book is as much about what I have learned from them as it is for them and the many other communities out there faced with the research tasks necessary to win political battles, secure funds, create local development, and build local pride.

# *One*

# "But I Don't Do Research"

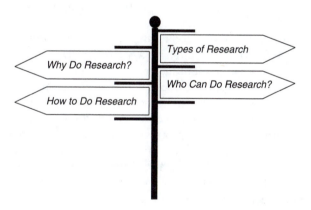

## "BUT I DON'T DO RESEARCH"

A few years ago I attended a workshop at the Highlander Research and Education Center in the Tennessee mountains. Highlander, if you are unfamiliar with it, is a famous place in American history. It was a primary influence in the development of a racially integrated union movement. It was centrally important in the civil rights movement, having spread the song "We Shall Overcome" throughout the world and provided education and training that impacted such luminaries as Rosa Parks and Dr. Martin Luther King, Jr. Most important, it has been a place where grassroots people come together to do the education and research necessary to win battles for social justice and equality.[1] Grassroots community activists and leaders travel from far and wide to this inspiringly beautiful rural setting to learn how to study, research, and tackle the important social issues of the day so they can return to their communities and make a difference.

To get to Highlander, if you fly into Knoxville as I did, you travel through the city and then out of town into the countryside. Eventually you turn onto a dusty gravel road that connects the main buildings of the Center, including the central meeting room, remodeled from an old round barn and furnished with a large circle of rocking chairs in the upstairs. It was in this meeting room, in our rocking chairs, where our group of academic researchers and community people met. For two days we talked, drew pictures representing our work, and developed models of how to conduct research that empowered grassroots communities. About halfway through the weekend, it became clear that the academics in the room were very comfortable using the word "research" to describe what we did. But the community members and community workers regularly prefaced their statements with "Well, it's not research, but . . ." or "It wasn't scientific, but . . ." After each "but" would come amazing tales of careful, sophisticated, sometimes unorthodox research practices that won victories in legislatures and courts.[2]

This sentiment is often echoed by my students, many of whom are community workers of various stripes—social workers, nonprofit managers, activists, community organizers, and community development professionals. When I ask them about their career aspirations, most of them plan to work "on the ground" in the nonprofit or government sectors, and some of them are there already. But very few can imagine doing any research in those professions. I have heard the phrase "But I don't do research" enough that it sounds like a mantra. Yet, when I probe, I find that many of them have to collect data on client outcomes, do case histories, conduct investigations, and engage in a wide variety of other things that are fundamentally research activities. Others have to write grant applications that require them to gather needs-assessment data, or conduct an evaluation. Our textbooks and syllabi, however, don't speak to these forms of research and thus don't prepare people entering the nonprofit and community organization world to do this kind of research.

It is a shame that only academics are seen as doing research, and that it has consequently developed an undeserved reputation of being at best useless and at worst a distraction from doing real work that matters for real people. Saul Alinsky, one of the 20th century's most famous community organizers, was fond of saying that "another word for academic is irrelevant."[3] And it is an even greater travesty that the research that real community workers and community members do on the ground does not get recognized as producing legitimate knowledge.

What is the research done on the ground in communities? One of the most important stories comes from the small community of Yellow Creek, Kentucky, where residents became concerned about the health of their livestock and even themselves. They began with a basic and admittedly unsophisticated public health survey of their community that found higher-than-expected levels of cancers and other afflictions. They began to suspect the upstream tannery of poisoning their drinking water but lacked the credibility to make the case stick. Needing assistance, they were able to enlist the services of faculty and students from Vanderbilt University, who helped them conduct a more detailed study. Together they established a link between the illnesses and the tannery, and eventually won their case in the courts.[4]

Neighborhood planning is another area where research occurs and often goes unrecognized. In the 1980s the Cedar-Riverside neighborhood of Minneapolis had just won an important battle preventing their community from becoming a victim of urban renewal which, in this case as in so many others, was literally urban removal. As a result of their victory, they attained the unenviable position of having to rebuild their dilapidated single-family housing, which had been left to atrophy by the original urban renewal plan. To rebuild the housing they had to do a complete housing study, determining which structures could be rehabbed with limited funds, which were too far gone to save, and where new homes could be built. To deal with the cold Minnesota winters, they did a sophisticated study of superinsulation, passive solar construction, and other cold-weather construction designs from around the world. Today, the neighborhood remains an important role model for neighborhood-based redevelopment and winter weather resistance.[5]

The arts provide another important source of unrecognized research practices. In the early 1990s in western Massachusetts, Mark Lynd helped organize a popular theater group composed of adults with developmental disabilities. Entitled *Special* and built on the experiences of the cast, the play was also built on research. The cast members interviewed experts in the field of developmental disabilities, and as the research progressed they began to explore more and more deeply the politics of the treatment, and mistreatment, they were receiving at the hands of professionals. The resulting performance then exposed and explored those treatment politics, changing forever the understandings of the cast members and, for many members of the audience, removing the stigma previously associated with developmentally disabled adults.[6]

Perhaps one of the most important examples of research that was only much later recognized as such comes from the very earliest stages of the modern women's movement. Suburban women, comparing experiences about their feelings of isolation, their interactions with Valium-obsessed physicians, and their lack of self-fulfillment, were some of the very first practitioners of the research and education practice of consciousness-raising that would coin the term "sexism" and transform American culture.[7]

## "SO WHAT IS RESEARCH?"

That gravel road leading up to the Highlander Center is symbolic of so many of these examples, for none of them was clean and easy research. They often challenged established political and cultural bases of power and developed new ways of doing research not readily accepted by established social scientists. And the process of doing and using the research in making social change did not go off without problems and challenges. In many ways, the entire process traversed a path of loose gravel. And it is on that loose gravel that much of this book will concentrate.

From the outside, things may look more like pavement than gravel. All of these projects began with the needs of real people trying to understand what was happening to them and what they could do about it. In some cases the people themselves did the research. In other cases they enlisted skilled outsiders to assist them. But in every case the research served a goal—eliminating a public health hazard, rebuilding a neighborhood, educating to combat discrimination, and achieving emotional health. On the face of it, these research processes are not that different from traditional academic research. They all began with a research question: Why are our livestock getting sick? How can we save our housing? How do we reduce discrimination? Why do we feel emotionally unhealthy? Now, those questions had to be refined to actually make them researchable, and this is where the research began to differ from traditional academic research. In contrast to what academics call *basic research*, this form of research is often referred to as *applied research*. And it is in traversing the gully between basic and applied research that you first begin to notice that you are driving on gravel.

What are the differences between basic and applied research? Applied research has historically been seen as research whose question comes from a practical problem that someone wants to solve. It typically involves working with some corporation, government, or other organization. Basic research has historically been seen as research with no immediate application, though of course having potential applications. In basic research the researchers are mostly in control of the research questions.[8] Think of research testing AIDS drugs as applied research and research to map the human genetic structure as basic research. AIDS drug research is directly tied to helping people with the disease or in danger of contracting it. Human genome research may have all kinds of benefits down the road, even potentially for treating AIDS, but the research is not driven by a specific practical concern.

**Basic Research**

- Driven by researcher interests
- Unrelated to immediate practical issues

**Applied Research**

- Driven by organizational interests
- Closely related to immediate practical issues

The belief among traditional academic researchers is that basic research is more *objective*, or less subject to being contaminated by the biases of the researcher. It is too easy, they fear, for a researcher trying to solve a problem to *bias* the results—set up the research to get the data they want to prove their point rather than find out what is really happening. Thus, they believe, basic research in which the researcher is *objective*—not hoping for any particular outcome—is actually more useful in the end, even if it doesn't generate immediate benefits. In addition, because basic research isn't tied to a particular set of circumstances, it is seen as more *generalizable*—applicable to a wide range of situations. Hence the common perception that people doing real research in real settings on immediate and pressing human problems are not really doing research—a belief that many community-based practitioners have bought into.

Over the past few decades, however, we have discovered both of these beliefs to be problematic. First, a number of people have shown that the standard of *objectivity* is a confused and self-contradictory concept. It is confused because objectivity was never meant to be more than a method for achieving accuracy. The approach of objectivity was to achieve as much emotional distance as possible between the researcher and the person being researched. This is the source of the famous "double blind study" so popular in drug research, where neither the patient nor the physician knows whether a patient is receiving the treatment or the placebo. By not knowing the research subject, proponents of objectivity believed, you could get more accurate information.[9]

But scientists gradually forgot that objectivity was but a means to accuracy and increasingly saw it as an end in itself. By distancing yourself from the research question, and consequently from the people you were researching—i.e., practicing objectivity—objectivity could be assured. What practitioners, particularly feminist researchers, showed was that the creation of emotional distance in fact often made the research less accurate. Because the researcher refused to build trust with the research subject, the research subject withheld information from the researcher, essentially spoiling the results. These feminists and other critics were able to show objectivity's self-contradictory nature and break forever the assumed link between objectivity and accuracy.[10]

Second, a number of research methodologists have called into question the assumed *generalizability* of basic research. Generalizability is closely related to objectivity. The idea here is that good research will be applicable to a wide variety of similar situations. If, for example, you want to know whether police foot patrols reduce property crime, you should design your research so the findings can apply in a variety of places. That is why so many traditional researchers rely on statistical studies involving large data sets. They believe that, if the data is gathered randomly from a wide variety of situations, the chances are greater that the findings will also apply to a wide variety of situations.[11]

As statistical studies took precedence over research involving fewer cases but more detail, the belief in the generalizability of statistical studies grew. But an important work by Andrew Sayer[12] showed the illogic of that assumption. He stood the usual distinction between *qualitative research* and *quantitative research* on its head. Qualitative research has typically involved interviews or document research or observation that a researcher then interprets rather than counts. There are usually only one or a few cases involved. Communities, organizations, families, and other social groups are favorite objects of those defined as qualitative researchers. Quantitative research typically involves counting characteristics of something and then conducting a statistical analysis to see if there are any patterns. Surveys, such as one to test whether level of education and amount of income are related, are a favorite tool of quantitative researchers. It is even possible to take qualitative data, such as interview transcripts, and turn them into quantitative data by counting the occurrences of specific phrases and thus turning a few interviews into a large data set. This form of research is also often called *positivistic,* since it tries to eliminate interpretation in favor of strict, predefined hypotheses and measurements.

Traditional positivistic researchers had assumed that qualitative research was only good for generating tentative cause-and-effect hypotheses that could then be tested by more sophisticated statistical research on large samples. Sayer, however, showed that *intensive research*—focusing intensively on one or a few cases—was better for studying cause and effect than *extensive research*—studying superficially a large number of cases. He argued that intensive research allows the researcher to actually follow a cause-and-effect trail in a specific situation, similar to how a criminal investigator follows a crime trail or how a physician diagnoses an illness. Extensive research, on the other hand, is particularly good for mapping the characteristics of a population. Consequently, large-sample extensive studies are useful for suggesting cause-and-effect relationships that can then be tested in real-world settings, much the same way that large-sample epidemiological studies are used by physicians in diagnosing an individual's illness. The research that community workers do is more in line with this division of labor between intensive research and extensive research than the division between qualitative and quantitative research maintained by traditional academics. Academic researchers have often seen qualitative research on a few cases as good only for suggesting variables that can be better studied by large-scale quantitative survey research. But community workers trying to find out what is causing a real community problem are more likely to use the general results obtained by such large surveys to suggest things to look for in tracing the causal path of crime, or housing deterioration, or teen pregnancy, or other problems in their own community using an intensive research model. Community

**Intensive Research**

- Focuses on one or a few cases
- Strives for detail and depth of analysis
- Good for causal analysis

**Extensive Research**

- Focuses on large number of cases
- Limits analysis to a few characteristics
- Good for mapping population properties

workers also conduct their own extensive model large-scale surveys when they are trying to understand neighborhood residents' perceptions or opinions, or trying to ascertain the extent of housing deterioration in a community.

The research model used in this book will use these distinctions between basic and applied research, and intensive and extensive research, as a basic foundation. But it will also go beyond them. For most research in community settings is not simply applied, but *project-based*. A project-based research model is one in which the research becomes an integral part of some social change project. The change focus can be an individual, an organization, a community, a region, or even a society. The important point is that the project is trying to create some difference in real people's lives, and the research exists in the service of that effort.

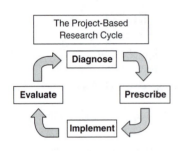

What is project-based research? If you consider how a typical social change project works, it begins with *diagnosing* some problem or issue. The change agents then develop a plan, or *prescription*, for intervening in the problem or issue. The next step is putting the plan into action, or *implementing* it. Then, those involved need to *evaluate* it to determine whether the desired change is occurring.[13] That could lead to a new round of diagnosing-prescribing-implementing-evaluating and so on, until we have achieved a perfect world. So our work is cut out for us.

As the subsequent chapters will show, it is possible that there will be research at every stage of this process. In the beginning stage of diagnosing, the research might be a needs assessment. At the prescribing stage, there might be a survey of the best practices available. At the implementation phase there might be a community history study. At the evaluation phase there will likely be an evaluation which, surprisingly, could actually begin at the diagnosing stage, as we will see in Chapter 7.

Because so much of this community practitioner research is project-based, it is often invisible, further contributing to its lack of respect in the research world. It doesn't get published. It doesn't get in the newspapers unless it is specifically designed to. It doesn't get presented at conferences. One of my goals for this book is to make visible the forms of project-based research being conducted in so many community settings today and to develop those forms of research to be more effective, better support their associated projects, and ultimately better serve the people they are intended to impact.

## "OKAY, SO I DO RESEARCH ALREADY.
## WHY DO I NEED TO LEARN ABOUT IT?"

While it is true that many community practitioners are doing amaz-ingly high-quality research, it is also true that many others are not. And the research has real consequences. The Toledo Community Foundation, which funds community change efforts, helped start up a new community organizing program in Toledo, Ohio a few years ago. They began by conducting an assessment of a select group of nonprofits they hoped could carry out the program. But they did not know what questions to ask in determining which nonprofits would best succeed in the program. Of the three organizations chosen for the program, one dropped out only a few months into the program, and another dropped out at the end of the training period. But the foundation also supported careful evaluation research along the way that allowed them to understand why the two organizations did not continue, and they developed diagnostic questions that could be used for better predicting success in future programs. Now they have much better diagnostic tools for future programs.

In today's fiscally austere environment, there are few resources to waste. Good research on the front end of a program can actually reduce waste further into the program. Research that goes into diag-nosing, planning, and assessing can make project dollars go further and have more impact. I was the person chosen by the Toledo Community Foundation to conduct the evaluation research for their new community organizing program. As few as six months into the program we were able to identify areas of success and areas of chal-lenge and make program adjustments that helped the project accom-plish more than it probably would have.[14]

Because the funding environment is so competitive, it is not only important for an organization to get the most out of the resources it has but also to put its best foot forward in getting new resources. Community agencies, and increasingly even government agencies, only survive if they can find outside sources of funding. Those com-munity workers who have pulled an all-nighter writing a grant pro-posal, wishing they had access to the poverty levels of their county, or the median income, or the crime rate, or any of a myriad of statis-tics that would strengthen the proposal, understand the importance of good research. Because maybe they didn't get that grant. And maybe if they had been able to do the research, they would have.

So research is more necessary than it has ever been before. Just as the rise of word processing made "white-out" an unacceptable garnish on final drafts, the rise of Internet-based data has made "lots of poverty" an unacceptably superficial measurement in a grant proposal. Today there is online Geographic Information Systems, or GIS, data that can map and display the characteristics of your neighborhood, city, county, or beyond. There is an amazing collection of online databases covering everything from census data to toxic sites.[15] And in contrast to a decade ago, when you had to get in your car and go from one government office to another, and then the library, and still not get everything you needed, today you can start up your Web browser and find nearly everything at your fingertips.

But, of course, it's not nearly as simple as it sounds. Being able to just find the sources is challenging enough (though Appendix D of this book will hopefully help). But knowing how to use the existing data and judge its accuracy, its relevance, and the effects of age on its applicability are also important. If you use the county-level poverty statistics for your grant proposal, and the target neighborhood for your grant is the poorest in the county, then county-level poverty statistics may not make your case. You might have to go to smaller census tract boundaries instead. Being able to design your supporting research for that grant proposal is as important as the information you ultimately get.

But this is perhaps not exactly the kind of "research" you were thinking about. For it sounds so much like college library research papers that seem to maintain an aura of boredom through the generations. It is research that doesn't really have a hypothesis, doesn't really have a data test, and doesn't really have findings. But wait. Rather than think of it as one of those what-am-I-gonna-write-about undergraduate research papers, think about it as a project proposal that uses research. The subsequent chapters and Appendix C will address this in much more depth. What is important here is that, when you are writing a project proposal, you are asserting that certain conditions exist in your community and that some intervention will change those conditions. Writing the proposal means doing the research necessary to convince the funder that your "experimental design" is well supported.

All this has been about the importance of doing research before the project even begins. What about research as part of the project itself? So much of the time, just doing the project takes up all of the staff time available in a small community organization. But funders are increasingly insisting that the project includes research, usually in the form of evaluation research, and are providing extra funding to support it. In the 2002 funding round for the federal government's Weed and Seed program, which is designed to combine local law enforcement with community development goals, groups could apply for extra funds to evaluate their work. As we will see in Chapter 7, a number of funders are even supporting what is variously called "empowerment" or "participatory" evaluation that is specifically designed to help program participants improve their practice rather than to just grade their mistakes.

There are a wide variety of other research activities that occur in the midst of a program and on whose accuracy the program depends. When the Austin Free-Net Neighborhood Network project began, one of their important activities was to develop a Web site with photos and descriptions of residents' favorite neighborhood spots to increase neighborhood pride and fight the corporate media's stereotyped portrayals of this inner-city African-American community. To do so, they needed to develop a research design that would put them in contact with neighborhood residents who could contribute their stories, make sure those stories got written down, and then organize them into a useful and proud Web site.[16]

Another important form of research that requires absolute accuracy occurs in the midst of an advocacy campaign. As we will learn in Chapter 5, when a community group goes into battle against a government or corporation, their facts need to be airtight. The ability of governments and corporations to hire expensive research consultants far outstrips the meager funds of community groups. But what groups lack in funding they can make up for in accuracy. As the Yellow Creek story early in this chapter notes, it took a partnership with an area university to ultimately win their battle, but it was a partnership they were able to achieve.

To win in the competition for grant funding, to win in the advocacy arena, and to win in designing and implementing programs that actually work, good research is central. We live in an era where torrents of information have become part of our daily lives. Good research is no longer a luxury but a necessity. It is always important to keep in mind that the project neither begins nor ends with research and that research is not even the largest part of the project. Research is often a necessary condition to success, however, and those working on the ground need to find ways to make it happen.

## "I'M ALREADY RUNNING FULL-OUT MANAGING OUR PROGRAMS. HOW CAN I DO MORE RESEARCH TOO?"

Those who work in the community sector have learned, like the rest of us, that they need to do more with less. And while we all know there is a breaking point where there is so much less that our only choice is to do less, funders and policymakers seem to pay little heed to the sounds of economic strangulation heard regularly in the non-profit world. Good research is a way to help do more with less because it helps assure better outcomes. It is also a way to help get more because it provides better support for funding proposals. But it has real up-front costs. Someone has to actually do the research. I have worked with a variety of nonprofit and community-based projects over the past couple of decades and, when push comes to shove, doing the work has to take precedence over doing the research. So what's a stressed-out community worker to do?

One strategy is to find ways to work research into the organization's staff time and even the volunteers' activities. Staff often are not trained in doing research, so doing it takes even more time. Spending time educating staff in doing research can ultimately save time. So make sure every staff member has a copy of this book! Volunteers, particularly in impoverished communities, can also gain employable skills through research training and experience. And when research becomes part of the program, as we will discuss in Chapter 5, there is no longer a trade-off between doing the work and doing the research. A community-needs assessment, conducted door to door by community volunteers, builds community relationships at the same time that it builds programming.

Creating in-house or in-community research expertise, however, is also time- and resource-consuming. And it can be another barrier to effective research, especially if you have to go out and find training. But the bright spot on the horizon of community research these days is the increasing interest being shown by college and university faculty and students. Over the past decade, higher education faculty and students have ventured further and further into their local communities. They did it first as *community service,* using students as a volunteer labor force to staff soup kitchens, poverty painting programs, literacy programs, and other similar projects. Then, the practice expanded into *service learning,* which provided entire classes of students doing community service linked to their course topics. Most recently, these student-based activities have been linked up with a much older practice of *participatory research,* which has historically involved expert researchers working collaboratively with community groups around a community

---

**Who Can Do Research?**

- Organization staff
- Community volunteers
- Students
- Faculty

cause.[17] As we will see in the next chapter, the combination of academic expertise, emphasizing abstract broad-based knowledge, with community expertise, emphasizing in-depth experiential knowledge,[18] is proving a powerful formula for success.

This new practice of community-academic collaboration can go a long way toward serving not just the immediate research needs of community organizations, as we will see in Chapter 2, but also serving community research training needs. The Trenton Center in Trenton, New Jersey is one of eight higher education–community networks that have been created around the country in the past decade. Each of these networks—located in Trenton, Philadelphia, Washington, D.C., Richmond, Virginia, Denver, Chicago, Minneapolis–St. Paul, and Appalachia—involves a collaboration between nonprofits and higher education institutions and serves an entire region.[19] The Trenton Center is unique in providing technical assistance, including research training, for nonprofit organizations. But it is not alone in offering research services specifically for nonprofit and community groups. Across the country (and listed at the end of Chapter 2) are a growing number of colleges and universities that provide this type of powerful collaboration.

## "I'M STILL NOT CONVINCED. BUT JUST IN CASE, WHERE DO I START?"

I understand how difficult it is to believe that research will be helpful for people already devoting all their waking hours to just getting the project work done. Even when I am working with academics engaged in project work, I have a difficult time getting them to free up time in their schedules to do the research that will help their projects succeed.

But if you've stuck with me this far, then I'm hoping it's because maybe you think all this research stuff isn't just snake oil. So your next question might be, "Okay, how do I do it with the least amount of disruption?"

Perhaps the best place to start is by thinking like a researcher. If you're not used to thinking that way, it's actually not all that difficult. There are five basic steps to any research process: choosing a question, designing the research methods, collecting data, analyzing data, and reporting the results.

> **Steps in Project-Based Research**
>
> - Choosing the question
> - Designing the research methods
> - Collecting the data
> - Analyzing the data
> - Reporting the results

## Choosing the Question

This can actually be the most difficult part of the entire process. Not just any question will do. It has to be focused enough to actually generate good data. Asking a question that is too general, such as "how do people feel about our community" carries the danger of eliciting answers that are all over the place. Some people may feel something about their neighbor next door, others may feel something about the corner liquor store, and yet others may feel something about the parish priest. Some questions may seem specific but actually are not. For example, to ask "how much crime is there in our neighborhood" requires asking what kinds of crime, during what times of the year or even what times of the day, with who as victims, and a variety of other potential qualifiers.

Another problem with choosing a question is to be careful of not having the answer already implied, or asking a "second-step" question. Asking "what is the best education program for reducing teen pregnancy" already assumes that an education program will reduce teen pregnancy. It may be helpful, instead, to ask how different programs to reduce teen pregnancy work in different contexts and then compare the results to the context of your community. It is possible that, in a particular community, a recreation program will work better than an education program. Likewise, asking "what are the best ways to reduce crime in our community" may be a second-step question that depends first on answering the question "what kinds of crime do we have in our community."

A useful strategy for developing a research question in a community setting, odd as it may seem, is to work backward. Remember, this is *project-based research*. As we will emphasize even more in Chapter 3, the outcomes of the project, not the results of the research, are most important. The research is important, but only in the context of the project. So if you are at the very beginning stages of the project, start thinking about what you want at end of the project, hopefully in a meeting of as many people as possible who will be affected by the project. Maybe the initial answer is "a better community." Working backward, you can specify what characteristics a better community would have. If the answer is more stores, you may work backward to research what kind of community retail exists and then what kind of retail people want.

## Designing the Research Methods

This is the step where that undergraduate research methods course can really help. For designing the actual research methods is both technical and artistic. The technical part comes in understanding what type of research methods fit what type of research questions. Some questions will be highly technical. For example, if you are concerned about the relationship between air quality and patterns of illness in your community, you may be looking at an advanced statistical study requiring expensive equipment and sophisticated data collection techniques. The research techniques and equipment can vary enormously from research involving childhood developmental testing, to environmental testing, community data collection, Geographic Information Systems mapping, structural engineering assessments, and almost anything else imaginable. The details of these techniques are beyond the scope of this book and are the points at which you may need to seek outside expertise or training. What we will consider here are ways for choosing research methods.

It is in choosing and adapting the research methods that the art comes in. Art is about emotion and meaning and intuition and those other intangible things. It is about understanding that, when your sinuses ache, it may be a sign of a change in the weather. It is about channeling your love, or anger, through a creative process and representing it in some unique form that communicates with others. It is easy to write a survey. It is extremely difficult to write a survey that is just the right length, with just the right tone in the questions, with just enough captivating language to pique the respondents' interest, and with just enough relational qualities to convince them that their response really matters. That is art, because it is about deeply connecting with the community and creatively connecting the technique of writing the survey with *knowing* the community. In contrast to traditional academic research, in project-based research the research directly matters, and that connection is crucial. And while that may seem rather New Age and abstract, for those people who are truly connected with the community the artistic side is often much less challenging than the technical side, as we will see.

Keeping this art/technique integration in mind, one of the first steps in designing the research methods is to decide whether you will be doing intensive research or extensive research. If you remember back to earlier in this chapter, intensive research involves studying one or a few cases intensively to trace causal patterns. Extensive research involves determining the characteristics of a population. In general, "why" questions imply intensive research methods, and "how many" questions imply extensive research methods. Asking "how many people are getting cancer in our community" requires doing a health survey of the community and may be a necessary first step to determine whether there is a cancer cluster. The "why" question, such as "why are people getting lung cancer in our community" may only be possible after first determining the extent and types of afflictions. Answering this "why" question may involve conducting intensive water and air testing or detailed case histories of individuals.

Once you've decided whether you are trying to determine "how many" or "why," it is time to look at specific research methods. Here is where art and technical knowledge combine. If the goal is to find out what the important issues are in the community, as a first step toward determining what kinds of programs people want, then an extensive research method is probably appropriate. The easy, quick method to employ is a survey, perhaps a one-pager that could be mailed out to residents with a stamped return envelope. Some technical expertise on survey design will be very helpful. But what if the community has a number of members who lack the level of written literacy needed to complete the survey? It may be better to do a phone survey, unless the poverty level of the community limits phone availability. This is another case where working backward may be helpful. If the goal is to get people involved in a voluntary effort, and the research is to determine what kind of things people may want to get involved in, then the best way of conducting the survey may be to go door to door to both get information and build relationships that can be mobilized in the volunteer effort. And that brings us to collecting the data.

## Collecting the Data

Once the research methods are in place, it's time to go out and get the data. And I must admit, most of what I have learned about collecting has not come from academic researchers but from community organizers. Doing a lot with very few resources is one of the hallmarks of a good community organizer. Before they go out to collect data, they ask "what data is already available, what data do we need to create ourselves, and how much work will it be to use the data." It may be that, in some cases, there is already a government agency responsible for compiling certain kinds of data. In many cities, groups who want to know which housing is owned by absentee landlords can get an electronic database of all the properties in the area, already compiled on CD-ROM. Other government agencies may be responsible for water and air quality testing. There may be public health data already collected on such things as food-related illnesses, sexually transmitted diseases, and others. There may also be university or college researchers who have compiled at least some of the data needed.

There are times, however, when those who have the data may be less than willing to share it. This is once again where the work of community organizers and advocates is instructive. For federal government data, the Freedom of Information Act, or FOIA (pronounced "foya"), is one way of getting information. Various other government levels provide laws that can force reluctant public agencies to cough up information they are not entitled to withhold.[20]

When the information is not available, however, the question becomes "who should go get it." There are four options available, and this is once again where art and technical expertise combine. The first option is to have an outside expert gather the data. That may be a necessary strategy in cases involving medical testing, or sometimes even environmental testing that requires strict sampling and measurement techniques. But those situations are relatively rare. In most cases non-experts with appropriate training can collect the needed data. Non-experts comprise the other three options. Organization staff are often an obvious choice because they may have some training in research methods through undergraduate degrees. But as we have seen above, staff are often already stretched to the limit in their jobs, and squeezing in data collection may do more harm than good. Those still receiving their undergraduate- or graduate-level training—students—are another option, particularly through some kind of formal service learning or community-based research program. They can do the work and receive credit for it, making it a lot easier to work into their schedules. But because they are students, having some kind of supervisory quality control process is important. The third option is using community members, and it has the potential benefits of building skills and relationships among individuals that we've noted above.

## Analyzing the Data

Data analysis can be a deceptive step in the process. On face level, it seems like it's just a matter of dumping all the data into a computer and spitting out findings. But interpreting data is also as much art as it is science. Statistical associations are the most befuddling. People often overinterpret what are really meager and tentative relationships. This is once again where Andrew Sayer's distinction between intensive and extensive research is useful. Too many researchers are using extensive research, which is best for determining the descriptive characteristics of a population, to do causal analysis. But the statistical causal relationships that those researchers find, except in rare cases, are often quite weak. When you read in the newspaper that researchers have found a "causal relationship" between stress and hair loss, for example, they are likely basing that finding on a statistical analysis that shows a small percentage difference in hair loss between highly stressed people and less stressed people. But that does not prove that stress causes hair loss. What is needed is intensive research to trace the causal sequence between stress and hair loss to see what else may be going on. Furthermore, because the data are usually collected at a single point in time, it is very difficult to tell for sure what is cause and what is effect. Is fear of crime a consequence of crime (people fear it because there is so much) or is crime a consequence of fear (because people are too afraid to report crimes they witness, the people committing the crimes are not caught)? If you collect a lot of data on crime and people's fear level all at the same time, you don't know which came first.

If the data are coming at you in statistical form, it is hopefully because you needed some descriptive data on your community. Be careful of trying to interpret the data as causal. Think of it as suggesting relationships that you can then use for digging more deeply. For example, if your data show both high joblessness and high crime, concluding that joblessness causes crime is overly simplistic. First, you don't know whether there is higher crime because jobless residents can afford less protection or because jobless residents need the extra income. And even if your statistics can show that jobless residents are more likely to be victimizers than victims, there is a long and torturous path from losing your job to committing a crime, and only a few people follow the entire route. And here is where intensive research is important. Bringing together a group of people who have lost their jobs and turned to crime to talk about their life courses can much more deeply inform the causal pattern. For it may be that job loss leads to family stress or self-esteem issues or substance abuse, and those things may variously lead to violent crime or property crime. The program you design to break the relationship between joblessness and crime may then provide quite specific interventions for the family, the self-esteem of the individual, and other things. This is a far cry from the jobs program that a simple statistical relationship would recommend.

And, similar to collecting the data, there are strategic choices to be made in analyzing the data as well. Certainly, it can be very efficient for an outside expert with access to students and computers and statistical analysis software to take a set of surveys and crunch the numbers out. But unless those outsiders know the community well, they may not be able to interpret the data. What if the data show a higher-than-average incidence of pediatric medical problems? Is it because of household hygiene deficiencies, lead paint, smog-choked air, poor prenatal care, or something else? Community members will be able to suggest, if not outright know, which of these things are most important for interpreting the data. It may, in fact, be useful for community members to be integrally involved at the data analysis stage so that they can add their interpretations to the analysis. This is another way, as we shall see, of building community relationships and skills.

## Reporting the Results

This is the most deceptive stage of the entire process, particularly if you are an academic researcher. For academic researchers have been trained to write formal reports of research findings for professional journals, which too often end up on people's bookshelves, becoming "shelf research." But project-based research is different. Project-based research may never be written down at all. It may be presented as community theater. It may be presented in photographic form. It may even be presented in a march on city hall. That doesn't mean it shouldn't be written down, only that there are many creative ways beyond words on paper to present the findings. Those of us in academia who do project-based research often need to retrain ourselves to write in an entirely different style, work with community coauthors, or use more interactive methods of presenting data.

Determining how to report the data once again involves working backward. The goals of the project will to a large extent determine the form of the research report. If the goal is policy change, written material is very important, but community education sessions and protests may also be an important part of the strategy. If the goal is community-building, then a community event with oral or visual reporting may be the most useful form of reporting.

Compiling and presenting the report is yet another area where doing research combines with building community relationships and skills. People who have had no community speaking experience, when they have been integrally involved with the research and are confident in their knowledge, can have their lives changed by getting up in front of a group. Community organizers know this and seek out every opportunity to have community members take leadership roles whenever possible. That can be a good rule for project-based research as well.

## "SO WHERE DO I AND MY COMMUNITY FIT IN?"

This book is intended as a resource for those who are already engaged in community work or see such work in their future. It is designed for those of you who are, or will become, professionally paid staff as well as volunteer neighborhood and other community leaders. And it is also designed for those researchers who will find themselves working with communities and their organizations.

We will spend more time in the coming chapters talking about communities and organizations, but it is helpful here to lay out some definitions. When I speak of *community,* I am using the term much more narrowly than is popular today. I even heard a national TV news anchor talk about the "athletic community" the other day, as if somehow everyone who exercised more than once a week belonged to a community. I hear other commentators talk about the "Black community" or the "disabled community." That is not accurate either. There are African-American and disabled communities, especially in particular places where members of those communities can interact face to face, trade favors, or attend meetings together. But to call a category of people a community just because they share a certain culturally defined characteristic makes the term meaningless. When I use the term *community* I am talking about a face-to-face group of people who share cultural characteristics, share resources, share space, and interact with each other on a regular basis.

I will also use the terms *group* and *organization*. An organization is at least semiformal, with some kind of specified leadership and a structure that is sustained over time. This can range from a formally established nonprofit organization with a board of directors to an ongoing neighborhood association with no legal standing. A group is generally informal and less sustained. It may be a collection of people who suddenly come together to deal with a crisis or to manage a single project or event, and then disband.

The lessons in this book apply to all of those levels of activity because, ultimately, all of them will be directed at the community in some way. Some groups or organizations will be more representative of a particular community than others. But all of them will be attempting to do projects in, on, or with one or more communities. And all of them will need research information to support the success of those projects.

The lessons in this book are also meant for you, whether you are a student, professor, community practitioner, or even a funder of community change efforts. At times it will seem like I am talking to only one of those possible "yous." I hope, however, that the rest of you listening in will still gain something from the conversation. What can each group take away from this book?

Community practitioners who have seen research as impractical, unproductive, or distracting can begin to see how research can help them and how students, faculty, and funders can help support their research needs. The project-based research model, emphasizing not research but social change projects, is written for the practitioner. All projects begin with a diagnosis, are derived from a prescription, eventually become implemented, and then are evaluated. This book will show how research is integral to all four of these steps and will show the wide variety of research practices that can be used at each step.

Students who have never imagined themselves moving into a career doing research can begin to see how research will be part of the career they imagine themselves moving into. In contrast to most of the research methods texts out there, this book emphasizes the integration of research and action, showing how research can improve the real work that real people in real communities do. Hopefully it will also give students ideas about research projects they can help with while they are still students and get valuable job training from at the same time.

Professors who have been providing valuable research methods training to their students, and have been frustrated at how little students seemed to care, will now have one means to help students better connect research and action. In addition, those professors just starting out in working with community change efforts, or wanting to make the leap, will hopefully find some useful material on the challenges facing community change efforts and the adaptations academics make to conduct research successfully in a community setting.

Finally, those who fund research, on the one hand, or community change efforts, on the other, will hopefully find some ways to consider funding more integration of the two activities. Too often, funders have lacked good models by which to judge proposals that bring research and action together. This book will provide a diversity of project-based research examples that they can use to consider the future proposals they receive. It may also help them consider ways of filling the current gaps in research resources needed by community organizations that have made so many grant proposals less than stellar.

Whatever your standpoint and experience, my main hope is that this book will help you to think more openly and creatively about the research process and how it can be put to use in a wide variety of community change efforts. For I am continuously haunted by the fear that "another word for academic is irrelevant," and I write this book partly to convince myself that I am not.

## CONCLUSION AND COMING ATTRACTIONS

With any luck I have left you with some ideas and lots of questions. This chapter has been but an overview of some of the possibilities and a way of thinking about project-based research. It has introduced the following ideas:

- Basic vs. applied research
- Intensive vs. extensive research
- The project-based research model: diagnosing, prescribing, implementing, evaluating
- Reasons to do project-based research: reduce waste, compete for funding, win on advocacy issues
- Ways to get research done: staff, volunteers, academics, students
- The steps in research: choosing the question, designing the methods, collecting the data, analyzing the data, reporting the results
- Definitions of community, organization, and group

The subsequent chapters will delve more deeply into the project-based research model and specific forms of project-based research. They will help you understand where you are in a project-based research cycle and the kinds of research that can further a particular cycle stage. In the next chapter we will talk about the importance of a participatory process, which will provide the foundation for everything else that follows. Chapter 3 will go into depth about understanding the project-based research model and how to use it in your own work. Chapters 4–7 each take one step in the project-based research model, discussing how research can help with diagnosing, prescribing, implementing, and evaluating. The final chapter tries to bring it all together, illustrating how to integrate research into the daily work of a community organization. Those of you interested in more information on the strategic planning process that I bring up in some of the chapters, research ethics in community settings, guides to writing grant proposals, and pre-existing data sets that you can use in community work will not want to skip the appendices, where all of those things can be found.

The coming chapters will also cover some of the controversies in conducting project-based research. As you have probably already noticed, I do not subscribe to a cookbook model of research. Research is not a clean process, nor is it a linear process. It is far messier than the average textbook presents it and messier than even this book will present it. Particularly when the research is combined with a social change project, the social change itself can occur unpredictably, with unpredictable consequences that require changing and sometimes even scrapping the research part of the project.

You will consequently find this book outlining processes of research—ways to organize people to do research, or models of research for particular situations. You will not find detailed information on how to collect or analyze data. Those are skills best learned from more traditional research methods texts. The models of project-based research are relatively unique. But techniques of data collection and analysis are common across all forms of research. In addition, because the road to good research is not smooth, you will find the controversies and challenges impacting various forms of project-based research covered in the "loose gravel" sections.

You may have also noticed my emphasis on community participation sneaking into this chapter. You will see it even more in subsequent chapters. That comes partly from my own research work with community organizers, for whom everything is participatory. It also comes from the benefits I've seen as community members have become engaged in project-based research. So if you are a public health professional, or a social service professional, or an academic who has been trained to do for rather than with, I will push you through this book to rethink your training. For the greatest contribution we as professionals can make is to literally work ourselves out of a job—to create opportunities for those normally shut out of access to skills, leadership, and self-confidence to achieve those goals so that we are no longer central or controlling.

Such a process builds community and democracy because it redistributes both power and responsibility, spreading it out, making us much more interdependent. Shame on us that we have not done more of this sooner, because without it we lack the collective capacity of even "lower" life-forms. We can learn a lot from a flock of geese, and we will in the coming chapters.

## THE GOOSE STORY[21]

Next fall, when you see geese heading south for the winter, flying along in V formation, you might consider what science has discovered as to why they fly that way: As each bird flaps its wings, it creates an uplift for the bird immediately following. By flying in V formation the whole flock adds at least 71% greater flying range than if each bird flew on its own.

People who share a common direction and sense of community can get where they are going more quickly and easily because they are traveling on the thrust of one another.

When a goose falls out of formation, it suddenly feels the drag and resistance of trying to go it alone and quickly gets back into formation to take advantage of the lifting power of the bird in front.

If we have as much sense as a goose, we will stay in formation with those who are headed the same way we are.

When the head goose gets tired, it rotates back in the wing and another goose flies point.

It is sensible to take turns doing demanding jobs with people or with geese flying south.

Geese honk from behind to encourage those up front to keep up their speed.

What do we say when we honk from behind?

Finally, and this is important, when a goose gets sick, or is wounded by gunshots and falls out of formation, two other geese fall out with that goose and follow it down to lend help and protection. They stay with the fallen goose until it is able to fly, or until it dies. Only then do they launch out on their own or with another formation to catch up with their group.

If only we could have as much sense as a goose.

## RESOURCES

### General Social Research Methods

Babbie, E., Halley, F., & Zaino, J. (2003). *Adventures in social research* (5th ed.). Thousand Oaks, CA: Pine Forge Press.

Mark, R. (1996). *Research made simple: A handbook for social workers.* Thousand Oaks, CA: Sage Publications.

Neuman, W. L., & Kreuger, L. W. (2002). *Social work research methods: Qualitative and quantitative applications.* Boston: Allyn & Bacon.

Neuman, W. L. (2004). *Basics of social research: Qualitative and quantitative approaches.* Boston: Pearson/Allyn and Bacon.

## Applied Research Methods

Bickman, L., & Rog, D. J. (Eds.). (1998). *Handbook of applied social research methods.* Thousand Oaks, CA: Sage Publications.

Thyer, B. A. (Ed.). (2001). *The handbook of social work research methods.* Thousand Oaks, CA: Sage Publications.

## Intensive and Extensive Research Models

Sayer, R. A. (1992). *Method in social science: A realist approach* (2nd ed.). New York: Routledge.

## NOTES

1. Adams, F., & Horton, M. (1975). *Unearthing the seeds of fire: The idea of Highlander.* Winston-Salem, NC: John F. Blair. Glen, J. M. (1988). *Highlander, no ordinary school, 1932–1962.* Lexington, KY: University Press of Kentucky. Horton, M., & Freire, P. (1990). *We make the road by walking: Conversations on education and social change.* In B. Bell, J. Gaventa, & J. Peters (Eds.). Philadelphia: Temple University Press.

2. Williams, L. (1997). *Grassroots participatory research: A working report from a gathering of practitioners.* Knoxville, TN: University of Tennessee, Knoxville, Community Partnership Center.

3. Alinsky, S. (1969 [1946]). *Reveille for radicals* (p. ix). New York: Vintage Books.

4. Williams, L. (1997). *Grassroots participatory research.*

5. Stoecker, R. (1994). *Defending community: The struggle for alternative redevelopment in Cedar-Riverside.* Philadelphia: Temple University Press.

6. Lynd, M. (1992). Creating knowledge through theatre. *The American Sociologist, 23,* 100–115.

7. See Friedan, B. (1963). *The feminine mystique.* New York: Norton.

8. Rossi, P. H., & Whyte, W. F. (1983). The applied side of sociology. In H. E. Freeman, R. R. Dynes, P. H. Rossi, & W. F. Whyte (Eds.). *Applied sociology* (pp. 5–31). San Francisco: Jossey-Bass Publishers.

9. See Acker, J., Barry, K., & Esseveld, J. (1983). Objectivity and truth: Problems in doing feminist research. *Women's Studies International Forum, 6,* 423–435.

10. Oakley, A. (1981). Interviewing women: A contradiction in terms. In H. Roberts (Ed.). *Doing feminist research* (pp. 30–61). London: Routledge and Kegan Paul.

11. Black, T. R. (1993). *Evaluating social science research.* Thousand Oaks, CA: Sage Publications.

12. Sayer, A. (1992). *Method in social science: A realist approach.* New York: Routledge.

13. Strand, K., Marullo, S., Cutforth, N., Stoecker, R., & Donohue, P. (2003). *Community-based research and higher education: Principles and practices.* San Francisco: Jossey-Bass. Strand et al. described a five-stage project model more applicable to a higher education perspective. The model described in this book is the result of my rethinking of the process from a community perspective.

14. Stoecker, R. (1999). Making connections: Community organizing, empowerment planning, and participatory research in participatory evaluation. *Sociological Practice, 1,* 209–232.

15. Please see Appendix D.

16. Rhodes, L., & Walden, J. (1997). *Virtual tours—reaching into neighborhoods.* Paper presented at the Directions and Implications in Advanced Computing (DIAC) conference, Seattle, March 1–2.

17. Stoecker, R. (2002). *Thinking about CBR: Some questions as we begin.* Keynote address given to Best Practices in Undergraduate Community-Based Research: Challenges and Opportunities for the Research University. March 22–23, Ann Arbor, MI. Retrieved September 15, 2004, from http://comm-org.utoledo.edu/drafts/cbrqs.htm

18. Nyden, P., Figert, A., Shibley, M., & Burrows, D. (Eds). (1997). *Building community: Social science in action.* Thousand Oaks, CA: Pine Forge Press.

19. Stoecker, R., et al. (2003). Community-based research networks: Development and lessons learned in an emerging field. *Michigan Journal of Community Service Learning, 9,* 44–56.

20. American Civil Liberties Union. (1998). *Using the Freedom of Information Act.* Retrieved July 15, 2004, from http://www.aclu.org/library/foia.html

21. The Goose Story is often attributed to "unknown" or "anonymous." In some cases it is attributed to Dr. Harry Clarke Noyes. (1992, January). *ARCS News, 7(1),* Hotel News Resource. Retrieved July 15, 2004, from http://www.hotelnewsresource.com/studies/study0195.htm.

# *Two*

# The Goose Approach to Research

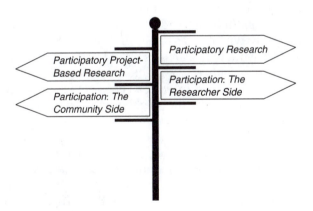

## HAVE YOU EVER FELT
## LIKE AN INTERLOPER?

Have you ever felt like an interloper?

I have.

When I was a graduate student, I decided to write a paper about the neighborhood I was living in at the time. It was a pretty fascinating place—an old, run-down area of small, single-family homes with an enormous 10-building high-rise development in its midst. Even more interesting was that a number of the old homes were undergoing renovation. I wanted to know why. So I gathered my courage and called the neighborhood organization office—making that first approach to schedule a research interview has always been hard for me. I arrived at the office for the interview and met Tim Mungavan, one of the neighborhood leaders and the community organizer/architect for the neighborhood redevelopment project. He looked a lot like me—blue jeans, ponytail, and wire-rimmed glasses. But there the resemblance ended. Before I could get a word out, he confronted me:

> We have students and reporters coming through all the time, asking neighborhood people to give their time and answer their questions. And we don't get so much as a copy of a paper from them. If I agree to talk with you, then I want you to agree that you'll give us a copy of the paper you write.[1]

Well, that did it. My first impulse was to run from the room, pack my bags, quit school, and find a nice, safe job sorting boxes somewhere. Thankfully, instead, I meekly promised to drop off a copy of the paper when it was done. Tim's words haunted me. Why was he so distrustful of researchers? Was I really just like them and couldn't be trusted either? Well, I thought about it and decided I didn't want to be lumped in with all those other researchers who had taken information from the neighborhood without any account-ability. I was going to be the exception.

So I returned a few days later and told Tim I wanted to con-tribute more than just a copy of a paper. I wanted to make sure that I gave something back to the neighborhood in return for the time neighborhood activists gave for my interviews. Well, Tim got this gleam in his eye and pointed to a door in the corner of the office. It led to a short hallway and an outside exit. It seems the city fire marshal was concerned because it had also become a storeroom and was so cluttered that it was almost impossible to get to the out-side door. Tim suggested I tidy it up. So there I was, a highly trained graduate student (well, at least that is what I thought) being asked to do menial labor. But I was intimidated enough to agree to it. The short and narrow hallway, barely six feet long, was filled with cardboard file boxes—the kind people use when they can't afford real filing cabinets—strewn helter-skelter about the hallway. Well, the first box I opened was filled with old neighborhood newspapers. By the time I finished sorting those boxes and clearing a path to the exit, I had all my research data organized exactly the way I wanted it, and I have been doing research projects with the Cedar-Riverside neighborhood in Minneapolis now for almost two decades.

The way I do that research, however, is very different from what I imagined when I first met Tim Mungavan. I didn't have a name for it then and, in fact, didn't have a label for it for a number of years after that. All I knew is that it felt better. I felt as though I was giving rather than just taking. And I no longer felt like an outsider, an interloper. If you just finished the first chapter, you remember the goose story. And that is what it felt like. I was part of the flock. My research became part of the neighborhood's reflection process, and even its planning process. As the neighborhood researcher, I could sometimes fly in the point position when the neighborhood most needed information and then fall back when other skills were needed. At other times, my research was "honking from behind," encouraging the neighborhood by reminding them of their victories in restoring the community. And when my neighborhood activist friends, so much in the thick of battles with city hall to get the funds and the freedom to rebuild their housing, occasionally fell out of formation with frustration and disillusionment, I could reflect with them on the history of all they had accomplished and help them develop new strategies to go back into battle.

This process of doing research *with* people, rather than on them, is the Goose Approach to research. For those of you who are students or professors, and often feel like interlopers when you do research, or avoid research altogether because of that feeling, the Goose Approach can help you feel as though you have something to contribute. In addition, because it involves the people being researched in the research process itself, it can help assure that the research makes a real contribution to the group, organization, or community. For those of you in community settings already who have only had research imposed on you, the Goose Approach— or, as it is more commonly known, the participatory approach— offers a way for you to take control of the research to serve your community.

This chapter will explore how to maximize participation in a research project. You will likely notice that, in doing so, I will describe the researcher as an outsider to the community or group. That is not always the case, but even a researcher who is a respected community member may face many of the same challenges of getting people involved in the research itself.

# PARTICIPATORY APPROACHES TO RESEARCH

Of course, as you've probably already guessed, this style of research is not really called the Goose Approach. Participatory approaches to research are called a variety of different things in different places: action research, participatory research, participatory action research, collaborative research, community-based research, community-based participatory research, and popular education. There are some important differences among these approaches, as we will see. But first let's explore what they have in common and how people doing research can use the general approach.

> **Participatory Approaches to Research: Common Elements**
>
> - Focuses on being useful
> - Employs diverse methods
> - Emphasizes collaboration

## 1. Focuses on Being Useful

One of the reasons participatory approaches work so well for people doing research in community settings is that they are designed to be useful. For those already working in community contexts who do their own research to help their projects succeed, this seems almost too obvious. The kinds of research we will learn about in this book—assessing needs, mapping resources, evaluating programs, and others—are by definition designed to be useful. Those of us in higher education, however, often need retraining to make our research useful.

But, really, what is the difference between research that is useful and research that is not? Isn't it possible that any research can be made useful by someone applying its findings? That is possible, but it requires making a leap from the context in which the research was originally done to the context where you want to apply the findings. This is particularly a problem with basic research that uses *cross-sectional data*, such as a survey, where you are collecting data from *across* a population rather than from just a few individuals. The danger is that you attempt to predict the course of events in any single situation based on research done on a broad cross section of situations, and your specific situation may be outside the typical range that cross-sectional research concentrates on. As we discussed in the first chapter, the probability that extensive research applies to any particular situation is difficult to know, and therefore such research is risky to rely on. Can statistical research on the quality of health care across urban communities in the United States apply, for example, to a working-class African-American community in Portland, Oregon? There is a lot that can go wrong between doing research on the general population and applying that research in a particular place with a particular group of people whose uniqueness might make general findings irrelevant.

The alternative is to custom-design a research project in the particular setting where it will be used. María Eugenia Sánchez and Eduardo Almeida[2] describe a two-decade research process with an indigenous community in Mexico called the Nahuat. For the first three years, the research team mostly got acquainted with the community, doing a few surveys and some field research to increase their own understanding of this unique culture. The women on the research team worked in the vegetable gardens alongside community women, and the men participated in outside economic craft and agricultural production. A number of them learned the Nahuat language. In this case, the researchers made themselves useful to the community before they tried to make the research useful. Eventually, they conducted legal research to help community members confront human rights abuses, and transportation research to get paved roads in the area. But the research and planning that went into these projects began from Nahuat cultural values and was guided by community members.

## 2. Employs Diverse Methods

In order to be useful, participatory approaches to research need to use methods that make sense to people. Most of us were trained to think about how well the research methods fit the research questions. A research question focused on understanding the opinions of the population in general, for example, implied a survey method, while a research question about the cultural characteristics of a small community implied field research.

Those standards still apply here. But there is an additional standard for determining which research methods to use—what methods will create research that will actually be used. Some of the communities I work with rely much more on talk than on writing, and one of my most embarrassing research moments came when I was working to write the history of a community organization in Toledo. We designed a project to recover the history of this once rowdy and confrontational community group on the east side of the city, in hopes of finding out why it succeeded for as long as it did and then why it folded. I ended up reading a lot of old newspapers and letters, but the most interesting part of the work was the interviews I conducted with neighborhood residents.

One method I use in such situations is to ask the people I interview to read and react to drafts of what I write. Validity—whether you are measuring what you think you are measuring—is one of the important issues in research. Returning interview transcripts to interviewees provides a validity check. I can find out whether I heard correctly and in the correct context. In addition, returning transcripts serves an educational purpose, engaging the people I interviewed in reflecting upon what they told me. This often works very effectively, both for correcting my mistakes and giving me new information as the people I interviewed begin to really understand what the research is about and then offer me even more information. In this particular case, however, I did not realize that some of the community people were illiterate. Sending them their interview quotes to review, followed by a 25-page draft, and then calling them for their reactions, placed those residents in terribly uncomfortable positions. I only found out about this gaffe indirectly through another resident, who quietly explained why her neighbor wasn't giving any corrections.

I learned through this experience that the written word is not the final word in research methods. In fact, some of the most interesting forms of research involve community theater and community art. Mark Lynd's[3] popular theater work, described in Chapter 1, is an example of project-based research that doesn't involve any writing. This project was designed for a group of adults with developmental disabilities to interview friends, family, and service providers and then use that interview data to create a play about living with developmental disabilities. The members of his group initially found the interview methods to be very difficult, especially when they interviewed experts on development disabilities, who often answered in jargon they could not understand. But, most important, they had decided to videotape the interviews. So they all sat down together to watch the videotapes and began to deconstruct the jargon. In doing so, they were able to compare the abstract language of the experts to their own stories. Then, rather than trying to write a report expressing the findings, they used the method of community theater. The play that resulted from this process allowed the cast members to present their experience in a creative form, informed by their new understanding of how others viewed them and their disabilities.

## 3. Emphasizes Collaboration

One of the best ways to make sure that the research will be useful, and that the research methods will fit the culture of the group or community, is for the people affected by the research to guide it. Knowing from the beginning that the people you are working with are not turned on by the written word can save a lot of headaches and embarrassment. And the best way to find out what kind of research methods will fit the community and produce the most useful outcomes is to ask.

Asking can be challenging, however. The researcher needs to spend some time getting to know the group or community. In many models of participatory research practiced in underdeveloped communities, this is called pre-research.[4] The researcher spends time learning what the power relations are in the setting—who the leaders are, what the power factions are, what issues are important to people. Because it is often impractical for the researcher to collaborate with everyone in the community or the organization, the researcher needs to know who is generally held in high esteem. Sometimes this is easy. In most of the research projects I do, I am invited in by some leader in the community or the program and am thus already associated with some group or individual. After just a few conversations with other people, I can fairly quickly determine whether my association with the inviter will help or hinder the work.

For the researcher entering the community without an invitation, establishing their own legitimacy can be more difficult. Recently I was involved in a project with neighborhood organizations in Melbourne, Australia. The goal was to conduct research assessing the information and technology needs of those organizations. The project had been developed between a local university and some of the organizations. But I was entering the situation cold, after a long 30 hours of cars, airports, and airlines to get there, and had no legitimacy in the eyes of these organization staff. The first few days were difficult. We couldn't get the neighborhood organization staff to commit to the meetings that had been set up before I arrived. So the first week there we spent a lot of time going out to the neighborhoods to meet people on their turf, on their schedule. By the end, we had begun to build up some interest and involvement from the organizations and are now looking forward to a "launch event" a few months down the road, where the organizations will take the lead in using the research to publicize their needs and then lobby for resources to fill those needs.

As with my early experience with the Cedar-Riverside community, described at the beginning of this chapter, "researchers" are increasingly distrusted out there as simply exploiting poor communities or disrupting organizations for their own professional advancement. Some community organizations now even require outside researchers to sign a contract stating what they will give to the community. A few years ago I became acquainted with the Corella and Bertram F. Bonner Foundation, which was sponsoring a project to create campus-based centers to support participatory forms of research. They were looking for someone to research the effectiveness of their efforts. It sounded like a fascinating project—doing participatory research to help participatory research.

Bobby Hackett, the Foundation vice-president, gave me his e-mail list to introduce the project to the faculty contacts on each of the campuses they were working with. I tried putting on my best participatory face and doing my pre-research through this e-mail list, but without much response. So I took the risk of approaching a gathering of all the participants, and the Bonner Foundation accorded me a space at the end of dinner the first evening. And it was a good thing it was at the end of dinner when there wasn't any food left to throw! I explained that the Foundation had asked me to research the lessons of the project and that I planned to do it in a participatory way, but I didn't get very far. Very quickly, up shot one of the professors, asserting that this didn't seem like a very participatory approach to him—the research project and the researcher (me, who by that time was trembling in my boots) had already been determined and, if this much had already been decided, how could the rest possibly be participatory? He was followed by another professor, who said: "I now know how community organizations feel—being required to participate in research they had no hand in designing!"

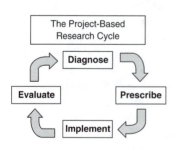

The Project-Based
Research Cycle

Diagnose

Evaluate

Prescribe

Implement

It was a tough crowd, and it was very clear I hadn't done my pre-research. The best I could do was to say that I was only there to offer the idea and plead that it would certainly be participatory from here on out, including a research planning meeting two days later, where they would determine what to research and how to use it. Well, they let me hold that meeting.

My most vocal critics, who are now among my best friends, decided to give me a second chance and attended the meeting. They not only made wonderful contributions but took the lead in making the research useful through a book we recently published (*Community-Based Research and Higher Education,*

2003). Even though the project has ended, we are still working together, advancing the cause of participatory forms of research. And they taught me a valuable lesson about the importance of doing effective pre-research and maximizing participation from the beginning.

## A PARTICIPATORY APPROACH TO PROJECT-BASED RESEARCH

How does the participatory approach work in a typical example of project-based research? It would be easy to say that there is no typical example of project-based research. They are as diverse as the groups, organizations, and communities that use them. They employ research methods ranging from water and air testing to mapping to large-scale surveys to in-depth interviews. And they engage academic disciplines ranging from anthropology to zoology. They range widely in the types and amount of participation they exhibit. They occur at different points in a project cycle, with some focused on diagnosing a situation, others prescribing solutions to a problem, others implementing interventions, and yet others evaluating outcomes.

They all have in common, however, the fact that they are doing research, whether it is surveying community attitudes, sampling air or water for pollution, counting abandoned houses, mapping crime data, documenting public health conditions, studying policy proposals, or others. And in doing research, they all follow the steps in project-based research outlined in Chapter 1. In the previous chapter, however, we focused on how to do each of these steps in terms of maximizing the accuracy of the research. Here we will focus on how to do each step in terms of involving participants and maximizing the usefulness of the research.

**Steps in Project-Based Research**

- Choosing the question
- Designing the methods
- Collecting the data
- Analyzing the data
- Reporting the results

## 1. Choosing the Question

Once the researchers have a good sense of the local power structure and issues, they can begin organizing a group to guide the research. Because of the contexts in which I work, there is often a predefined board or steering committee with whom I work initially. My first meeting with that group outlines the possible research questions, which at that point often are issues the group is concerned about. I then take that list of ideas and check them with people outside of this initial group. In my most recent work with the Cedar-Riverside neighborhood, for example, the local non-profit community development corporation (called a CDC)[5] invited me in to see if I could help design research to bridge some of the cultural and political divisions in the neighborhood. One of their research questions was concerned with how to overcome conflicts between residents of CDC-owned housing. As I talked with other community members, however, it became clear that some residents blamed the CDC itself for those conflicts. Since the CDC was sponsoring the research, we began to realize that if I did research on the housing conflict, I might worsen rather than resolve the conflict. Instead we ended up choosing a research question that focused on studying the community organizing potential across the neighborhood. In the last decade, Cedar-Riverside has become a very diverse community of white, Korean, Vietnamese and Hmong, Ethiopian, Oromo,[6] and Somalian residents. We decided to research the diversity of community organizations representing these communities, and their interrelationships, to build a broad-based neighborhood coalition.

## 2. Designing the Methods

The next step was to design the research itself. In traditional research, the main concern would be what methods best served scientific standards. Those standards are important and are the contribution the researcher makes to the research process. From a participatory project-based research perspective, however, it is also important to design the research methods for maximum impact. In this case, because the CDC was attempting to reach out and unify the community, part of my job became not just interviewing neighborhood organization representatives but linking organizations with each other. So one aspect of the research method involved interviewing organization representatives to find out their organization's history, mission, current projects, and interorganizational linkages. But a second aspect of the research involved encouraging organization representatives to meet with each other. In each interview I disclosed the purpose of the research and asked permission to provide the CDC with the organization's contact information. The research process itself helped to establish informal relationships called "weak ties"[7] between organizations in the neighborhood. At the same time I was doing the research project, the CDC was doing their own outreach. And while CDC staff were already aware of many neighborhood organizations, my initial compilation of contact information for the 40-plus organizations helped their efforts to organize two neighborhood events and recruit participants across the community's ethnic groups.

## 3. Collecting the Data

Many proponents of participatory research prefer that community members be as involved as possible in every stage of the research, including collecting the data. This is particularly the case for the popular education model, which emphasizes that community members themselves should do the research to build their own research skills and knowledge base.[8] There are lots of situations where that is impractical, however. Community or organization members are often too busy to collect the data, and few grants provide enough money for people to take time off from regular jobs or afford childcare so they can do research. The tight timelines that often confront project-based research, along with the training required for lay researchers to do the work, also don't mix very well. In many cases, then, the researcher ends up carrying out the research. But it is still very important to get as much participation as possible. In the case of Cedar-Riverside, I was able to spend time with a former Peace Corps volunteer with experience in East Africa. She provided me with an initial introduction to the Somali, Ethiopian, and Oromo communities. Among the things she taught me was to visit the organizations in these communities personally instead of calling to schedule an appointment. Doing so initially doubled my anxiety about making that first contact, as I have learned to start slowly and from a distance with most nonprofit organizations so they don't feel belabored with yet another researcher. But in each case, I walked into the office, introduced myself, was met with exceeding warmth, and offered a seat and as much time as I wanted right then and there. The first time I was shocked. I figured I would shake hands, set a time for a future interview, and be on my way. I had to do the interview on the fly. It actually helped, because this Somali man was so gentle and warm that I immediately reconfigured what I was doing to seek his advice on how to organize the research so that it would be useful to him as well. And I did that with every subsequent interview.

## 4. Analyzing the Data

Similarly to collecting data, many proponents of participatory research advocate the involvement of community or organization folks in analyzing the data. If the people affected by the project are involved in doing the analysis, they will receive educational and skill benefits and also be more likely to use the research. There are many ways to accomplish this. My preference, partly because most of my project-based research is with community organizations, is to start small. In research such as the Cedar-Riverside project, which is inter-view-based, I use the interview transcript validation process described above, giving each person I interview a transcript (when I am confident they are literate in written English) to review for accuracy. I also emphasize that the transcript is private until they approve it. I received comments from about a third of the people I interviewed, made the changes they suggested, and sent every person interviewed a rough draft. Again I asked each person to review it and add their own comments agreeing or disagreeing with the analysis. While I was doing this, I was also meeting with the CDC board each month, and they accorded me space at each of four monthly meetings. At the first meeting we organized an education session on different types of community organizing and then distributed a brief questionnaire asking board members about the community organizing goals they thought the CDC should pursue. At the next meeting I presented the results of that brief questionnaire, showing that the board preferred a cooperative community-building approach across the ethnic communities more than a confrontational approach of pitting the community against some outside target like city hall. We discussed this in terms of what types of community organizing CDCs may be best suited for. At the third board meeting I presented the rough draft of the research report. The discussions informed their own analysis of what the CDC should do, and during this time the board supported two cross-cultural, community-building events, both of which featured food from each of the neighborhood's communities. I'd never before attended a Somali-Ethiopian-Vietnamese-Korean-Anglo potluck.

## 5. Reporting the Results

As I've mentioned, reporting the results can occur in many creative ways—community theater, quilting, street demonstrations, oral storytelling, and who knows how many others. In this case the reporting occurred in writing, with the research report going on the Web. In addition, as the research progressed we also decided to create a neighborhood directory with the contact information for all of the neighborhood organizations that gave their permission, and we put that on the Web. It may seem odd that we would emphasize Web-based reporting in a neighborhood of poor immigrant and refugee communities. Indeed, at the beginning of the research the CDC board and staff and I thought that was out of the question. But here again, the advantages of community participation in the research process made themselves known. It turns out that many members of the Somali, Oromo, and Ethiopian communities were avid and skilled Internet users, partly because it was the best way to keep in touch with friends and family in their homelands and partly because of their desire to succeed in their new home. Every organization representative used e-mail regularly, and most even preferred receiving electronic copies of the research rather than paper copies. So we put it all on the Web. In addition, the CDC continued its strategic planning around its growing interest in supporting community-building in the neighborhood, expanding its outreach for its annual meeting and electing its first Somali board member in December of 2002.

## BUILDING PARTICIPATORY RELATIONSHIPS: THE RESEARCHER SIDE

This Goose Approach to research, as you may have surmised by now, rests on relationships. If, like me, you have ever feared imposing yourself on a community or organization, or felt like an interloper, it may be because you haven't really developed any relationships with the flock. Particularly, we professional researchers often feel caught between thinking we know what's best for the community or not contributing our own perspective for fear of being too influential. Both responses, however, are symptomatic of not having built those relationships and misunderstanding what collaboration and community-based expertise mean. I remember being brought up short a few years ago while working with an African-American community in Toledo. I was at a meeting, not contributing because I was stuck in the "fear of undue influence" trap, when one of the neighborhood leaders asked me directly what I thought. We'd worked together for about a year by that time, and while I hemmed and hawed, Rose Newton, in her wonderfully confrontational way, said: "Just tell us what you think and don't worry about it—if it's a stupid idea we'll tell you."

So, for those of us researchers with no community base, or communities/organizations with no available researcher, how does one build those relationships? The process has to begin by finding each other. At the end of this chapter you will find a list of resources that can help researchers and communities to find each other.

Researchers and communities trying to find each other face different kinds of challenges and opportunities. In many ways, it is easy for researchers to find partners. While researchers who want to work collaboratively in community and organization settings are still relatively rare, communities and organizations are everywhere. In urban areas, city governments often maintain directories of area non-profits and community organizations, as do university social work departments. In rural areas, local newspapers often list meetings of area groups, and county governments can sometimes be good sources of contact information. The challenge is finding the right organization or group to work with. Researchers not only need to find an organization willing to accept help but one that has the capacity to guide that help and use the end product of the research. How can a researcher assess a potential community or organization partner before investing time and resources that may only lead to failure? Here are some questions to ask about the community/organization side of the equation:

> **Questions the Researcher Should Ask**
>
> - Does the community/ organization have the capacity to participate?
> - What resources can the community/organization contribute?
> - Does the community/ organization have research needs you can fulfill?

## 1. Does the Community/Organization Have the Capacity to Participate?

If the research is going to actually be used, the community or organization needs to have the capacity to use it. In some cases it is possible to find out something about an organization's history before even meeting them, including things like the stability of the board and staff, its funding, and the kind of projects it has been responsible for. This doesn't mean that small, unstable organizations, or disorganized communities, should be avoided altogether. Indeed, a good participatory research project can help build and stabilize a weak community or organization. But using research in this way takes special skill and effort, and the researcher either needs to have good community organizing skills or needs to be working with a skilled community organizer. It is also okay to take a risk on a small project that may not lead to anything. There are those out there who compare developing a collaborative research relationship to dating. You can't know everything about your potential partner before taking some risks, so make the risks small at the beginning.

## 2. What Resources Can the Community/Organization Contribute?

For those of us who do our community research on the side, because our university values only research that produces journal articles, it is often difficult to do this kind of research pro bono. As the community-based research model becomes more popular, and we develop a better understanding of how to engage students in such research projects, the research resource gap is becoming less problematic. But there are still resources that must come from the community side. Depending on the project, they often need to make time for interviews, open their files, read drafts, provide office space and computer access for students, and even help with training and supervising students on occasion. They may also need to be responsible for organizing meetings around the research part of the project. One of the most difficult challenges I have faced is working with a community organization that is already going full out. I become responsible for contacting all the relevant community people to encourage them to participate in the research planning, finding a place to meet, and making the reminder phone calls. It is important to know at the beginning whether there are staff resources or money available to support these research organizing tasks.

## 3. Does the Community/Organization Have Research Needs You Can Fulfill?

The community/organization needs to come up with a research question the researcher has some background in. I hesitate to think what may have happened in Cedar-Riverside had I not understood the thorny issues involved when CDCs try to move beyond their usual mission of building housing to building community. Most community organizations have a lot of expertise to begin with, and they are looking for advanced information. Of course, there are cases where the community or organization is entering uncharted waters as well, in which case a researcher's methodological expertise may be more important than their substantive expertise. I remember my second participatory research project in Toledo. The community development coalition that formed out of our first project decided it wanted a study of how philanthropic foundations give away money. At the time I didn't know what a foundation was, much less how to study them. But then I found myself and an extraordinarily dedicated graduate student ruining our eyesight reading microfiche tax records of Toledo-area foundations. For me personally it was the most tedious research I have ever been involved with, but, for the community, it was the most popular and influential research project I have ever contributed to.

## BUILDING PARTICIPATORY RELATIONSHIPS: THE COMMUNITY SIDE

Communities or organizations trying to fill a particular research need not only have to develop their own understanding of what they need but they also may need to really hunt to find a researcher who can fill that need, as there are often no lists of available researchers. Additionally, because time and resources are tight, it is important to find help that actually helps. There are still horror stories out there of researchers who didn't follow through on a promised project, didn't complete it in time to do any good, or didn't do quality work. And if you're not a research expert, it's difficult to judge someone who claims to be. It's also difficult to demand a résumé from people who are essentially volunteering themselves and their students for your cause—though you still should. So, what are the standards by which offers to help should be judged? There are a set of questions community members and workers, as well as academics themselves, can ask.

> **Questions the Community/ Organization Should Ask**
>
> - Is the researcher willing to follow the community/ organization's lead?
> - How good is the researcher at meeting deadlines?
> - Can the researcher communicate in a community context?
> - What experience does the researcher have?

## Is the Researcher Willing to Follow the Community/Organization's Lead?

Any community organization being approached by a researcher should have a test ready. If you remember back to the beginning of this chapter, the first time I approached a community organization with my research question, as a graduate student, they instead asked me to clean their storeroom. Trying to be a good citizen, I accepted the task. I discovered that they were testing me not only to see if I could truly collaborate with them but also to see how far I would dig for the gold mine of data that their storeroom contained. Have a casual meeting and discuss what kind of participation the community will have throughout the research process. Discuss whether the researcher plans to publish anything from the research and whether you will have any input in their writing. Discuss who owns the data. The "A" answer will be "the community/organization owns it." Some community groups have gone to writing up contracts with their academic partners, which hold both the academic and the community accountable and are also helpful in planning the overall project.

## How Good Is the Researcher at Meeting Deadlines?

Community projects and academic projects are as different as any two things called "projects" could be. Community projects almost always have strict deadlines tied to absolute funding or legislative dates. Academic projects often have no deadlines except for the faculty member who needs to have an article published before the tenure decision deadline. Many of my academic friends chafe at the implication that they can't meet a deadline, and of course many of them are very responsible, but the academic environment is very lax about deadlines, allowing students and faculty to treat those deadlines more as suggestions. It is important to understand that, in academia, it is almost always possible to turn a paper in late. In the case of submitting articles to academic journals, there is no deadline at all. But when a foundation says your funding proposal must be in their hands by 5 p.m. on March 15, they mean it. It doesn't matter if you suffered a heart attack on the way to the mailbox. When I served on the review board for neighborhood grants made by the City of Toledo, one of the proposals arrived at the city at 5:15 p.m. on the appointed day—15 minutes late. By city policy, we had to refuse it. So make sure the researcher understands the project schedule. If students are involved, and the project extends beyond the end of the course, develop a plan for how the research will be completed after the students are gone.

## Can the Researcher Communicate in a Community Context?

Remember that last article you read from a professional academic journal? Remember how much of it you understood? Remember how many times you had to put it down before finally finishing it (if you actually did finish it)? And don't think those questions apply only to community people and students. When I was a graduate student and a new assistant professor, I had some wonderful community mentors who taught me how to write for community audiences. It wasn't about "dumbing down" my writing but about making it interesting—shorter sentences, more common language, catchier phrasing, a more storybook tone, with more real people. Academics and community members need to discuss how they will report on the research and how collaborative the process will be. Another way to assess how well a researcher can communicate is for them to attend a community meeting and find out whether everyone speaks the same language or at least can translate.

## What Experience Does the Researcher Have?

It is not enough for a researcher to be good at collaborating, meeting deadlines, and communicating. They ultimately also must be able to do the work. Do they have expertise in the type of research needed for your project? Do they have any past experience with similar projects? If they will be using students, what kind of training and expertise will the students have?

Regardless of these questions, most important to community-academic collaboration is the relationship. Project-based research is time-consuming, unpredictable, and often politically messy. The relationship needs to stand up through all of that. If you are not sure the relationship will be strong enough, then the research may not be good enough.

# LOOSE GRAVEL

The path to participatory research is pretty clear—the more participation the better. If the researcher engages community or organization members at every step of the research, the chances for success
are high. It's actually not hard to do. It just feels hard because, for
many of us, it requires working across class, race, and cultural
boundaries. But it is ultimately the relationships that matter, especially when you hit some of the loose gravel on the way to a successful participatory research project. There are three kinds of loose
gravel that are important to understand from the beginning: understanding who the "community" is; determining whether the situation you are researching is characterized by conflict or cooperation;
and dealing with charges of researcher bias.

## 1. Who Is the Community?

This patch of loose gravel may not apply as much to those working strictly in bureaucratically defined organizations. But those of
you in such situations may still confront concerns that the people
most affected by the research are not really involved in guiding it.
Especially if you are working with a service organization located in
a poor community, but not controlled by its residents, this section
can be particularly important.

It is interesting to me how reluctant people are to talk about the
question of who is the community. Some don't want to talk about it
because they fear that the conversation will be divisive. They would
prefer to think about us as all one big community, and to talk about
*the community* as separate from those of us trying to help will rein-
force divisions and cause conflict. Another reason some don't want
to talk about it is because, at some level of consciousness, we "on the
outside" know that the community is not us. And that applies not
just to academics but to foundations, United Ways, government
agencies, and even most nonprofits. Because, by and large, those
organizations are not controlled by people who live, eat, and sleep
with the problems that participatory research models are designed
to attack. And that is where I begin in thinking about the community
in participatory research.

To me, "the community" is the people with the problem: The
economically disinvested neighborhood trying to get respectful and
effective police protection; the gay/lesbian community trying to get
fair marriage and adoption laws; the Latino or African-American

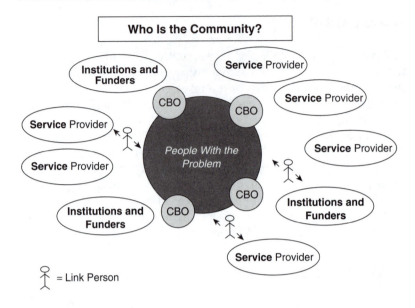

Who Is the Community?

= Link Person

community trying to stop employment discrimination; the disabled community trying to get better health care; or the rural community trying to get clean drinking water. The community may be spatial or may span spaces. It may be well organized or disorganized. In some cases people may not even define themselves as a community—until a good community organizer brings them together so they can discover their common issues and complementary resources. When they do understand their issues and resources they sometimes form their own community-based organizations (CBOs)—groups that they as a community control, either by a majority hold on the board of a formal organization or by their mass membership and participation in an informal group. In the Cedar-Riverside neighborhood project described earlier, I found myself working with the neighborhood community development corporation (which is run by an elected neighborhood board), the Confederation of Somali Community in Minnesota, the Oromo Community of Minnesota, the Korean Service Center, and an informal Vietnamese group, among the many other non-community-based nonprofit organizations.

A step removed from the community are those organizations that are not controlled by the community but are connected to it by staff or board members who come from the community. Those "link people," or "bridge people," or "translators," as they are variously called, are special. In multicultural situations they are the people who not only speak multiple languages but also understand the rules of multiple cultures. In Cedar-Riverside I worked with a Vietnamese community leader, a Somali community leader, a leader in the Oromo community, and a leader of the local Korean community. All were members of their respective ethnic communities, and were also running formal community-based service organizations in the neighborhood.

Two steps removed are those organizations with no direct connection to the people with the problem. Their staff or boards may share some structural characteristics—of class, race, gender, sexual orientation, disability, or other important characteristic—but they do not share the experience of the problem. Service providers, institutions, government, and other similar organizations trying to help a community—when they have no community base, no community participation or control, and no bridge people—are often suspect in a community. And yet it is with these twice-removed groups that so many academics partner—something I call working from the middle.

This situation confronts us with a number of questions. First, what does a researcher do in a divided community when there are divisive CBOs? This can often seem like the most difficult situation to deal with. But it may not actually be as difficult as it seems. For researchers often occupy a special status in community settings. Similar to newspaper reporters, many people see researchers as people who can help them tell their story. In my many years of working with the Cedar-Riverside neighborhood, perhaps one of the most contentious (though thankfully still nonviolent) neighborhoods in the country, I have learned a number of lessons in working with divisive neighborhood factions.

The most important lesson is that, if you don't take sides, you have to keep secrets. In the many neighborhood disputes I have witnessed over the years, I have more than once been told of the strategy one side planned to get the other side. I've kept that information secret, following my basic code that I don't distribute anyone's information before they have had a chance to review and revise it. Consequently, they had to work out the disputes themselves. And they were much better at it than I would have been.

The second lesson is that there are situations where your own values compel you to choose sides. I have just finished yet another research project with the CDC in Cedar-Riverside, looking at the strategies they have used to successfully create over 250 units of housing in the neighborhood. I agreed to the project after two years spent avoiding the housing conflicts in the neighborhood. But I eventually came to see those opposing the CDC as such a grave threat to the neighborhood housing that I felt compelled to give up my neutrality. That doesn't mean I don't still keep secrets, particularly because those opposing the CDC are community residents rather than outside actors. But my research is focused on helping the CDC reorganize the affordable cooperative housing they created rather than helping its opponents find a way to transform it into privately owned houses that they could buy low and sell high.

A more challenging situation than an organized, but divided, community is one that is disorganized, where there are no CBOs with any effective capacity. In some cases the researcher gets approached by a service organization working in such a community. The organization itself serves people in the community but has no community members who participate in the organization's programmatic or governance decisions. Think, for example, of homeless service organizations. Partly because of the level of deprivation of homeless individuals, and partly because of the level of mental illness such a situation can exacerbate or cause, it seems unimaginable to do participatory research with homeless individuals guiding the research. Yet that is exactly what happened with Project South's work in Atlanta in preparation for the 1996 Olympics, as the city demolished public housing near downtown and tried to sweep the homeless off the streets.[9] Ian Landry has also been conducting participatory research with homeless individuals in Canada toward building participation of the homeless in program development.[10] These are admittedly rare situations. But they provide lessons for how a researcher and a service organization can work together to increase the participation of people normally thought of as only recipients of those services.

Thinking of ways that the community (defined, remember, as "the people with the problem") can be involved in the research also provides an important test of a service organization. Some service organizations have such a long history of not engaging recipient participation in program design and implementation that they cannot imagine how to do it. If you are a researcher approached by a service organization, you can propose a method that involves recipients in decision making about the research, and then suggest how such participation can continue when the research actually gets put to use. If you are experienced in such a process yourself, you may even help a traditional service organization make the transition from simple service provision to building the sense of power and efficacy in those people it formerly thought of only as recipients. This becomes even more important if you are approached by a foundation to evaluate a program. My experience with the Bonner Foundation, described earlier, taught me that a research project appearing to be imposed from the "outside" will become little more than shelf research. In the case of the Bonner Foundation, it wasn't even being imposed, but the fact that even the idea for the research came from outside the program participants was immediately suspect.

The most important lesson in working from the middle, or with a disorganized community, is to do it with a skilled organizer. We researchers particularly—for some reason—see the research we do as extremely complex and requiring extensive training to carry out. But we don't see the skills involved in organizing a group, running a meeting, and managing the flow of interpersonal relations in moving from research to action as also requiring extensive training and a high level of expertise. One of my embarrassing failures in participatory research came while working with a Hispanic community in Chicago, who had experienced some successes in getting their local schools to be more culturally sensitive and supportive of parent involvement. The organization sponsoring the effort wanted to document their work and its outcomes so they could apply for grants to expand the project. My colleague and I agreed to do the research but wanted the parents to do the interviews—neither of us were fluent in Spanish or experienced in Hispanic culture and hoped that involving parents would assure that the research truly reflected the community's experience. What we didn't know, however, was how much organizing was involved in making this happen. We had funds to pay the parent interviewers, but our first meeting with them recruited only a few parents. We had a difficult time explaining the purpose of the project and how to do it and didn't realize how important it would be for us to keep the project moving by calling subsequent meetings, checking in regularly with the parent interviewers, and expanding the circle of parent participants. Ever since then I have realized the benefit of working with a skilled community organizer who could do those things.

## 2. Is the Situation Characterized By Conflict or Cooperation?

As we will see beginning in the next chapter, project-based research can occur across an incredibly wide range of issues. But one of the most important ways that such research can vary is across situations of conflict or cooperation. At one extreme is an organization that is organizing its membership to attack a target—a bad-guy corporation or government that has excluded or damaged the community in some way. At the other extreme is a unified organization or community developing a new, noncontroversial program to serve its own members. These two types of projects come from two very different worldviews and illustrate the distinction between what sociologists call functionalist theory and conflict theory.

Functionalist theory argues that healthy societies tend toward natural balance and naturally sort people into jobs and positions according to their individual talents and societal needs. This theory also assumes that people have common interests even when they have different positions in society. Healthy, persistent societies change gradually rather than abruptly. Thus, a group organizing to force change can throw off equilibrium, and cooperation to produce gradual change is a better alternative.[11] In contrast, conflict theory sees no natural tendency toward anything but conflict over scarce resources. In this model, society develops through struggle between groups. Imbalance is the normal state of affairs. A false equilibrium is only achieved temporarily, through one group dominating the other groups. Conflict theory sees society as divided, particularly between corporations and workers, men and women, and whites and people of color. The instability inherent in such divided societies prevents elites from achieving absolute domination and provides opportunities for those on the bottom to create change through organizing for collective action and conflict.[12]

Different types of organizations often tend toward one of the two models. The community work industry, for example, can be divided into the practices of advocacy, service delivery, community development, and community organizing. Advocacy—the practice of trying to create social change on behalf of others (such as children or trees or illegal immigrants who are unable to advocate for themselves)—and service delivery—what we normally think of as social services—both tend to occur through midrange, non-community-based organizations. Community development—providing housing, business, and workforce development—and community organizing—building powerful self-advocacy organizations—are more likely to occur through true community-based organizations. Advocacy and community organizing are based more on conflict theory, while service delivery and community development are based more on functionalist theory.

The question becomes how to use participatory forms of research with each situation. Historically, the practices of participatory research and popular education have been seen as more consistent with conflict theory, and action research has been seen as more consistent with functionalist theory.[13]

Participatory research and popular education were influenced by the Third World development movement of the 1960s. Academics, activists, and indigenous community members collaborated to conduct research, develop education programs, and create plans to counter global corporations attempting to take over world agriculture. Their research, education, and planning processes led to sustainable, community-controlled agricultural and development projects. The "participatory research" and "popular education" models resulting from this movement across India, Africa, and South America have been the leading models around much of the world.[14] These models also emphasize people producing knowledge to develop their own consciousness as a means for furthering their struggles for social change.[15] Consequently, the highest form of participatory research is that which is completely controlled and conducted by the community. It is interesting in this regard that the most well-known practitioners of this model, such as the Highlander Research and Education Center, the Applied Research Center, and Project South, are all organizations outside of academia.

The origin of action research is most associated with Kurt Lewin.[16] He and his colleagues focused on attempting to resolve interracial conflicts, along with conducting applied research to increase worker productivity and satisfaction. Action research emphasizes the integration of theory and practice and does not challenge the existing power relationships in either knowledge production or material production. It has been used in education settings and in union-management collaboration in research to save jobs and improve worker satisfaction.[17] Action research values useful knowledge, developmental change, the centrality of individuals, and consensus social theories. The point of reference for action researchers is the profession more than the community, and the practice is very similar to the models used by professional planners. The action research model emphasizes collaboration between groups and does not address the structural antagonism between those groups emphasized by the participatory research model. Action research instead seeks to resolve conflicts between groups, reflecting the basic worldview of functionalist theory.

It is important for the researcher and the community/organization to understand this distinction. In Cedar-Riverside, the survey we did with the CDC board showed clearly that they disliked conflict and wanted to work from a more functionalist world view. There were many issues they could have taken on by using a conflict approach. For example, the city had suspended a major source of funding for redevelopment in the neighborhood, leaving Cedar-Riverside the only neighborhood in the city not receiving such funds. But CDC board members wanted to emphasize strategies for bringing the community together around working *for* something rather than working against something, perhaps because they had become worn out by all the conflict over two decades of rebuilding and defending their community.

If the researcher works from a worldview that reflects functionalist theory, and the community worldview reflects the opposite, and they don't talk about it, each side could actually be working toward a different kind of outcome. And they may not realize it until it's too late. I was, in fact, used to Cedar-Riverside being a rough-and-tumble, confrontational neighborhood always up for a fight. But I did not realize how heavy a toll the neighborhood's internal conflict had taken, since I now lived 700 miles away and maintained my involvement through monthly site visits. I was all ready to provide research support so that they could organize a big confrontational campaign. Thankfully, we talked about this very issue, which led to research supporting a community-building strategy rather than a community organizing strategy.

## 3. Is the Participatory Approach Biased?

Doing research in a way that involves community or organization members often invites charges of bias. How accurate can research be, after all, if non-experts direct it? How accurate can it be if a researcher with a commitment to support a particular community or organization does it?

This particular patch of loose gravel will carry different risks for communities compared to researchers. Communities and organizations need to worry if foundations, judges, legislators, and community members will take their research seriously. These audiences assume that the research is conducted with some degree of one-sidedness. Their main question is whether the research is accurate. And while being armed with research that looks objective can sometimes help win a policy issue, more important is having research that can survive the criticisms of the opposition.

For university- or college-based researchers, however, the appearance of objectivity can be as important as the degree of accuracy. We saw in Chapter 1 that there is no necessary relationship between objectivity and accuracy and that the distinction between the two has been lost. But when it comes to getting tenure, if the academic's research appears too passionate, it doesn't matter how accurate it might be. It is still labeled and discarded as biased.

In addition, project-based research doesn't fit cleanly into higher education. When I got my first professor job, it was split half and half between a regular department and a university-based applied research center. I used this position to do participatory research with community organizations. After the third year, however, I had to give up my work through the research center. Half of the department faculty didn't like it because they thought I was supposed to be doing research and interpreted my work as service projects. The other half thought just the opposite. In addition, much of this kind of research is descriptive and involves counting things. It is often much easier to get community permission to publish their data than it is to get an academic journal to accept an article based on such descriptive data. Some academic journals are becoming more interested in publishing articles on how to do participatory forms of research, but we still have a ways to go in gaining legitimacy for participatory forms of research.

So the first challenge for academic researchers involves explaining what they are doing. That is becoming easier thanks to the growing popularity of service learning and community-based research in higher education.[18] But even when faculty review committees understand it, they may not respect it. That is because so much of this kind of research disregards the reified version of objectivity that demands the researcher remain dispassionate and distanced, and that the research remain in the control of professionals at all times.

What are the defenses against this? First, as we have already discussed, is the critique of objectivity itself and returning objectivity to its status as a strategy rather than a goal in itself. More difficult to deal with is the charge of the researcher "going native"—becoming overidentified with the community's values. But here, too, it is important to separate commitment to a community from commitment to a particular research outcome. Just as objectivity and accuracy are not the same, neither are going native and researcher bias. The question is not the extent to which the researcher identifies with the community but how skilled they are at conducting research that can accurately reflect reality. Of course, researchers helping an organization evaluate a program need to check their desire to make the organization look good. But it is no less difficult for experimental researchers to check their desire to confirm their own hypothesis.

The final issue the academic researcher has to deal with is the charge that unskilled community members are making too many decisions about the research and therefore threatening its accuracy. On the face of it, this seems difficult to defend against. But Phil Nyden and colleagues[19] have shown that the combination of the abstract knowledge of academics and the experiential knowledge of community members is more powerful than each alone. The most powerful illustration of this point comes from a deadly disease that struck the Navajo community in 1993. When the Centers for Disease Control tried to investigate what was killing members of the Navajo Nation in New Mexico, they went in without understanding the cultural norms of mourning the dead and community privacy standards. As a consequence, the people they interviewed told them anything just to get them out of the way, and the CDC ended up, unknowingly, with useless data. In the interim, more people died. Eventually, a Navajo public health researcher, consulting with a local Navajo medicine man, helped manage the cultural differences, and they discovered the killer was the mouse-borne hantavirus. It appears, however, that this virus had already been diagnosed through Navajo "myth," which told of the relationship between excess rainfall and growth in the mouse population and the bad luck one would receive if a mouse ran across your clothing.[20] The Centers for Disease Control now cites the knowledge of traditional Navajo healers in its information on hantavirus[21] and has established community advisory committees around the country to link community-based knowledge with scientific knowledge.[22] Lives were lost by ignoring community knowledge, and were saved by treating that knowledge as legitimate.

## CONCLUSION

This chapter has focused on the process of doing project-based research with community members and organizations, emphasizing how to increase the participation of community and organization members in the research. It is important to remember, however, that this is not participation for participation's sake. The next chapter will focus on the project-based research model and will show how participation fits into that model. The purpose of participation in a research context is to support the project work of the organization. So, remember that participatory forms of research:

- Focus on being useful
- Employ diverse research methods
- Emphasize collaboration

Community and organization members can participate in, contribute to, and guide every step of the research process, including:

- Choosing the research question
- Designing the research methods
- Collecting the data
- Analyzing the data
- Reporting the results

When project-based research involves a collaboration between professional researchers and community groups or organizations, the two parties need to ask some questions of each other. Researchers should ask:

- Does the community/organization have the capacity to participate?
- What resources can the community/organization contribute?
- Does the community/organization have research needs you can fulfill?

Community groups or organizations should ask:

- Is the researcher willing to follow the community/organization's lead?
- How good is the researcher at meeting deadlines?
- Can the researcher communicate in a community context?
- What experience does the researcher have?

Finally, there are some potentially tricky issues that researchers and organizations need to face in project-based research:

- Who is the community? Is the organization or group sponsoring the research representative of the community or connected to it?
- Is the situation characterized by conflict or cooperation? Do the partners in the project agree on the characterization of the situation and the strategies to use in that context?
- Is participatory research biased? Will it be taken seriously in policy and legal contexts?

# RESOURCES

## Community-Based Research
## Networks Based in Higher Education

Community-Campus Partnerships for Health, http://www.ccph.info
Coral network, http://www.coralnetwork.org/
Just Connections, http://www.justconnections.org
Neighborhood Planning for Community Revitalization, http://www.cura.umn.edu/programs/npcr.html
Policy Research Action Group, http://www.luc.edu/curl/prag/
University Community Collaborative of Philadelphia, http://www.temple.edu/uccp

## Popular Education Centers Based in Higher Education

Center for Popular Education and Participatory Research, University of California Berkeley, http://cpepr.net/

Centre for Popular Education, University of Technology Sydney, http://www.cpe.uts.edu.au

## Popular Education and Participatory Research Centers Outside of Higher Education

Applied Research Center, http://www.arc.org/

Highlander Research and Education Center, http://www.highlandercenter.org/

Paulo Freire Institute, http://www.paulofreire.org/

Participatory Research in Asia, http://www.pria.org

Project South, http://www.projectsouth.org/

## Books and Edited Collections

*Michigan Journal of Community Service Learning, special issue on community-based research, Vol. 9(3)*, 2003.

Nyden, P., Figert, A., Shibley, M., & Burrows, D. (1997). *Building community: Social science in action.* Thousand Oaks, CA: Pine Forge Press.

Park, P., M. Brydon-Miller, B. Hall, & T. Jackson (Eds.). *Voices of change: Participatory research in the United States and Canada.* Westport, CT: Bergin and Garvey.

Strand, K., Marullo, S., Cutforth, N., Stoecker, R., & Donohue, P. (2003). *Community-based research and higher education.* San-Francisco: Jossey-Bass.

Stringer, E. T. (1999). *Action research: A handbook for practitioners* (2nd Ed.). Thousand Oaks, CA: Sage.

Wallerstein, N., & M. Minkler (Eds.). (2002). *Community-based participatory research in health.* San Francisco: Jossey-Bass.

## How-To Guides

Ritas, C. (2002). Speaking truth, creating power: A guide to policy work for community-based participatory research practitioners. Community-Campus Partnerships for Health, http://depts.washington.edu/ccph/pdf_files/ritas.pdf

Stoecker, R. (2003). The CBR FAQ. The Bonner Foundation, http://www.bonner.org/campus/crp/faq.tml?keyword=&s=1

# NOTES

1. Stoecker, R. (1994). *Defending community: The struggle for alternative redevelopment in Cedar-Riverside.* (p. 25). Philadelphia: Temple University Press.

2. Sánchez, M. E., & Almeida, E. (1992). Synergistic development and participatory action research in a Nahuat community. *The American Sociologist, 23,* 83–99.

3. Lynd, M. (1992). Creating knowledge through theatre. *The American Sociologist, 23,* 100–115.

4. Escarra, C. (2002). Participatory research. Presentation at the University of Toledo, August 28.

5. In the United States, community development corporations are nonprofit organizations that focus on rehabilitating or building housing and developing small-scale local economies.

6. Oromo is an ethnic group that comes from the area now called Ethiopia.

7. Granovetter, M. (1973). The strength of weak ties. *American Journal of Sociology, 78,* 1360–1380.

8. Freire, P. (1970). *Pedagogy of the oppressed.* New York: Continuum.

9. Project South. (1996). *The Olympic Games & our struggles for justice: A people's story.* Atlanta: Project South.

10. Landry, I. (2002). The homeless men of Halifax: organizing for action. In COMM-ORG Papers. R. Stoecker (Ed.). Retrieved July 15, 2004, from http://comm-org.utoledo.edu/papers.htm.

11. Morrow, P. C. (1978). Functionalism, conflict theory and the synthesis syndrome in sociology. *International Review of Modern Sociology, 8,* 209–225. Eitzen, S., & Zinn, M. B. (2000). *In conflict and order: Understanding society* (9th ed.). Boston: Allyn and Bacon.

12. Morrow, P. C. (1978). *Functionalism, conflict theory, and the synthesis syndrome in sociology.* Boston: Allyn and Bacon. Eitzen, S., & Zinn, M. B. (2000). *In conflict and order: Understanding society* (9th ed.). Boston: Allyn and Bacon.

13. Brown, L. D., & Tandon, R. (1983). Ideology and political economy in inquiry: action research and participatory research. *Journal of Applied Behavioral Science, 19,* 277–294.

14. Ibid. Freire, P. (1970). *Pedagogy of the oppressed.* Also see Paulo Freire Institute. (n.d.). Retrieved July 15, 2004 from http://www.paulofreire.org. Hall, B. (1993). Introduction. In P. Park, M. Brydon-Miller, B. Hall, & T. Jackson. (Eds.). *Voices of change: Participatory research in the United States and Canada* (pp. xiii-xxii). Westport, CT: Bergin & Garvey.

15. Gaventa, J. (1991). Toward a knowledge democracy: viewpoints on participatory research in North America. In O. Fals-Borda, & M. Anisier Rashman (Eds.). *Action and knowledge: Breaking the monopoly with participatory action research* (pp. 121–131). New York: Apex Press.

16.  Lewin, K. (1948). In Gertrude W. Lewin (Ed.). *Resolving social conflicts: Selected papers on group dynamics.* New York: Harper & Row.

17.  Whyte, W. F. (Ed.). (1991). *Participatory action research.* Newbury Park, CA: Sage.

18.  Strand, K., Marullo, N., Cutforth, N., Stoecker, R., & Donohue, P. (2003). *Community-based research and higher education: Principles and practices.* San Francisco: Jossey-Bass.

19.  Nyden, P., Figert, A., Shibley, M., & Burrows, D. (1997). *Building community: Social science in action.* Thousand Oaks, CA: Pine Forge Press.

20.  Suzuki, D. (2000). Hidden killer: portrait of an epidemic. *The Nature of things* [television broadcast]. CBC Television, Sunday, June 18. See also Alvord, L. A., & Van Pelt, E. C. (1999). *The scalpel and the silver bear.* New York: Bantam.

21.  Centers for Disease Control. (2000). Navajo medical traditions and HPS. Retrieved July 15, 2004, from http://www.cdc.gov/ncidod/diseases/hanta/hps/noframes/navajo.htm

22.  Centers for Disease Control and Prevention. (2002). Chronic disease reports and notes, 15 (1). Retrieved July 15, 2004, from http://www.cdc.gov/nccdphp/cdnr/cdnr_winter0207.htm

# *Three*

# Head and Hand Together

## *A Project-Based Research Model*

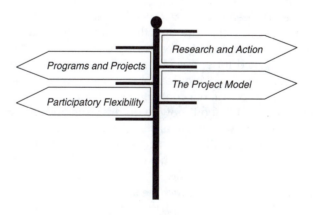

## THE HEAD AND HAND SPLIT

I grew up in a working-class family, with one of those fathers who came home dirty from head to toe every evening from fixing furnaces, repairing pipes, digging foundations, or any manner of other highly skilled but dirty, body-wearing activities. My mother, along with managing the home and at times managing a full-time clerical job, also was a skilled tailor for the family and for extra income. I was the first person in my family to go to college, and when I would come home brimming with excitement about the course I was taking in aesthetic philosophy, it was all but impossible for me to find a way to communicate all that "head work" I was doing with parents whose lives had been spent doing "hand work."

This head-hand split or, more commonly in philosophy and psychology, the "mind-body split," has been a troubling theme in Western culture for nearly as long as there has been Western culture.[1] But especially since World War II, the split has become pronounced in dividing our class system. The rise of a managerial class who does only head work, against a working class who are supposed to do only hand work, has limited us perhaps as greatly as any division in society. Those of us in higher education also experience the pressures of this split, as the emphasis on pure research often puts many roadblocks in the way of academics striving to make research useful.

There are also hopeful signs, however. The previous chapter showed new models for bringing head and hand together in the research process itself. The rise of service learning and community-based research models is transforming higher education in important ways. But we still have a ways to go. For it is not enough to change the way we do research. We also need to develop ways of linking research and practice that can directly confront the head-hand split. Doing so goes beyond fields like medicine where, even though the research is designed for application, there is still a division between medical researchers and medical practitioners, who communicate mainly through professional conferences and journals.

We can learn a lot about how to do this from all those working-class folks out there who have mastered the integration of head and hand, often without realizing it. Many of them, particularly skilled craft workers like my parents, must be able to do intellectual work in order to do their craft work. And every once in a while they become aware of just how much head work they are doing. When the Toledo Museum of Art and the University of Toledo commissioned the famous architect Frank Gehry to design a new addition to the museum that would house the university art program, he created one of his signature designs. There wasn't a right angle in the place. And he didn't provide detailed specifications on how to install all the utilities—plumbing, heating, and electric. The craft workers were nonplussed. How were they supposed to install utilities in such an oddly shaped structure? But as they worked on

the problem and came up with the plans, they began to realize how much intellectual work they were doing, and how much they were enjoying it. Instead of engaging in cookie-cutter designs they had done dozens of times before, they were actually employing, and enjoying, their craft. They had to make their "research" process conscious—understanding the building; discovering new ways of fitting pipe, running cable, and hiding conduit; testing design options.

Except among those academics in the fields of service learning and community-based research, there is no parallel to the head and hand integration of the "hand" professions. Formal research and practice are still separate. So when those trained in academia enter fields of community and organization practice, they find themselves running programs, on the one hand, and then trying to do the research necessary for writing grant applications and conducting evaluations on those grant-funded programs, on the other.

This chapter will explore the head and hand split between research and practice, building an integrated model of how to bring the two together. Here we will explore the "project-based research model" in all its glory, looking at how project cycles work and how research may fit in at each phase of a typical project cycle.

## FROM HEAD AND HAND
## TO RESEARCH AND ACTION

The version of the head and hand split that occurs out there in the field of community and organization change is the split between research and action. Making change involves action, whether that is organizational restructuring, community organizing, or broad-scale social movement action. Of course, effective action depends on good information, whether for understanding the possibilities and barriers to organizational change, or the possible allies and opposition around a policy issue. But rarely are these two things brought together as fully as they could be.

Practitioners often avoid doing research because they see the world from the perspective of doing programs. You choose a need among the many available out there. You write a grant proposal. If you get the grant you try to figure out how to do the work with so little money. You accomplish what you can, and when the money runs out you stop. Research takes too long, has too many up-front costs, and provides too little payoff.

In contrast, academics are increasingly trying to do useful research but often do it wrong because they see the world from the perspective of research as an isolated and independent activity. You choose a question that interests you. You write a grant proposal. If you get the grant you try to figure out how to do the research with so little money. You hopefully get your data collected and analyzed and write an article. Application is something that comes down the road, if at all, and is almost always done by someone else, who is supposed to take your general findings and apply them to a specific situation.

One of the reasons that both practitioners and academics are reluctant to see research as helpful is because they have been trained in research as an isolated activity, disconnected from any actual application. This is a disability for many of us when we need to conduct research that is useful.

For those of you who see the world first through the eyes of a researcher, we will begin from an unexpected angle—the project. For it is important to understand that research plays only a supporting role in the project-based research model. When I do training workshops in community-based research I often discuss the difference between how academics see the relationship between action and research and how practitioners see it.

Academics first approaching project-based research tend to see the project as a research project with only a few minor implications for application or action, whereas practitioners and other community members see it as a social change project where the action is most important and research is secondary. This has some important implications. First, the research can't exist independently from the project itself. Second, and even more important, the project is not a result of the research. The research is in fact a result of the project. That does not mean the research findings are determined by the project in a kind of "here are the conclusions, now get me some facts" way. Rather, the goals and the aims of the project, however general they may be, shape what the research question is, what kinds of methods will be used, how data will be collected, how it will be analyzed, and what will be done with it.

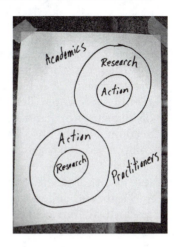

Furthermore, the research is but a small part of the project. There are so many other things going on. Take, for example, how the Association of Community Organizations for Reform Now (ACORN) has been approaching the issue of predatory lending—the practice of unscrupulous lenders loaning money at inflated interest rates to people whose credit is not good enough to qualify for a conventional loan, and then repossessing the home when the loan defaults. This practice threatens central city neighborhoods with continuing instability and housing inflation. When ACORN took on this issue, one thing they did was a national study of predatory lending to identify the worst offenders. But that was just a small part of the action. The bulk of their work was with residents in at-risk communities, educating them about the risks of predatory lenders; organizing them to do actions on legitimate lenders to pressure them to do more lending in those communities; and lobbying for changes in government policy and predatory corporate practices. The research is a crucial part of the campaign, but it is also a small part, and it exists only for the purpose of furthering the goals of the campaign. There is a small research staff working on the national predatory lending study. There are thousands of people working to change government policy, increase the flow of traditional lending dollars into excluded communities, and attack predatory lenders. Of course, those separate aspects of the campaign also require research—to identify the victims of predatory lenders in a community; find out the "CRA" ratings of local banks, which tell how carefully they are following the guidelines of the federal Community Reinvestment Act; and to develop policy alternatives.

How might this program look different if it was action guided by a research project? First, the scope of the project would likely be much more limited and its trajectory much more tentative. Research, as those of us in the profession have learned, rarely offers up certain findings across wide-ranging questions. It would also likely take much longer, and action would be restricted until the findings were secure and strictly verified. The research would likely also be developed independently of the project goals, and could even determine the project goals.

The shorter timeline, greater flexibility, and dependent nature of project-based research doesn't mean it is sloppier or less valid than traditional research. Remember, accuracy is paramount in any kind of change effort, and especially if the change effort is likely to encounter opposition. What it does mean is that the timeline is often compressed, the research question is often limited to something that is easily countable, and the presentation of results often occurs in less formal (and less lengthy) brochure or policy brief format.

To better understand how the project guides and shapes the research, then, we need to spend some time understanding how such community and organizational change projects are developed.

## OF PROGRAMS AND PROJECTS

What is the context in which project-based research operates? That depends on whom you ask. The further you get from the community, the more players you have who are invoked as "stakeholders" in any social change effort. Community members, unless they are local leaders intimately involved in the project, usually see only themselves and the ground-level workers involved with them. To the extent that they see anyone else as relevant in the context, it is often as the enemy or opposition. But move up to the level of the organization staff sponsoring an initiative, and they see an intense interconnection of agencies and organizations contributing. In the healthy communities model,[2] for example, you can find social service agencies, health clinics, hospitals, and colleges and universities. Funders may also be included among the stakeholders here, and when that happens the interlocking elites that control foundations can also be included among the players.

When we distinguish between programs and projects, we can better understand the roles of all these players in project-based research. A *program* is a more comprehensive social change initiative and often is a more abstract set of goals. A *project* is a specific implementation of one or more program goals.[3] In a comprehensive community initiative, the program attempts to simultaneously combine strategies to address social ills such as crime and unemployment with community-building activities and "bricks and mortar" community development activities.[4] Within a comprehensive community initiative program, individual projects may include general

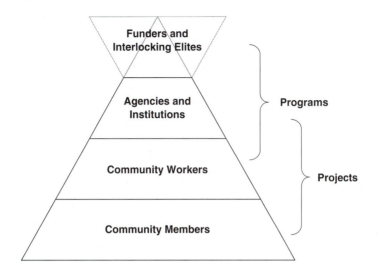

educational development (GED) classes, job training, neighborhood block watch, etc.

There is often a gap between the development of programs and projects that creates difficulties for both the success of the social change initiative and the conduct of any research supporting that initiative. Funders and elites, either because they sit on the boards of community organizations or because they control their purse strings, are often involved in developing or reviewing program goals. But they often know little about the specific projects implementing those program goals. Community members are much more likely to be involved in developing projects, through either direct participation or providing information to organization staff. But they typically are not involved in shaping the broader programmatic goals. Research, whether it is needs or asset assessments at the beginning of a project or evaluations at the end, is much more intimately connected to the project than to the program. This can create internal political problems if the research begins to lead individual projects in a direction different from the original program goals. This is particularly the case with funder-driven and regulation-driven programs. The main problem with such programs is that they are inadequately justified, guided, and monitored. It's not clear they fill a real need, serve an identified population, or succeed. The reason for this lack of clarity is that they were not developed, implemented, and evaluated through a careful research process with the involvement of the people they are purportedly designed to impact. One of the most interesting cases of an outsider-driven initiative that became a community-driven initiative occurred in the Dudley Street neighborhood of Boston. The Riley Foundation, in conjunction with a consortium of social service agencies, devised a plan and created an organization to revitalize Dudley Street in 1984. But at the first community meeting where they announced their plan, they were met with a firestorm of resident protest. The good news is that the community and the consortium then worked together to create the Dudley Street Neighborhood Initiative, becoming one of the model programs in the United States for doing projects with significant resident involvement.[5]

It is called *project-based research,* then, because it focuses on the development of concrete projects guided by people at the grassroots. Rarely in community and organization change efforts does support research study the upper levels of stakeholders except as targets of a social change effort. A main goal of project-based research is to amplify the voices and information of those who are rarely heard, so those voices and information can be used in designing specific interventions or organizational components that fit the expressed needs and desires of the constituency targeted by the program. The project comes first in such a model, and the research serves a support function, with one exception, which we will discuss in the next section.

## THE PROJECT MODEL: DIAGNOSE, PRESCRIBE, IMPLEMENT, EVALUATE

Social change projects, whether they occur at the level of an organization, community, or even society, go through identifiable stages. They begin with an attempt to diagnose a condition. Based on that diagnosis, the change agents choose a treatment or prescription. The treatment is implemented, and its impact is evaluated. Depending on the impacts, a new round of diagnosis, prescription, implementation, and evaluation may be required.

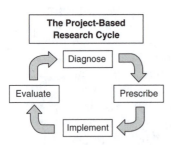

If we work with this medical metaphor for a moment, there are a number of different situational contexts where this model can be employed. First is the patient who displays sudden and acute symptoms and finds their way into the emergency room. The diagnosis, prescription, and implementation of treatment may need to occur quickly under such circumstances. Research support, in such circumstances, needs to be on-call and rigorous. This is the situation community organizations find themselves in with a sudden community disaster. When disaster relief organizations such as the Red Cross or the Federal Emergency Management Agency move into a community devastated by a flood, tornado, or other disaster, they need to do more than provide relief. They also must quickly research infrastructure needs—is there safe water; how long will it take to restore electricity; how many people need shelter and how much available shelter is there; and what other kinds of aid are available? That research determines whether water is trucked in, generators are set up, temporary shelters are constructed, and other services provided.[6]

Another metaphorical scenario is the patient who comes in for their annual checkup. If it is part of a regular checkup, the physician not only provides a general exam but also may order specific tests based on the patient's history. For many community organizations, the annual strategic planning process, described in Appendix A, fits this scenario. This process is a time for the organization to review its goals for the past year, determine what was achieved and what was not, and set goals for the next year. Because these planning processes are often scheduled far in advance, there is a lot of time to research goal achievement (in an evaluation framework) and/or to research changes in the resource environment that may provide new opportunities.

The third scenario, regrettably all too common in the fields of community practice and community health, is the chronic patient requiring continuing care for specific conditions. These are conditions about which the patient can make decisions that help control the effects of the condition, but the condition itself is outside of the individual's control—diabetes, asthma, and other such conditions cannot be blamed on the individual, just as economic disinvestment and lack of educational opportunity cannot be blamed on the individual suffering community. Yet, just as the patient with diabetes can make choices about what they eat, the community can make choices about how it responds to disinvestment. Research, in such cases, can help communities learn what the best practices may be in other places; what resources are available to implement various strategies for controlling some of the effects of disinvestment; and occasionally whether it is possible to attack contributing environmental factors at city hall, the local corporate headquarters, or even the federal government.

All of these communities, however, engage projects based on the diagnose, prescribe, implement, evaluate model. It is to that model that we now turn.

## 1. Diagnosing

What does it mean to diagnose a condition in a community or organization? In general, diagnosis involves identifying a "change opportunity." The community or organization might express concerns about various conditions, problems, needs, or issues.[7] From that list one or more problems need to be identified[8] and developed into a problem statement.[9] As we will see in the next chapter, this can happen in various ways and depends on whether the problem is being diagnosed in a social work, public health, education, community organizing, community development, multidisciplinary, or other context. The diagnosis of the internal community or organization components involves determining who is involved in defining the problem; who must be involved in implementing any change; who may or may not benefit; who may support or oppose change; and how open the community or organization is overall to change.[10] Most important, however, the diagnosis involves more than simply understanding the organization or community internally. It also involves understanding the external context or "macro reality."[11]

It is at this stage of diagnosis where the relationship between practice and research may be reversed.[12] In cases of disorganized community settings, where there is no identifiable and broadly legitimized community leadership, the research may precede the action. This is often the case in the field of community organizing, where the organizer conducts research through a door-knocking process, learning what concerns residents have. The organizer then uses that research to find out what the most pressing issues are and recruits residents to build an organization to address those and other problems. Once the organization is built, however, the research moves to a secondary position, determined by the organization's trajectory and history.

What kinds of research are done at this stage of the project cycle? Most popular are needs assessments, where a community or organization studies its own shortcomings, service gaps, or problems. But rising in popularity is the complementary model of asset mapping, where the focus of the research is not on problems but possibilities. While these two approaches are clearly complementary, the need vs. asset approach also generates a fair amount of controversy, as we will see in the next chapter. There are also many other more specific research procedures conducted to determine or verify the extent of an already determined need, such as studying the numbers and types of offenders being released into a community to determine the scope and quantity of services that may be needed to support their reentry. And one of the other important research processes is the "who-done-it" detective-style analysis of understanding the causal sequence of events that may have created a community cancer cluster, or caused housing abandonment, or led to skyrocketing truancy.

## 2. Prescribing

Once a situation has been diagnosed, it is time to begin exploring ways to impact it. This is often the most difficult part of program design and the most difficult part of the cycle to design research for. For at this stage the group managing the project is often engaging in a planning process. It may be strategic planning, where the group is charting a course for an organization. It may be program planning that involves a number of interconnected projects. It may be community land use planning limited to a specific, set land area and a limited set of development options. Or it may be limited to planning a narrowly defined project.

Another complication is that there may not have been careful research done to diagnose a problem, which is particularly the case with funder-driven projects. An organization may be implementing a program without knowing much about the need. A public health smoking-cessation program done without careful research to learn the extent of smoking, the situational factors contributing to smoking, and other details of the community where the program will be implemented will make program design all the more difficult.

There are nonetheless a number of information categories that need to be addressed at this stage of the project cycle. Most important, a group or organization may not know what project options are available to address the diagnosed problem or issue. In that case the first research project needed is a best-practices analysis. This may be as simple as a library or Web search, but it is often more complicated. As Chapter 5 will show, developing comparative research standards may be crucial to developing an effective prescription. Just as a physician will not prescribe certain antibiotics to patients with certain allergies, certain intervention projects won't work well in certain settings.

The other kind of information needed to make a prescription has to do with understanding the local resource base. One of the main tasks will be designing the details of the project, including how many personnel with what kinds of skills are needed to do the work, how long it will take, and what materials will be necessary.[13] It is helpful to know at the beginning of project planning whether the resources necessary to implement a particular prescription are available. This analysis goes beyond just seeing whether the money is available to also looking at what barriers to implementation may exist, including political opposition or risks.[14] If the goal is to create a community policing program, but the community is highly distrustful of the police, then that issue may need addressing before implementing any new program.

At this stage of the project cycle, then, a group or organization may be using a wide variety of research practices. They may do comparative research to judge the fit of different interventions from other places. They may conduct a community power study to judge local support for a particular intervention. They may use various forms of brainstorming or visioning processes to find out what solutions community members can come up with. They may also do policy research, particularly if the goal is to change a government or corporate policy. And in contrast to the diagnosis stage, where the research may occur somewhat independently from other organizational processes, at the prescription stage the research is carefully integrated with a planning process, with information gained from the research informing the planning process along the way, and the planning process informing what research is needed.

## 3. Implementing

We often think about the implementation stage as that part of the project cycle beyond research—after all, implementation is the *hand* part of the project cycle. But that is actually not the case at all. Especially if you are following a participatory research model, research may in fact *be* the project.

There are a number of cases where research is the project. Community theater and art projects provide the best examples of research as the project. Community theater, as a practice used to interpret community conditions, celebrate community characteristics, or present community problems, is integrally based on research into those conditions, characteristics, or problems. In some cases the art may be the result of diagnostic research, but often a group or organization chooses performance, visual, or other art as a medium and then conducts research to supports its development. A number of communities, as we will see in Chapter 6, have also developed community Web sites involving intensive community research.

What types of research are typically conducted to support community art/performance projects? The possibilities are innumerable, ranging from analyzing census statistics, or using Geographic Information Systems software, to digging through old historical records and conducting oral history interviews, to photography and other alternative data collection procedures. But there are a couple of research methods that show up regularly in community art and performance projects. One of those is oral histories, which are especially popular in cross-generational community art projects. Such projects typically involve youth interviewing community elders as part of a community history recovery project, or members of indigenous communities interviewing speakers of the indigenous language to preserve it. The other is case study analysis, where a group charts the causal sequence of a community issue or problem, using the data to present the information in artistic form.

Another set of examples where research becomes part of the project itself is in advocacy campaigns. A group that may have diagnosed a problem, and traced the cause to a government policy or a corporate practice, then engages in an advocacy campaign to change that policy or practice. In such situations the group needs more than good data about the problem. They also need data about the target of the change. In the case of a corporate target, that may involve who the major investors are, what the economic health of the corporation is, and what competitors there are. In the case of a government target, the research focuses on what the bureaucratic regulations and processes are for a policy change, as well as what the political vulnerabilities of public officials may be.

This form of research, often called *target research,* is also multi-methodological. It is the most challenging ethically because it sometimes involves clandestine research done undercover or through informants and closeted whistleblowers. It can also use a number of publicly available records, such as annual reports and tax records in the case of corporate targets and, in the case of government targets, employ the Freedom of Information Act.

## 4. Evaluating

Perhaps the most misunderstood part of the project cycle is the evaluation phase. Too often the evaluation phase is something required but not supported by funders, and the results are too often used to determine whether the project gets continued or renewed funding, rather than to actually improve the project design and implementation. In addition, evaluation is often conducted by outside researchers who may be only marginally familiar with the organization and/or the community and do their research only at the end of the project. And, finally, the preferred evaluation model is one that concentrates on *outcomes.* Measuring outcomes, such as changes in teen alcohol abuse, is challenging enough. Then attempting to determine whether the teen alcohol reduction project had any impact on those measured changes is even more difficult.

Consequently, those doing the hand work of project implementation often resent funders imposing evaluation requirements and outside researchers conducting those evaluations. Under such circumstances, especially when funding is on the line, getting good information can become a cat-and-mouse game. Organization staff try to "spin" the data they present to put on their best face, and may even withhold some information because they distrust the outside evaluator. This serves no one's purposes. Funders don't get good information on which to base funding decisions. Project managers don't get good information for planning successful implementations. And researchers lose credibility with both parties.

There are other evaluation models, however, that contrast with traditional evaluation in a number of important ways. First, they are designed to be used by those managing the project rather than by funders. In such *utilization-focused* evaluation[15] the goal is to provide information to those doing the project hand work so that they can make corrections along the way rather than only learn what worked and didn't work at the end of the project. Second, such evaluations are increasingly guided by those doing the project work rather than being designed by disconnected outside researchers. Such *empowerment* or *participatory evaluation*[16] models assure that the information collected will be directly useful to the people actually doing the work. Third, in these new evaluation models, the research starts when the project starts rather than being tacked on at the end. Chapter 7 will explore how the evaluation becomes part of even the diagnosis, prescription, and implementation stages of the project cycle. The more quickly the data is collected, analyzed, and reported, the more quickly the project managers can identify potential problems and unexpected successes and make any needed midcourse corrections.

As we will see, employing a utilization-focused, participatory evaluation method does not mean eschewing any concern about outcomes. Indeed, it is impossible to determine whether to make midcourse corrections without having good outcome measurement. What is different from traditional outcome evaluation, however, is that the project process is studied as rigorously as the project outcomes, focusing on understanding the causal path from the intervention to the outcome. And the measures are determined in close consultation with the people doing the project work, bringing hand and head together.

# THE PROJECT MODEL AND PARTICIPATORY FLEXIBILITY

Most of my focus so far has been on projects that occur at the local level. And indeed, that is where most project-level work occurs. But there are also many projects that occur on a much larger scale. Take the Kyoto Protocol on global warming, for example.[17] This is a global-level project attempting to reduce greenhouse emissions blamed by many for increasing global average temperatures and creating increasingly volatile climate changes. The research attempting to diagnose the extent of the problem and the validity of the theorized connection between global temperature rise and greenhouse gases is terribly complex. Then imagine attempting to evaluate the relationship between strategies and outcomes. There is not just a single project occurring at the level of the nation or world. Instead, there is a collection of separate projects occurring in many different locales. They may even have different goals. In Brazil, the global warming problem is more about the destruction of the Amazon rain forest. In the United States, the problem is much more about automobile emissions. But even in the U.S., there are places where the problem is much more about coal-fired power plants than about cars. Ultimately, then, the unit of analysis is often at least partly local. It may mean studying the emissions of a single coal-fired power plant and attempting to separate that plant's emissions from emissions drifting over hundreds of miles from other sources.

The need to both understand and separate the global and the local struck the public health field in the spring of 2003 with the discovery of Sudden Acute Respiratory Syndrome, or SARS. It was certainly not the first time that global and local had come together in a public health crisis, as acquired immunodeficiency syndrome (AIDS) had already created a model for studying the global transmission of disease. But SARS struck at a time of mass movement of people across the globe through airplanes. Interestingly, however, the main source of transmission did not seem to be airplanes. In fact, those most at risk of contracting the disease were medical staff, and it took some time for public health researchers to understand hospitals as a primary source of transmission. Once they did, new protocols for isolating patients, and standards for infection control, dramatically changed the way many hospitals approached a patient with a cough and fever.

The important point of this discussion is the need for flexibility. This book will present many cookie-cutter approaches to research at each phase of a social change project. But those cookie-cutter approaches will work only as well as the process that designs the research. Research fads put the research before the project. Take, for example, the explosion of interest in "social capital" in the 1990s. Made most famous by Robert Putnam's "bowling alone" thesis[18] that argued people were no longer engaged in collective community activities, therefore depriving the community of "social capital," projects sprang up to build social capital. But too few of those projects did adequate diagnostic research to understand the relationship between social capital and real capital—the lack of good jobs, fair mortgage rates, and locally owned commercial activity. In many poor communities, a lack of social networks was a consequence, not a cause, so interventions designed to build social capital started at the wrong end of the problem.

Another fad that puts method before process is the "logic model" framework being promoted by numerous foundations, including the United Way.[19] This model is propelled by the right motivation—to get community groups to think systematically about the relationship between goals, strategy, and the information needed to determine goal achievement. But from there, too many of the efforts degenerate into telling groups what their goals should be, what strategies they should use, and what measures are acceptable. Consequently, the logic models become fill-in-the-blank templates that restrict groups from custom-designing intervention processes and experimenting with new possibilities. And to the extent that groups are given less and less flexibility in determining their own goals, strategies, and measures, the logic model actually diminishes the role of research in determining what is best for a particular group facing a particular situation.

Project-based research requires a more flexible research process, less dictated by fads and more guided by community members. It uses the participatory research process outlined in Chapter 2 that involves community members at every stage of the research—from choosing the research question through reporting the results—to create projects that more accurately identify and target causes as well as consequences.

At each project phase, then, any research supporting it needs to go through the steps of choosing the question, designing the methods, collecting the data, analyzing the data, and reporting the results as collaborative activities. The more collective and participatory the process at each step, the more likely the research will take into account the uniqueness of the setting in which the project occurs and the context surrounding it.

# WHERE ARE YOU IN THE PROJECT CYCLE?

While the project cycle outline seems straightforward, determining where a group or organization is in that cycle can be more difficult than it may first appear. And, consequently, determining what research may be useful to a project can also be difficult. One of the things I do when I am working with a group is to ask them what activities they are engaged in and what kinds of information they need in doing those activities. We can often generate a very long list that would easily budget out to a six-figure grant application. Filling all of those information needs all at once is unrealistic, of course, so we then prioritize those needs by a series of questions:

1. What kinds of information are easiest (in terms of time, skill, and money) to get?
2. What kinds of information will provide the greatest immediate benefit to the project?
3. What kinds of information is the group or organization in the best position to use?

The answers to these questions can vary tremendously depending on where a group or organization is in the project cycle. A project designed to reduce teen alcohol and drug use would benefit tremendously from solid baseline research on the extent of alcohol and drug use among a specified teen population. But such information is extremely difficult to get. Imagine how long it would take to identify and develop trusting relationships with every teenager in a community to get reliable data on their alcohol and drug use to establish a baseline, and then do a follow-up after the program is finished. Instead, the need to finish the project on a certain schedule may only make it possible to do research with the teens in the project. A group that has already begun a breast cancer screening program is not in a position to second-guess whether the program is actually needed or appropriate. It may be in a position, however, to do an evaluation that can backtrack and compare project activities to a needs analysis of the target population.

Organizations involved in ongoing service activities will find it most difficult to decide where they are in the project cycle. Often, such organizations seem to be in a perpetual implementation phase, adapting to changes in laws and base budgets but otherwise providing a steady state of services. These are the organizations discussed in Chapter 1, who are so busy just providing services that they cannot imagine doing research to change or expand their activities. But those organizations often also go through regular internal reviews, or prepare annual reports, that require reflecting on their activities. Those providing direct services may also find new situations walking through the door on a regular basis but will only know that if they have a tracking system in place to help them identify new common issues arising in their constituency.

For those organizations not certain where they are in the project cycle, or what research may be most beneficial, the boxed list below may be of some value.

---

**Where Are You In the Project Cycle?**

*1. Diagnosis*

- We are noticing our clientele seeking different services than they used to.
- We know that X is a problem but are not sure why.
- We want to know what is going on in our community.
- We are redoing our strategic plan.

*2. Prescription*

- We want to know the best practices for dealing with situation X.
- We can get funding to do program X but don't know if it will work in our community.
- We need to know whether there is anything we can do about situation X with our resources.

*3. Implementation*

- We want to restore, preserve, or celebrate some aspect of our community/group.
- We need to find where the political opportunities are in our city government to win a policy issue.
- We need to find the leverage points to get a corporation to change its practices.

*4. Evaluation*

- We need to know if we are having any impact.
- We are trying to decide if we should change our mission or strategies.

---

This collection of statements is neither exhaustive nor mutually exclusive. It is possible, for example, that an organization revising its strategic plan—the document that sets the organization's goals and strategies—may wish to start with an evaluation of the success of its current strategic plan. But it may also be that the organization has accomplished the goals in its strategic plan and is trying to decide what to do next. That is the case with a number of community development corporations who have found themselves in the problematic position of having achieved their housing production goals. Now that they have no more vacant neighborhood land, and no more units to restore, they must find new needs to keep the organization going. Similarly, at the prescription phase, determining whether an intervention will work depends on an accurate diagnosis.

## LOOSE GRAVEL

Understanding the project cycle and where you are in it is not just important to deciding what to research. It is also important to deciding, literally, what to do. Knowing whether you have done an adequate diagnosis before beginning a program; have carefully studied all the options before making a final prescription; are following through on what you said you were going to do in the implementation; and are paying careful attention to evaluating your progress is crucial to project success. Research, remember, is but a single component of a much larger and more complex process, and it exists only as support for the project itself. That complexity becomes enmeshed in the relationship between the research and the project itself, leading to two types of loose gravel along the way. One is about time and the other is about politics.

### Of Timelines and Deadlines

A few years ago a couple of my graduate students worked with one of the local community organizations here collecting data to support a $50,000 grant proposal to build a community policing program. Their job was to go through pages and pages of crime reports and victim evaluations from the neighborhood, determining the frequency of various types of crimes and average scores for police response. The information had to be available, on a strict deadline, so the organization could submit their grant proposal. It was, and the organization got their grant. It was a proud moment for me as a professor because the students had committed themselves to the project's timeline rather than to the semester timeline (which didn't fit the project at all).

As we saw in the previous chapter, deadlines in community work are often much more strict than they are in academic work. But the conditions under which community organizations work are often also much less stable. The loose gravel here is how to determine and meet strict deadlines at the same time that the project timeline is shifting like sand blowing in the desert. I recently did research with the West Bank Community Development Corporation in Minneapolis's Cedar-Riverside neighborhood, introduced in the previous chapter, to support their strategic planning process. Strategic planning processes normally take a few months. But in this case, a rapidly deteriorating economy and local political conflicts disrupted the CDC's housing development timeline, delaying the sale of CDC-owned houses in the neighborhood and disrupting its cash flow. In addition, a lawsuit between the CDC and a group of residents stalled the planning process and detoured other CDC funds to lawyers. In the midst of this, quite understandably, the CDC director suffered a heart attack. Only now, two years later as I wrote the first draft of this chapter, did we return to the strategic planning process that the original research process was to support. A lot has happened since the summer of 2001, far beyond terrorist attacks and wars.

Had we been able to foresee all that would happen, we would have delayed the research. Some of the original research, documenting which other organizations operate in the community that the CDC can partner with, needs to be updated. But the need to get the strategic plan in place quickly, once houses were being sold and the cash flow improved, made that impractical.

This is not an unusual circumstance. Matching the flow of the research to the flow of the project cycle is tricky, and a bad match can be costly. If the research gets too far ahead of the project cycle it can become out of date by the time it is used. If the research gets too far behind, the project may have to move ahead without it. This is where the need to combine research expertise with project expertise becomes crucial. To the extent that no one in the project can predict either how long the research will take or how long the project will take, one of the first research activities involves determining the time and money resources needed for certain kinds of projects and certain kinds of research.

What I often do to organize support research for a community change project, which will be outlined more in the coming chapters, is a "backward" planning process. I work most often with neighborhood organizations, and we often start by bringing together

**Planning Research Backward**

1. What are the goals and desired outcomes of the project?

2. What are the activities needed to achieve those goals and outcomes?

3. What information is needed along the way, at various points in the project cycle, to support those activities?

4. How can that information best be obtained?

neighborhood residents with organization staff for a planning process. We look at where in the project cycle the group or organization is to see what kinds of research are most beneficial. We then discuss what the goals of the project are (or should be if they are not yet determined)—essentially looking a year or more down the road. Starting from that future, we move back in time to discuss the steps needed to reach those goals and what is involved in achieving each step. We then focus on outlining what the research will involve, based on where in the project cycle the group or organization needs the research. I can bring some experience on how much time different kinds of research require (though I am still surprised sometimes when we actually do the research). By the time we are done, after a couple of hours, we have a pretty good idea of what is needed to do the research and the project.

This "backward" planning process is common in the strategic planning field.[20] What is not common, however, is the integration of research with the strategic planning process. It is, in fact, possible for highly resourced projects to integrally plan the project and its needed support research at each step of the project cycle.

## The Politicized Research Process

Community change projects, even those being done as social service, are often political. Making social change means disrupting stable patterns of power and interaction. And those patterns, however unhealthy they may be, often also feel comfortable even to those suffering.

What are some of the sources of research politicization? Well, they come primarily from the politicization of the project. The organization doing the project may be politicized as a competitor in a multi-organizational field or a politically factionalized community. Those doing the project may be politicized as "outsiders" by community members. A social change effort may be politicized by threatened elites or public officials. And an organization may be politicized internally by research that may expose organizational weaknesses or other problems.

One of the most interesting examples comes from El Paso, where a group of high school students, in partnership with a community organization, researched the lending practices of area banks. The research generated intense publicity even before it was finished. As the publicity increased, banks' willingness to participate in the research decreased. This was a political minefield for the local university, even though it was only indirectly connected to the research at the time. But careful negotiations between university representatives, bankers, and local businesses actually produced funding for a university-led study seen as having less bias but still involving the students.[21]

This form of target research often produces the most dangerous political situations and is one of the most important examples of why the project needs to take priority over the research. Without an already organized group building political power to take on powerful institutions like banks, an individual piece of research, and particularly an individual researcher, can be extremely vulnerable. But organized groups can counter the power of money with the power of people, preserving the integrity of research and allowing it to support the power-building process.

While the politicization of target research can make life difficult for community change efforts, in some ways an even riskier form of research focuses internally on a community or organization. The issues involved in doing community history recovery or internal project evaluations will be treated in depth in the chapter on implementation and the appendix on ethics. For our immediate purposes, it is important to understand what the general risks are. Any research that focuses inwardly, using a participatory approach, on the history and culture of a community carries with it the risk of letting skeletons out of the closet and cats out of the bag, consequently rekindling old feuds and resentments. More than that, it carries the additional risk of creating new feuds and resentments. What happens when the research documents the failure of a past community project and names names in assigning cause to the failure? What happens when the research documents differences in power and prestige, however minute, between community members?

There are those in community settings who will commission the research for their own ends and purposes rather than for community ends and purposes, and who want to control the flow of information. Thankfully, these individuals are relatively easy to identify. They are the ones who do not want to share information within the organization or among their constituency. And this is one of the challenges of "working from the middle," discussed in the previous chapter, where the organization is not connected to its constituency in any substantial way. Some service organizations want to be more connected to their communities and welcome the opportunity to employ research as a way to develop that connection. Others have more of a social control orientation and refuse to share information with their constituency, or argue that "they" wouldn't be able to understand it or wouldn't be interested in it.

For those of us who do project-based research—either from the inside as organization members or from the outside as researchers for hire—the politics of community change requires that we often add a step to the research process. Before we engage in community-based research processes, we need to do adequate "pre-research." The pre-research process involves studying the community itself to understand its leadership structure, resource distribution, organizational infrastructure, and culture. By doing so, you can identify factions, uncover actual or potential resentments, and begin to get hints of what closeted skeletons and bagged cats may be lurking in the corners of the community.

In addition, the pre-research process also begins to build relationships in the community. Indeed, learning who will and will not talk to you as the researcher is one way to quickly begin to understand where the trust lines are drawn. In a recent research project I engaged in, involving door-to-door interviews as part of a project evaluation, one of the things we began to learn about was a neighborhood faction angry at a prominent community organization. Some community members, in hearing this organization was one of the research sponsors, even refused to talk to me. Others gave me an earful about how they believed the organization had bypassed them for benefits or shortchanged them in favor of another perceived community faction. At this point our research project became a pre-research project, helping us reconsider how to get accurate information. Thankfully, because the research was being sponsored by a number of community organizations in coalition, we could emphasize the research as serving the coalition, which was less well known in the community but also not politicized.

Pre-research does not have to be a highly sophisticated process, but there are a set of questions that can guide the researcher's information-gathering:

1. How is formal power distributed in the community or organization? Who is most influential in determining who gets and who doesn't get? Who is connected to power holders outside of the community or organization, impacting how resources flow across those boundaries?

2. How is informal power distributed in the community or organization? Who is seen as a strong role model or source of advice, regardless of whether they occupy any formal leadership position?

3. If formal leaders and informal leaders are different people, what is the relationship between them? What is the history of their relationships? Are there long-standing resentments or unfriendly competitions?

4. What are the controversial issues in the community or organization and how do people line up on those issues? Are people deeply polarized on any issues? Are formal and/or informal leaders deeply polarized?

5. Where does the proposed research project fall in this web of power and relationships? In what ways could it contribute to increased polarization or conflict between community or organization leaders and members?

Often the most convenient place to start addressing these pre-research questions is within the group or organization sponsoring the research, asking for a sense of the community. They will typically identify other individuals to speak with. When the research will focus on a community, asking about what service organizations, churches, and businesses are important in the community will provide a lot of information. In an organization setting, asking about how the organization was founded and how it has changed will provide information on its stability and potential points of internal conflict. Old newsletters or newspapers, especially at the micro- community setting, often identify influential individuals and organizations. None of this needs to be done clandestinely. In fact, I find that I develop the most trust when I am the most honest, explaining how the research, and the project it is supporting, can go awry if all parties concerned don't have a shared understanding of the political fault lines in the community or organization and how those may impact the research process. Of course, if you are an outside researcher, you don't just blurt out that you need to know what the factions are at the first research planning meeting. Trust and relationships are as crucial at the pre-research stage as they are at all stages of the project-based research process itself.

## Head and Hand . . . and Heart?

It is true that being able to reflect on the work of community change—bringing head and hand together—is a luxury. Funders will still not often pay for the information-gathering activities necessary to make the most of community change projects. Community groups and organizations still lack the capacity to take on such support research themselves. But we will see that there are numerous examples of groups and organizations employing community-based research, often with the aid of pro-bono researchers from colleges and universities.

While skepticism remains that research can support social change, there is also significant hope that it can. Community change is about more than just integrating hand work and head work. It is also, fundamentally, about heart work. The hours are too long, the pay too low, the risks too high, and the sacrifices too great to do community work for solely practical or intellectual reasons. In the many project-based research activities with which I have been involved, I have sat around the table with mothers who have lost their teenagers to gunfire, coal miners who have lost their health to coal dust, parents who have lost their homes to corporate disinvestment, residents who have lost their neighbors to carcinogens in their water, and many other people suffering many other losses and indignities. Their commitment to doing everything possible to create a better future for themselves, their neighbors, and their children starts in the heart. And it is their heart that requires us to find ways to make sure their efforts succeed. They have the heart and they are doing the hand work. What they often need is support for the head work. Sometimes that simply means having extra hands to collect information. Other times it means having expertise to gather accurate information. But when brought together, the heart-hand-head combination does more than support community change. It also helps make all of us more whole.

## CONCLUSION

These past three chapters have focused on the foundation of project-based research. Chapter 1 looked at the general underpinnings of applied research. Chapter 2 looked at the processes of participatory research. This chapter has tried to bring those principles together in outlining the model of project-based research, which included:

- Reconnecting head and hand, or in this case research and action
- Distinguishing programs and projects, and focusing project-based research at the project level

- Specifying what happens at each of the stages of project-based research: diagnosis, prescription, implementation, and evaluation
- Practicing participatory flexibility
- Judging where you are in the project cycle

We also looked at some of the difficulties involved in project-based research, including:

- Managing timelines and deadlines
- Doing research in politicized contexts

These first three chapters have been the building blocks, the foundation, for what is to come. Next we will move into the details of each step of the project-based research cycle, beginning in Chapter 4 with diagnosing.

## RESOURCES

### Developing and Designing
### Programs and Projects in a Community Setting

Kettner, P., Daley J. M., & Nichols, A. W. (1985). *Initiating change in organizations and communities: A macro practice model.* Monterey, CA: Brooks/Cole Publishing Company.

Netting, E., Kettner, P. M., & McMurty, S. L. (1993). *Social work macro practice.* New York: Longman.

Kirst-Ashman, K. K., & Hull, G. H., Jr. (2001). *Generalist practice with organizations and communities* (2nd ed.). Stamford, CT: Brooks/Cole.

Alinsky, S. (1969). *Reveille for radicals.* New York: Vintage.

Alinsky, S. (1971). *Rules for radicals.* New York: Vintage.

Bobo, K., Kendall, J., & Max, S. (1991). *Organizing for social change: A manual for activists in the 1990s.* Washington, DC: Seven Locks Press.

Beckwith D., with Lopez, C. (1997). Community organizing: People power from the grassroots. COMM-ORG Working Papers Series, 1997 Working Papers, http://comm-org.utoledo.edu/papers.htm

## NOTES

1. Plato. (1974). *The Republic.* Translated by G. M. A. Grube (Trans.). Indianapolis: Hackett Publishing Co.

2. Hancock, T. (1993). The evolution, impact and significance of the healthy cities/healthy communities movement. *Journal of Public Health Policy, 14,* 5–18.

3. Kettner, P., Daley, J. M., & Nichols, A. W. (1985). *Initiating change in organizations and communities: A macro practice model* (p. 33). Monterey, CA: Brooks/Cole Publishing Company.

4. Smock, K. (1997). Comprehensive community initiatives: a new generation of urban revitalization strategies. In R. Stoecker (Ed.). *COMM-ORG Papers*. Retrieved July 15, 2004, from http://comm-org.utoledo.edu/papers.htm

5. Medoff, P., & Sklar, H. (1994). *Streets of hope: The fall and rise of an urban neighborhood.* Boston: South End Press.

6. Board on Natural Disasters, National Research Council. (1999). *Reducing disaster losses through better information.* Washington, D.C.: National Academies Press.

7. Kettner, P., Daley, J. M., & Nichols, A. W. (1985). *Initiating change in organizations and communities: A macro practice model* (p. 26).

8. Kirst-Ashman, K. K., & Hull, G. H., Jr. (2001). *Generalist practice with organizations and communities* (2nd ed.) (p. 298). Stamford, CT: Brooks/Cole.

9. Meenaghan, T. M., Washington, R. O., & Ryan, R. M. (1982). *Macro practice in the human services: An introduction to planning, administration, evaluation, and community organizing components of practice* (p. 21). New York: Free Press.

10. Netting, E., Kettner, P. M., & McMurty, S. L. (1993). *Social work macro practice* (p. 224). New York: Longman. See also: Kettner, P., Daley, J. M., & Nichols, A. W. (1985). *Initiating change in organizations and communities: A macro practice model* (p. 26).

11. Kirst-Ashman, K. K., & Hull, G. H., Jr. (2001). *Generalist practice with organizations and communities* (p. 298).

12. Stoecker, R. (1999). Are academics irrelevant? Roles for scholars in participatory research. *American Behavioral Scientist, 42,* 840–854.

13. Kettner, P., Daley, J. M., & Nichols, A. W. (1985). *Initiating change in organizations and communities: A macro practice model* (pp. 28–29).

14. Netting, E., Kettner, P. M., & McMurty, S. L. (1993). *Social work macro practice* (p. 224). See also: Kirst-Ashman, K. K., & Hull, G. H., Jr. (2001). *Generalist practice with organizations and communities* (p. 298).

15. Patton, M. Q. (1997). *Utilization-focused evaluation: The new century text* (3rd ed.). Thousand Oaks, CA: Sage Publications.

16. Fetterman, D. M., Kaftarian, S. J., & Wandersman, A. (Eds.). (1996). *Empowerment evaluation: Knowledge and tools for self-assessment and accountability.* Thousand Oaks, CA: Sage Publications. Also see Stoecker, R. (1999). Making connections: Community organizing, empowerment planning, and participatory research in participatory evaluation. *Sociological Practice, 1,* 209–232.

17. The United Nations Framework Convention on Climate Change. (2004). *The convention and the Kyoto protocol.* Retrieved July 15, 2004, from http://unfccc.int/resource/convkp.html

18. Putnam, R. D. (2000). *Bowling alone: The collapse and revival of American community.* New York: Simon & Schuster.

19. United Way of America. (2004). United Way of America outcome measurement resources. Retrieved July 15, 2004, from http://national.unit edway.org/outcomes/resources/. See also W. K. Kellogg Foundation. (n.d.). *Logic model development guide.* Retrieved July 15, 2004, from http://www .wkkf.org/Programming/ResourceOverview.aspx?CID=281&ID=3669

20. See Appendix A for more information on strategic planning.

21. Staudt, K., & Brenner, C. T. (2002). Higher education engages with community: new policies and inevitable political complexities. In R. Stoecker (Ed.). *COMM-ORG papers.* Retrieved July 15, 2004, from http://comm-org. utoledo.edu/papers2002/staudt.htm

# *Four*

## Diagnosing

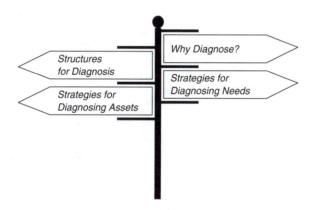

## HOW TO SURVIVE ON A DESERTED ISLAND

There is an old joke in academic circles about the physicist, the chemist, and the economist who find themselves suddenly shipwrecked on a deserted island with only a case of canned beans to eat. The problem is, they need to find a way to open the cans.

> *Physicist:* Well, I can calculate the amount of force needed to split the seam of the can based on the mass and trajectory of the object we use.

So we can just find a big enough rock and throw it hard enough and that will do it.

*Chemist:* That's too messy. I can tell you how hot of a fire to build in order to heat the contents of the can so that the seam will split.

*Economist:* Wow, that would really be messy. I have the perfect solution. Let's just assume we have a can opener!

For those of you who never had an economics course, or slept through it, economists are regularly criticized for ignoring reality. And that would be a good enough start to this chapter. But the joke is actually even more telling of the wrong way to approach project-based research. Here are three people stranded on a deserted island, and their first thought is how to behave as if they are not. In project-based research, the first task would be to *diagnose* the island—carefully exploring its potential risks and resources. Maybe the island is teeming with easily identified and safe fruits, vegetables, roots, and herbs that would make all those baked beans seem pretty second-rate.

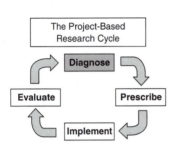

Even more important than what to do when you find yourself suddenly stranded on a deserted island without a can opener is what to do when you find yourself immersed in an inhabited community. This chapter is about what to do if you find yourself in the position of choosing and starting a project in a community. It is about the most creative stage of project-based research. The next project stages—prescribing, implementing, and evaluating—are often constrained by what happens in the previous stage. But at the very beginning, the diagnosis stage, the research is as much art as craft. At this earliest stage of project development, it is often the case that nothing is formed. The "community" may not even exist as such—it may just be a conglomeration of individuals sharing a common geography but not interacting or defining themselves as a group. There may be no representative organization to work with. Of course, it may also be the case that the community is highly organized and already has a history of successful project cycles, in which case they probably don't need anyone's help. But those are rare circumstances. The old adage that the goal of social workers is to work themselves out of a job is seldom realized, and examples of poor and excluded communities that have transformed themselves into stable, middle-class strongholds are extremely rare.

So the "research" process of this initial stage of project development is about much more than research. It is about bringing people together to think about, understand, and reflect on their situation. This chapter is about how to bring people together and how to use diagnostic research in the service of bringing people together.

## THE IMPETUS FOR DIAGNOSIS

What starts a diagnostic process? Interestingly, the impetus often comes from outside the community. Perhaps the most famous case of outsiders attempting to diagnose a community was the Dudley Street Neighborhood Initiative. Remember, from the previous chapter, that DSNI began as a collaboration between the Riley Foundation and area social service providers who were going to revitalize this disinvested and declined section of Roxbury, in Boston. But when they entered the community they hadn't done their diagnostic homework and were surprised to find a large group of energized residents who saw the outsiders as invaders. The reaction forced the outsiders to begin working collaboratively with community members, eventually building a community organization board controlled by community members.[1]

Another model practiced by outsiders entering a community comes from the age-old practice of community organizing. Made famous by Saul Alinsky[2] in the middle of the 20th century, community organizing is the process of bringing people together to build an organization that can help them increase their influence over public decisions. Saul Alinsky was best known for helping poor and working-class people organize entertaining disruptions that forced governments and corporations to finally listen to those communities. In one case he helped a Chicago group organize a "shit-in" at O'Hare Airport, back in the days when you didn't need a ticket to get to the concourse and you had to put a quarter in a slot to use a toilet. With just a quarter you could bring some light reading material and occupy a toilet all day. A relatively small group could occupy every toilet at the airport. Horrified

> **Why Do Diagnostic Research?**
> - To fix a problem
> - To make a change
> - To oppose something
> - To propose something

public officials, when they caught wind of this carefully leaked plan, immediately entered into negotiations with the community organization.[3]

There is great diversity in the field of community organizing today, with a wide variety of models. Some emphasize working with neighborhoods, while others emphasize working with identity communities.[4] Some have a confrontational style, using actions and protests against those they see as harming the community,[5] while others practice a cooperative style of working with power holders in government and corporations.[6] But they all share the characteristic of using specially trained community organizers who bring people together to build a strong, stable organization.

One of the first tasks of the community organizer is to get to know the community, and that often involves doing diagnostic research. As the community organizer knocks on residents' doors, the main question they ask is "what are the issues and concerns in this neighborhood?" This process is often not formal research that follows all the rules of reliability and validity, but it gives the organizer a pretty good idea of what concerns people and who is the most concerned. The organizer then invites people to a neighborhood meeting discuss those concerns. That first meeting creates the initial core group that builds the organization. They choose an issue to work on and build a plan for tackling that issue.[7]

Once the group has chosen an issue, they almost invariably find that they need formal diagnostic research, even for simple things. In community organizing, one of the golden rules is to start with an issue that is relatively easy to win. The symbolic starter issue used to be the stop sign. A new community group would find a dangerous, uncontrolled intersection with a history of accidents and incidents and organize to get a stop sign for it. Today the starter issue for many groups seems to be speed bumps—those asphalt humps on residential streets that will ruin your shocks if you go over them at more than 15 miles an hour. Where I live, getting a speed bump requires intense diagnostic research. You either have to get the traffic department to come out and put a traffic counter on the street, or you have to count the cars that go by yourself. It also helps if you can get the police to come out with a radar gun to document the number of cars speeding down the street. Further research can involve documenting the number of children who live on the street, or who cross it during the day. Armed with that research, the group then goes to city hall to lobby for a speed bump, or perhaps a stop sign.

On issue-based organizing like this, the process seems straightforward enough. Some group identifies a problem and then sets to work on it, doing whatever research is necessary to address the problem. But there are other, more challenging situations. Not all community projects begin with a problem. If we stretch the medical metaphor a bit, we will see that there are a number of reasons to visit your family physician. One is because you are sick. But you may also be going for an annual exam just to make sure everything is working the way it should. Or maybe you want to start an exercise program and need some physician advice. Or perhaps you are traveling overseas and need some inoculations. Diagnosis, in these cases, may find a problem you didn't think you had, or may focus on understanding your tolerance for a particular drug or fitness routine. In the social research world, such diagnoses may include determining the suitability of an area for certain kinds of development, or to find previously unknown community resources and resident skills. So you may be doing diagnostic research because you have identified a problem you want to change. Or you may be doing it in the hopes of finding opportunities that can be built upon. These different motives will lead to different processes and produce different structures to guide the diagnostic research process.

## STRUCTURES FOR A DIAGNOSTIC PROCESS: THE CORE GROUP

Who decides in diagnostic research? Answering this question requires us to bring in one of those over-misused words: *stakeholder*. Most of the applied researchers out there say you need to have some kind of advisory group that represents the various interests at stake in a project. What is a stakeholder? In brief a stakeholder is a person, group, or organization that has a "stake" in the outcome of a decision. In other words, they are likely to gain or lose something depending on which way the decision goes. It is pretty easy to get carried away with this, however. Take the question of building new housing in a working-class neighborhood. Certainly those who live next to those houses have a stake in what kinds of houses are built and how they are marketed. Likewise, local businesses that depend on the neighborhood, like corner carry-outs, have a stake in the housing. Government has a stake in the housing, either because it may have to pay for it or because it may generate additional property taxes. Contractors who might build the houses, lenders who might make loans to buy the houses, and insurers who might insure the houses also have stakes. And what about other neighborhoods, which might lose population to those new houses? You can see how out of control it can get.

Thankfully, in most of those projects, most of those people aren't interested in being involved. In fact, unless the project involves millions of dollars, the problem is recruiting people to plan the project rather than keeping them away. But it is always helpful to keep in mind who the "indirect stakeholders" (those who might be theoretically impacted sometime in the future of the project) might be, since at least some of those people will be in the position of deciding whether to fund the project or approve it on some level. And those are the people your diagnostic research will need to convince.

Instead of concentrating on stakeholders, then, I have found it useful to think in terms of forming a *core group*. There is not a lot of difference between the two, except that a core group is more likely to be recruited from those who are directly impacted and are also interested in the research process. So how do you create a core group to guide a diagnostic process? That depends on what you are trying to diagnose and the political landscape.

When Lois Gibbs started worrying about the health problems affecting her neighbors in the Love Canal neighborhood near Niagara Falls, she helped found the Love Canal Homeowners Association. Their diagnostic research included testing their homes, water, and resident health, as well as researching the history of land use in the area, which showed they were basically living on a toxic dump. The residents formed LCHA to publicize the results of their diagnostic research and get help from the government to relocate residents. When government-sponsored research disputed their contention that they were being poisoned, it became all the more clear that the residents had only themselves to rely on. So confrontational did it become that LCHA members even held officials from the federal Environmental Protection Agency "hostage" at one point to show how strongly they felt about the issue.[8]

In a situation like this, where a community is pitted against outsiders, the universe of possible stakeholders obviously includes people on both sides of the issue. But it is also clear that the people on one side (usually government or corporate actors) have a lot more power than people on the other side. And the self-interests of the two sides clash. In such situations it often does not make sense to include stakeholders from the other side. The people with the problem need to populate the core group to guide and organize around the diagnostic research effort.

Other stakeholder groups come together across political boundaries. The federal Community Outreach Partnership Center (or COPC) program supports projects led by stakeholder groups that include academics, bankers, government officials, and neighborhood residents in the belief that it is possible to work together.[9] The asset-based community development (or ABCD) model also emphasizes the involvement of a wide cross section of stakeholders in the method of asset mapping that we will discuss below.[10] The Healthy Communities model, which focuses on developing community-based health education and treatment programs, also builds stakeholder groups across political boundaries.

There is no one model for building an effective project stakeholder or core group, and it is beyond the scope of this book to look at the many thorny issues of project management. But we need to deal with the question of stakeholders to the extent that it impacts project-based research because at least some subset of the stakeholders will likely be involved in guiding the research. In forming a stakeholder or core group to guide the research, there are a set of important questions to take into account:

> **Forming a Research Stakeholder or Core Group**
>
> 1. Is the context of the project characterized by conflict or consensus?
>
> 2. Do you embrace or avoid conflict? Does your approach fit the situation?
>
> 3. Is there already a formal or informal stakeholder group formed?

## 1. Is the Context of the Project Characterized By Conflict or Consensus?

The pre-research process will already have given you some indication of how comfortable or volatile the context is. And the importance of understanding this cannot be underestimated. Bringing together a group of people who will only fight and sabotage each other, or at the very least will not trust each other, can not only prevent helpful research but disrupt the project itself. If the situation is one of powerless insiders against powerful outsiders, it may be better to work with just the powerless insiders and use the research to help equalize the power. There are other circumstances where the conflict is between insider factions, and both must be present. One of my early project-based research undertakings—studying the relationship between community organizing and community development activities for a coalition of community organizations, community development corporations, and funders—ran headlong into a conflict between a faction that wanted new funds to go to development only and a faction that wanted to use money to promote community organizing. Far from bringing the factions together the research contributed to the ultimate demise of the coalition.[11] I am still convinced that this was the only desirable outcome because it prevented the funders from taking over the coalition, but it was an unpleasant reality.

## 2. Do You Embrace or Avoid Conflict?
## Does Your Approach Fit the Situation?

Knowing yourself in project-based research is crucial. If the situation is rife with conflict, and you are a conflict avoider who wants to bring everyone together to hold hands, you may need to control your impulses. Conflict, especially in group settings, often has to be worked through rather than avoided, and that takes a highly skilled facilitator. Likewise, if you are regularly on the lookout against conspiracies and cabals, make sure you don't overinterpret the disgruntlement of one or two people as deep factions. They may be only a faction of one or two. While there are conflict creators out there, they tend to lose legitimacy in a group pretty quickly. More challenging are the conflict avoiders, who are so nice that they often don't realize how unequal the power imbalances are in many stakeholder groups. I have sat around a number of research planning tables and have watched the "principal investigator" carry on long and friendly discussions with the people around the table occupying powerful positions, virtually ignoring community residents, and then wondering why the residents stop coming. And I have spoken with those residents, who do not see everyone around the table as one big happy family. A traditionally structured stakeholder group may need to go through some confrontation and truth-telling before everyone can get down to business.

## 3. Is There Already a Formal or
## Informal Stakeholder Group Formed?

Regardless of what the ideal group may be, you may have to begin by working with an already formed stakeholder group. There is often nothing wrong with that. Sometimes, however, when you commence the research, you begin to find people who resent being left out. I have had two recent experiences where, as I began conducting interviews in a community, certain community leaders who were left out of the research stakeholder group deeply questioned its legitimacy. In one case, they organized a small group to attend the meeting where the research results were to be presented, causing a bit of a stir when they began asking why the research did not include questions about their concerns. In the event that there is already such a stakeholder group formed, it may be useful for the group itself to answer questions 1 and 2 above.

# STRATEGIES FOR A DIAGNOSTIC PROCESS: PROBLEMS AND OPPORTUNITIES

This theme of conflict vs. consensus effects more than the structure of the group guiding the research. It ultimately affects the research strategy itself. Remember that old proverb that a problem is just an opportunity turned inside out? Well, that always seemed a little disingenuous to me. If your child has just been murdered in a drive-by shooting, stopping the killing is not an opportunity—it is an imperative. Problems and opportunities are different things, and they lead to different kinds of diagnostic research. The main form of diagnostic research that centers on problems is the needs assessment. In needs assessment, the focus is on understanding the difference between a current condition and an ideal condition.[12] Needs assessments diagnose what is *missing*. The main form of diagnostic research dealing with opportunities is asset mapping. Asset mapping involves understanding the array of capacities and social networks, what some call *social capital*, on which social change projects can be built. Asset mapping diagnoses what is *present*.

Before looking at how to use each of these models, we need to spend a few moments on the argument between them. Ever since asset mapping became popular in the mid-1990s, it has been embroiled in controversy. John Kretzmann and John McKnight, the founders of the method and its associated model of asset-based community development, evoked the ire of many by criticizing the dominant needs-based approach to community development. The old approach, they argued, portrayed poor communities as helpless and powerless. Consequently, resources were directed to outside experts and service providers rather than to the community itself, reinforcing the perception that the community was incapable of helping itself.[13] The influence of their model was quite dramatic, as funders and agencies jumped on the asset-based bandwagon and started doing asset mapping in poor community after poor community. For many, asset-based community development epitomized the pull-yourself-up-by-your-bootstraps philosophy that had hung on from the 1980s, placing the responsibility for community change—appropriately, they believed—on the shoulders of community members.

The critics of the asset-based model, and its emphasis on social capital, were vocally opposed to what they saw as a right-wing turn in the asset-based model. Focusing on a community's social capital implied that the community bore sole responsibility not only for its own improvement but for its deteriorated condition to begin with. The asset-based model, they charged, absolved government and corporations for disinvesting from those communities. Looking at poor communities through rose-colored glasses, the critics argued, allowed funders to turn their backs, government to shrug its shoulders, and corporations to escape blame.

Sadly, however, much of the argument has been misdirected. Part of the problem is that Kretzmann and McKnight's original critique of the needs-based model overshot its target. The risks of disempowering communities occurred with the social service approach to community change, not with the community organizing approach. Indeed, from a social service approach, needs are something to be filled by outside experts. But from a community organizing approach, needs are caused by outsiders, not fixed by them, and it is up to the community to organize and demand that those needs be filled. In addition, the many advocates of the asset-based model were so taken by it that they neglected to heed Kretzmann and McKnight's warning that focusing on assets does not mean communities can develop independently of outside resources. Of course, less than one page of discussion on needs in a 376-page manual didn't help to make the point!

We are left, then, with polarized approaches to needs assessments and asset mapping. In the next sections we will focus on the application of each approach and then look at a combined method.

## THE PROBLEMS APPROACH: NEEDS ASSESSMENT

In conducting a needs assessment, remember, the focus is on understanding the gap between what is and what people want there to be. Getting to that point is the interesting part. One thing that makes it interesting is that it is often possible to find many needs in any community or organization, and choosing one to focus on is the challenging part. Additionally, nailing down what people want, in order to establish the scope of the need, is often a very difficult task.

Consequently, needs assessments can begin in two different ways. A group or organization at the beginning of a strategic planning process, where they are trying to set goals for their work for the next year or longer, often begins with a wide coverage approach to find the universe of needs out there. Following this initial step, the group will choose one need to diagnose. In many cases, however, a need arises in a community without a broad survey, and the social change project begins with researching the specific, identified need.

These correspond to the distinction between intensive research and extensive research discussed in Chapter 1. Remember that extensive research uses a large number of cases to understand the characteristics of a population, while intensive research studies one or a few cases in depth to understand cause and effect. Each of these models follows the basic research steps outlined in Chapter 1: choosing a question, designing the methods, collecting the data, analyzing the data, and reporting/acting on the results.

## Extensive Needs Assessment

Conducting an extensive needs assessment is similar to the community organizing process described earlier in this chapter, in which the organizer goes door to door in the community and finds out what gripes people have, but is more formal. The purpose is to find out the universe of needs in a community or organization. It is typically done in a survey format—by mail or phone or in person. Often the researchers have some suspicions of what the needs may be, and the survey questions ask people to rank possible needs against each other or to assign each need a ranking score. In other cases, however, the questions are more open-ended, asking people to respond to the question "What do you think are the three most important problems in this community?"

One of the leading regions of the United States for all kinds of project-based research is rural Appalachia. In the Meadowview community, located in Washington County in the western corner of Virginia, faculty and students from Emory and Henry College partnered with an emerging community organization to conduct an extensive needs assessment of the community. They planned the research as a door-to-door survey, done jointly by college students and community residents, trying to keep the total length of the survey to under three minutes. To promote the research, they designated the day they were going as "community survey day" and advertised on the local radio stations and in newspapers. They got over a 75% response rate. Among the strongest results from the survey was the need for health care. Not only did many residents lack medical insurance, but the community did not have a physician, and many residents didn't have the means to get to the nearest doctors ten miles or more away. The project that grew out of this survey then involved negotiating with a faith-based mobile medical service to visit the community on a monthly basis. The community's longer-term plan, for which they are now actively fund-raising, is to redevelop an abandoned commercial district and start their own medical center.[14]

Another form of extensive needs assessment occurs in what is commonly known as a SWOT analysis, which stands for strengths, weaknesses, opportunities, and threats. SWOT analyses can range from highly formalized procedures that last for months to informal procedures that take only hours. Regardless of the formality and length of SWOT analysis, the basic process involves gathering information about an organization's activities and outcomes covering a certain time period, often a year. A group of people who have experience with the organization and its activities, sometimes with the assistance of professional researchers, sifts and sorts that information. This is often done using a popular education process, where group members compare their perceptions and conclusions with each other along the way to develop a list of the organization's strengths and weaknesses, and the broader context's opportunities and threats, to explain the organization's successes or failures over the previous time period. The goal is to develop a list of strategies to help the organization maximize its strengths, overcome its weaknesses, make the most of the available external opportunities, and neutralize the external threats.[15]

I have used a less formal version of this method with community-university partnership programs, community development corporations, and community technology networks. It's not difficult to do with the right group of people in the room. There are some important conditions needed for a successful SWOT analysis. First, you need people—10 to 20—who are knowledgeable about the organization and its programs, and you need to spend some time making sure the participants have common knowledge. Second, you need an atmosphere of relative safety, particularly to discuss weaknesses. Third, you need adequate time—a minimum of one two-hour session, but often as many as three or four sessions if the organization is involved in a number of activities. I typically start the discussion with developing a list of the most important outcomes, or lack of outcomes, of the past year. Some groups will want to try and process each of those outcomes rather than just develop a list, sometimes to feel better about failure. This is where it is important to help people feel comfortable with not moving into the analysis until the data is collected, as a group can get bogged down for hours analyzing one failure. Once the list is developed you can move into the

**A Model SWOT Analysis**

1. Recruit research group of 10–20 stakeholders or core group members for one to three meetings lasting approximately two hours each.

2. Generate a list of successes and failures of the group or organization over the past year. Allow for some limited discussion of each, without dwelling on any.

3. Generate lists of the group's or organization's strengths and weaknesses, and the external environment's opportunities and threats, based on the understanding of successes and failures.

4. Brainstorm ideas for maximizing strengths and minimizing weaknesses while taking advantage of the environment's opportunities and neutralizing its threats.

SWOT analysis itself. I have worked with groups who have analyzed each outcome for strengths, weaknesses, opportunities, and threats; and I have worked with groups who just start making lists of strengths, weaknesses, opportunities, and threats and just briefly reference the outcome they are deducing a strength or whatever from. Generally, the second method goes faster, but the first method produces a bit more depth. Out of this list comes the raw material for drawing up a strategic plan. For example, the SWOT analysis I did with the Coalition to Access Technology and Networking in Toledo (CATNeT) showed that the organization was very strong in building relationships across the city but weak in getting computer hardware into the hands of poor people. It helped identify a need that eventually turned into a plan to develop a computer recycling project.

Whether by SWOT analysis or some other method, once an array of needs have been identified, the group needs to decide what to do next. This often means ranking the identified needs by some criteria so that the group can choose which needs to address. It is at this point that the group often turns to an intensive needs assessment.

## Intensive Needs Assessment

In contrast to the broad brushstrokes of the extensive needs assessment, the intensive needs assessment takes an identified need and fully explores how important and broad that need is, where it came from, and what caused it. This form of needs assessment is not as popular as extensive needs assessment. Once people have identified a set of needs, they often want to get right to dealing with them. But, given that time and money are limited, it is nearly always necessary to select from the list of needs identified. And that is where intensive needs assessment comes in.

There are lots of methods to use in deciding needs priorities. Each member of the stakeholder or core group can choose their top three, and then you can see if any particular needs rise to the surface. They can also use a "paired comparison," in which they compare each need in pairs, until they are all in rank order. You can also use a Q-sort methodology, a more sophisticated version of ranking items.[16] In most situations, however, at this point in the process people want to talk about the needs and are uncomfortable being stuffed into a specific method for ranking them. I've nearly been laughed out of rooms for suggesting time-consuming methods of ranking needs when the priorities were apparently obvious to everyone but me.

What is important in ranking needs, however, and is neglected often in even sophisticated paired comparison methodologies, is the development of ranking criteria. If one person ranks needs according to what is cheapest to address, and another ranks needs according to what could produce the greatest impact, your results could be a mess, even if they don't look that way. Generally, needs assessment researchers seem to emphasize the criteria of importance and feasibility.[17] *Importance* can be defined by how deeply people feel about the need, how much impact it has, how many people it affects, and other criteria. Feasibility is usually defined by the capacity of the group or organization to actually do something about the need. There are lots of other potential criteria, however. In fractured communities, another criterion may be how controversial the need is. A gathering place for gay members of the community may be extremely important and may even be doable within an organization's budget. But it may also be controversial in the broader community. Of course, just because it's controversial doesn't mean it shouldn't be done, but that aspect of the need should be taken into account.

Often it is helpful for the group itself, using a popular education methodology, to determine its own set of criteria. Not only will this create criteria that the group itself buys into, but the discussion that generates the criteria will also help make sure everyone is using the criteria consistently.

It is in determining the importance, feasibility, or other criteria of judging each need where intensive research comes in. Studying each need to find out what it will cost to develop a project around it, how much impact successful programming will have, and other aspects of the need takes care and thought. And while it is possible for this step to get intermingled with the prescription stage, where a plan of action is chosen, at this point the research is not so much developing a detailed plan for filling the need as it is looking at the scope of the need and potential resources required to fill it. It is here that a force field analysis can come in handy.

Force field analysis was developed by Kurt Lewin[18] over a half century ago but is still used widely in strategic planning circles and in fact is applicable at many points in the project cycle. The basic concept is simple. The group gathers data on the forces impeding or facilitating change. You can get pretty creative with it. Mosaic.net International calls it fishes and boulders and has people draw a stream on a big piece of butcher block paper and then paste boulders signifying the impeding forces and fishes signifying the facilitating forces.[19]

Determining the indicators of a force, and measuring it, can be more challenging. The better defined the ranking criteria, the easier the measurement. If, for example, feasibility is defined as degree of staff expertise and time, or funds to buy expertise and time, the force field analysis can look for data indicating available staff expertise and time and/or available external funds and expertise.

Taking each need in turn, the group looks at the relative strength of facilitating vs. impeding forces to judge the feasibility of meeting a particular need. Those forces can be wide ranging but, like SWOT analysis, should include attention to forces within the community or organization and those outside it. In many ways, force field analysis treats each need as a separate case to which traditional case study techniques can be applied.[20]

The West Bank Community Development Corporation (WBCDC) in the Cedar-Riverside neighborhood of Minneapolis used force field analysis in their recent strategic planning. They looked back on their past accomplishments in the areas of housing, economic development, and community organizing, and analyzed the outcomes in each arena using a force field analysis. They used a combined staff and board process for this—with staff experts presenting their analysis of the positive and negative forces affecting their accomplishments, and then inviting board participation in developing that analysis further. The housing, economic development, and community programs were framed in a set of needs-based goals. After analyzing their outcomes, they had an understanding of how positive and negative forces in the neighborhood, city, and broader economy influenced the organization's successes and failures. Their success in developing housing, for example, was facilitated by extraordinarily low interest rates, even overcoming the impeding force of the district city council member opposing their work. The less successful economic development work, they found,

**A Model Force Field Analysis**

1. Recruit research group of 10–20 stakeholders or core group members for one or more meetings lasting approximately two hours each.

2. Review the list of needs developed through a SWOT analysis or other procedure. Allow for some limited discussion of each, without dwelling on any.

3. Develop criteria for rating the feasibility of meeting needs.

4. Using the feasibility criteria, collect information on facilitating and impeding forces inside the group or organization and outside it. This can be done through separate data collection or in a meeting if the stakeholders are well informed.

5. Apply the data to determine the feasibility of meeting each need.

was hindered not just by a slow national economy but also by a lack of connection between the neighborhood's East African shop owners and a large potential clientele of white college students nearby. They then used this information in developing the criteria for evaluating future projects, as we will see in the next chapter.

# THE OPPORTUNITIES APPROACH: ASSET MAPPING

Asset mapping is part of the asset-based community development (or ABCD) model made famous by John Kretzmann and John McKnight. Like needs assessment, the basic idea is pretty simple. You find out what talents and resources are available in the community and then you find ways to develop them. Perhaps there are people with construction skills, and you get a grant to put them to work rebuilding houses in the neighborhood. Perhaps there is cheap storefront space available to start small businesses (otherwise known as abandoned commercial space in the problems approach), and you develop plans and write grant proposals to fill them.

The actual process of asset mapping almost always follows an extensive research model, since the idea is to develop an inventory of skills, organizations, and physical resources. The research can also be quite involved. In mapping individual skills, surveyors go door

---

**Ways to Use Asset Mapping**

1. Do a door-to-door survey to find out residents' talents. Then link individuals with common talents with each other, and link individuals with organizations and businesses.

2. Research existing community organizations and associations through library records, resident interviews, and newspaper sources. Develop coalitions of organizations to do projects.

3. Develop a list of physical assets in the community, such as parks, diners, and churches, that can be used by community members. Design projects that put these resources to better use.

---

to door in a community with a seven-page survey asking people about their skills, interests, and business acumen.[21] It can be quite challenging to get community residents to give their time to such a survey, particularly when some of the questions can be rather personal and the survey itself is not anonymous. It is important to assure residents that the information will be used, and perhaps even couple the interview with an invitation to a subsequent planning meeting. Following up with residents is also important, since the asset map can be used to link individuals with each other or with organizations and businesses that can employ their skills.

Another form of asset mapping in a community focuses on organization and association assets. The goal here is to develop a list of the formal organizations and less formal associations in a neighborhood, along with their missions and activities. The methodology for doing this is less laid out than for mapping individual capacities. It is helpful—especially if you are trying to recruit a group of organizations to join a coalition project—to conduct interviews with the organization directors or presidents. But you first need to locate the organizations themselves. Libraries will sometimes have directories of organizations, as will newspapers. But the best way I have found to get a list of neighborhood organizations is to use a snowball sampling approach. Some of the community organizations will be quite public and well connected in the neighborhood. Their board and staff members will also often be connected to the other organizations. By the time you have interviewed half a dozen of the larger, more public organizations, you will have pretty close to a complete list of organizations for the neighborhood.

Perhaps one of the most important ways to use asset mapping is in the service of a particular project. Kretzmann and McKnight outline the use of asset mapping in developing a local park. In thinking about how to develop the park, the sponsoring group can map the local associations and organizations that could provide expertise or other resources; local institutions such as schools, churches, police, and other city services that could make use of and/or help maintain the park; sources of for-profit support; and the talents of residents. Once the array of talents and resources is known, they can be brought together to plan and implement the development project.[22]

I conducted an organization/association mapping project with the West Bank Community Development Corporation a couple of years ago when they were interested in developing a community organizing project. We concentrated on finding those organizations and associations that might be interested in collaborating on such a project. It didn't take long to develop a list of nearly 40 organizations and associations, though it took somewhat longer to interview their representatives. Quite amazingly, the list included everything from offices at the University of Minnesota, bordering the neighborhood, to small townhouse associations with half a dozen members. At the same time we were conducting the research, the WBCDC was recruiting these identified organizations to participate in community events that began building stronger cross-organizational relationships. The research led to a Web site listing all of the organizations with their contact information. Regrettably, local political and funding challenges disrupted the project, but the WBCDC was still able to organize a neighborhoodwide picnic and a community art mosaic project with participation from a number of the identified organizations.

As we've discussed, this opportunities approach contrasts rather starkly with the problems approach. It is also distrusted by many community workers because of its association with an unrealistic and conservative self-help mentality that seemingly ignores the realities of structural class, race, and even sex discrimination. But it also poses some important challenges to the problems approach. Needs assessments can be backward looking—studying what has been lost or what is missing based on what used to be. Asset mapping provides for the possibility of coming up with new ideas and strategies, moving beyond looking at what is missing to what is possible. The problems approach can also, as we've discussed, be disempowering if it is too closely allied with a social services strategy to filling needs. But even when the problems approach is connected to a community organizing strategy, it can suffer for lack of knowledge about the community resources that can be mobilized.

This complementarity of needs assessment and asset mapping hasn't been developed to its full potential. The next section will attempt to do just that.

# OF NEEDS AND RESOURCES

How does one combine needs assessment with asset mapping? The combination is not quite as unique as it might seem. Particularly when you use a participatory approach through the entire research process, the two go together quite naturally. One of the most developed methods of combining research on needs and assets comes from the participatory rural appraisal literature. Developed mostly in a rural Third World context, participatory rural appraisal (or PRA) is a research process designed to simultaneously discover the needs of a community and the community resources that will help determine what strategies will best meet those needs. For example, in rural communities lacking a stable electricity generation or distribution infrastructure, bringing in electricity-intensive technology to meet community needs is impractical. But those same communities may have access to power generation from wind, sun, or water that will allow for some small-scale electric devices to be used. Essentially, the model is about developing strategies to meet local needs that fit the context.[23] This is E. F. Schumacher's *Small is Beautiful* thesis put into a research methodology framework.[24]

The PRA folks like to say that there is no such thing as a "typical" research outline for their practice. They also emphasize that it is the process, not any specific techniques, that is most important in conducting a successful PRA procedure. The process is very much focused on bringing together a core group to participate in designing, carrying out, and using the research. The process of constructing the core group emphasizes including residents. And in some ways it is natural that including residents would lead to an emphasis on needs and assets, since residents would want solutions they could actually afford and maintain.

We have already discussed the participatory research processes in Chapter 2. Here we will concentrate more on the techniques of combining needs and assets. In PRA the emphasis is on a popular education approach to research, so the techniques emphasize activities that involve community members. One of the most commonly used is community mapping, where groups of community members go out and construct pictorial maps of their community based on their observations. Another method derived from agricultural contexts is seasonal mapping, where resident groups develop maps based on seasonal changes. An extension of this is historical mapping, to show changes in the community over time. PRA also employs a method called the community inventory, which is similar to asset mapping except that the inventory focuses more on the physical infrastructure and includes an assessment of the quality of what is being inventoried.

In underdeveloped rural areas, for example, the inventory includes the presence of wells and assessments of the availability and potability of water from each well. A final category of methods involves wealth and power charting, where resident groups construct Venn diagrams (circles of various size showing size and power, and with overlapping boundaries to show intersections of groups) to better understand where wealth and power may be concentrated in a community.[25]

A technique like this is also applicable to urban settings. My very first project-based research activity when I became a new assistant professor involved working with a community organizer and a group of neighborhood-based community development corporations (CDCs). The CDCs, which as a group were not very productive at the time, knew they needed better funding, better training, and better technical assistance. But what they mostly needed was documentation of those needs that also showed that they were worthy of having their needs met. So my collaborator, a community organizer named Dave Beckwith, brought together a core group of the CDCs and we collectively designed a research project to show what the CDCs were trying to do with what little they had. I conducted a mixed intensive-extensive study of the CDCs, trying to collect as much in-depth information as possible on each CDC's budget, staffing, activities, and outcomes, and what they needed to be more productive. The result was a report describing what assets the CDCs had, what they were accomplishing in terms of housing and economic development, and what they needed to become more productive. Dave then organized a day-long conference featuring the research report and bringing together local government and funders with CDC directors to discuss what to do about the situation. The result was a new coalition called the Working Group on Neighborhoods that successfully brought in $2 million to support the core budgets of CDCs and their training and technical assistance needs.[26]

I was involved in a second project more recently trying to assess and develop the information and communication technology (ICT) capacities of community organizations across the seven largest cities of Ohio. In this case we built core groups in each city composed of local researchers and interested community organization members. We used an initial statewide meeting to draft a survey and then revised it with feedback from the core groups in each city (which mostly involved shortening the survey from four pages to two). The survey focused on the computer and Internet assets already available to the organizations and their information needs. This was in the mid-1990s, still the infancy of the Internet, and we quickly found

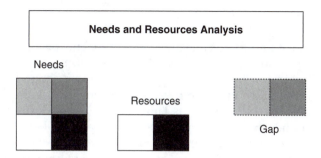

**Needs and Resources Analysis**

Needs

Resources

Gap

that the organizations had very few technology assets—their computers were old and almost none of them had even dial-up Internet access at the time. After a two-day conference, presenting and planning around these results, we began attempting to develop programs to meet the needs, though most of the successes occurred from the efforts of the local core groups rather than from the state-wide network.[27]

The difference between this *needs and resources* analysis approach and the needs assessment and asset mapping models is that the needs and resources analysis studies both needs and assets from the beginning. A needs and resources analysis also starts with an identified issue. Both asset mapping and needs assessment start with the goal of identifying one or more issues through the research process itself. The research is then designed to more fully explore the issue as a need or set of needs and at the same time to study the resources currently available for meeting the need set. It is possible in a needs and resources analysis, just as in asset mapping, to find that existing resources are not being effectively deployed. In contrast to asset mapping, however, it also highlights what resources are lacking. The goal of the needs and resources analysis is to identify the *gap* between the identified needs and the documented resources.

## LOOSE GRAVEL

There is a lot of loose gravel on the road to a good diagnosis. Regrettably, it is not just a matter of doing a nice piece of research, determining a list of community needs and assets, and developing projects. Indeed, doing diagnostic research at all may be called into question, especially if it is needs- or problems-focused. And the results can become quite contentious.

## The Pressure for Solutions

The most important challenge to good diagnostic research may be getting community members into the mood to do a good diagnosis. Remember the beginning of this chapter about the three academics stranded on a desert island? Remember how they immediately defined the problem as "how do we open a can of baked beans?" rather than as "what is there to eat around here?" That is often a challenge in the diagnostic stage of project development. In fact, it is often even worse than that, as funders put out requests for proposals, called RFPs, that already specify the solution. The community's job in such cases is to come up with a diagnosis that fits the solution which, in my mother's mid-20th-century, family-appropriate language, would be called "bass-ackwards."[28]

So the pressure is on, not just from inside the community to "solve" the problem even before it is understood but also from outside the community. And it is understandable that people would want to leap into solutions. When your youth are dying from gunfire or being jailed at alarming rates; your adults are unemployed; your houses are falling down; glass litters the sidewalks; and hopelessness litters the culture, the demand for immediate solutions is intense. Asking people to step back and study the problem seems almost disrespectful. And yet, it is an effective diagnosis that can make the difference between a solution that works and one that does not. Just as a physician wants to make sure your sore throat is the result of a bacterial infection instead of a virus before prescribing antibiotics, a community project needs to be based on an accurate diagnosis of the problem.

Convincing people to do a careful assessment of needs, assets, or both before leaping into doing projects is not easy. It is sometimes possible to combine an immediate crisis intervention strategy with longer-term diagnostic research, helping to reassure people that at least something is being done in the short term. Getting increased police patrols immediately while studying a sudden increase in neighborhood crime helps convince residents that action is being taken while research is being conducted. It also helps if there is money to pay for the diagnostic research so that it doesn't have to come out of an existing budget line.


## Needs vs. Neediness

Another challenge facing needs assessments in particular is that, since the growing popularity of asset mapping, people increasingly object to needs-based language. More and more I find both community residents and service providers objecting when we start talking about what the community *needs* or what *problems* exist in the community. They then immediately invoke the language of *assets* or *social capital*—though, interestingly, they often say things like "this community needs to develop its social capital." I believe, however, that this objection to talking about needs and problems comes from two kinds of misunderstandings. The first misunderstanding is that, for too long, talking about needs came to mean *being needy*. Community residents got sick of being portrayed as needy—i.e., incompetent and helpless—by service providers and other outsiders. When asset-based community development came along, people didn't have to talk about needs at all anymore. But, as even Kretzmann and McKnight acknowledge, poor communities have needs. The challenge is separating a discussion of needs from a discussion of being needy. That is what is so useful about needs assessment—it is possible to research the needs themselves and discover that those needs are not the result of the residents' shortcomings but are more likely the result of discrimination, disinvestment, and other unfair treatment by governments and corporations. The second misunderstanding comes from seeing a poor community *as a problem*, vs. seeing that community as *having a problem*. In discussions with those who live outside of disinvested communities, it is interesting how often they talk about how "that community is a problem." It is very much the outsider's perspective, painting with broad brushstrokes. Again, however, good diagnostic research can get beyond the stereotyping of communities to learn what the specific problems are in a community, as well as what resources the community can build on in attacking those problems.

We need to separate having needs from being needy, and having problems from being a problem. And those of us who are outsiders to such communities may not be in any position to impose language. People do have their pride, and they often don't want to admit to outsiders that they have problems and needs. But they will admit such things to each other, and that is why it is so important to develop a strong core group. They can support each other in looking at needs and problems. In addition, developing an analysis of those needs that helps community members understand the broader forces at work, such as government and corporate policies, helps hold at bay the deficiency stereotype and provides identifiable issues they can organize around. We can't simply throw out needs-based language and substitute asset language because too many communities still have a lot more needs than they do assets. And that isn't their fault.

## The Blame Game

Speaking of whose fault it is, dealing with the issue of fault and blame is where the next slippery spot comes in when attempting to do diagnostic research. Especially when attempting to diagnose needs or problems, the question of fault is inevitable. The popular approach these days is to avoid assigning blame and move directly on to solutions. Part of this comes from a desire to avoid conflict. Finding blame means confronting those who are at fault. Especially when fault is unclear, this can cause a lot of conflict. Diagnostic research ventures attempting to pinpoint the cause of cancer clusters, for example, often get caught in conflict between those who diagnose the nearby corporate-owned chemical dump as the cause and those who diagnose the lifestyle behaviors of the residents as the cause. The difficulty in winning a battle between researchers in such a case is difficult indeed and often rests on the skills of organizers and lawyers as much as the skills of researchers, reminding us that the research is but one part of the overall project. Good research is a necessary, but not a sufficient, condition of winning a battle of blame.

Is such a battle necessary? Isn't it enough to just move on to solutions? There may be times when it is possible to just develop solutions. But in many cases, particularly public health problems, it is necessary to find the cause of the problem. In the case of a community cancer cluster, which is it—the high-fat, heavy-smoking lifestyle of residents, or the toxic dump leaching chemicals into the land around them? It is probably both, but we all know that the default solution will be a smoking cessation clinic unless there is a hard-fought campaign focusing on the toxic dump. Determining the cause, in cases like this, is a life-and-death necessity.

## CONCLUSION

This chapter focused on doing research supporting the first stage of the project cycle, the diagnosis stage. We covered:

- Motivations for diagnostic research
- How to structure a diagnostic research process using a stakeholder or core group
- Strategies for diagnostic research, including needs assessments, asset mapping, and the combined needs and resources approach

We also looked at the challenges in diagnostic research, including:

- The pressure to find solutions quickly
- Focusing on needs rather than neediness
- Addressing questions of cause and blame

# RESOURCES

## Needs Assessment

Witkin, B. R., & Altschuld, J. W. (1995). *Planning and conducting needs assessments: A practical guide.* Thousand Oaks, CA: Sage Publications.

Altschuld, J. W., & Witkin, B. R. (1999). *From needs assessment to action: Transforming needs into solution strategies.* Thousand Oaks, CA: Sage Publications.

Work Group on Health Promotion and Community Development. (2003). Chapter 3. Assessing community needs and resources: The community tool box, http://ctb.ku.edu/tools/en/chapter_1003.htm

## SWOT Analysis

Tellus Consultants. (n.d.). SWOT Analysis for participatory research in the Pacific, http://www.tellusconsultants.com/swot.html

Dept. of Urban and Regional Planning. (n.d.). *SWOT Analysis: Urban Design Project Manual.* University of Illinois Urbana-Champaign, http://www.urban.uiuc.edu/Courses/Varkki/up326/manual/swot.htm

Balamuralikrishna, R., & Dugger, J. C. (1995). SWOT analysis: A management tool for initiating new programs in vocational schools. *Journal of Vocational and Technical Education,* http://scholar.lib.vt.edu/ejournals/JVTE/v12n1/Balamuralikrishna.html

## Force Field Analysis

Iowa State University Extention. (2001). Force field analysis, http://www.extension.iastate.edu/communities/tools/forcefield.html

Accel-Team.com. 2004. Team building - Force field analysis, http://www.accel-team.com/techniques/force_field_analysis.html

New England Regional Leadership Program. (1998). Exercise 3: Force field analysis. Center for Rural Studies, http://crs.uvm.edu/gopher/nerl/group/b/c/Exercise3.html

## Asset Assessment

Asset-Based Community Development Institute, (2004). http://www. northwestern.edu/ipr/abcd.html

Kretzmann, J. P., & McKnight, J. L. (1993). *Building communities from the inside out*. Chicago: ACTA Publications.

Madii Institute. (2003), http://www.madii.org/

## Participatory Rural Appraisal

Chambers, R. (1999). *Whose reality counts?—Putting the first last*. London: Intermediate Technology Publications.

Institute of Development Studies. (2004). *Our work on PRA*, http:// www. ids.ac.uk/ids/particip/research/pra.html

# NOTES

1.  Medoff, P., & Sklar, H. (1994). *Streets of hope: The fall and rise of an urban neighborhood*. Boston: South End Press.

2.  Alinsky, S. (1969). *Reveille for radicals*. New York: Vintage. See also Alinsky, S. (1971). *Rules for radicals*. New York: Vintage.

3.  Alinsky, S. (1971). *Rules for radicals* (pp. 141–144).

4.  Delgado, G. (1994). *Beyond the politics of place: New directions in community organizing in the 1990s*. Oakland: Applied Research Center.

5.  Cortés, E., Jr. (1998). Reclaiming our birthright. *Shelterforce Online*. Retrieved July 15, 2004, from http://www.nhi.org/online/issues/101/cortes.html. See also Fellner, Kim. (1998). Hearts and crafts: Powering the movement. *Shelterforce Online*. Retrieved July 15, 2004, from http://www.nhi.org/online/issues/101/fellner.html

6.  Eichler, M. (1998). Look to the future, learn from the past. *Shelterforce Online*. Retrieved July 15, 2004, from http://www.nhi.org/online/issues/101/eichler.html

7.  Bobo, K., Kendall, J., & Max, S. (1991). *Organizing for social change: A manual for activists in the 1990s*. Washington, D.C.: Seven Locks Press.

8.  Gibbs, L. (1998). *Love Canal: The story continues*. Stony Creek, CT: New Society Publishers.

9.  Community Outreach Partnership Centers Program. (2004). Retrieved July 15, 2004, from http://www.oup.org/about/copc.html

10.  Kretzmann, J. P., & McKnight, J. L. (1993). *Building communities from the inside out*. Evanston, IL: Center for Urban Affairs and Policy Research Neighborhood Innovations Network, Northwestern University.

11.  Stoecker, R. (1997). The imperfect practice of collaborative research: The Working Group on Neighborhoods in Toledo, Ohio. In Nyden, P., A. Figert, M. Shibley, & D. Burrows (Eds.). *Building community: Social science in action* (pp. 219–225). Thousand Oaks, CA: Pine Forge Press.

12.  Witkin, B. R., & Altschuld, J. W. (1995). *Planning and conducting needs assessments: A practical guide.* Thousand Oaks, CA: Sage Publications.

13.  Kretzmann, J. P., & McKnight, J. L. (1993). *Building communities from the inside out.*

14.  Stanley, T. (2003). *Celebrating the Meadowview community.* Presented at the Just Connections Conference, Emory, Virginia, June 5–7.

15.  Balamuralikrishna, R., & Dugger, J. C. (1995). SWOT analysis: A management tool for initiating new programs in vocational schools. *Journal of Vocational and Technical Education, 12.* Retrieved July 15, 2004, from http://scholar.lib.vt.edu/ejournals/JVTE/v12n1/Balamuralikrishna.html. See also Jones, B. (1990). *Neighborhood planning: A guide for citizens and planners.* Bigtown, IL: Planners Press, American Planning Association. See also Dept. of Urban and Regional Planning. (n.d.) *SWOT analysis.* University of Illinois Urbana-Champaign, Retrieved July 15, 2004, from http://www.urban.uiuc.edu/Courses/Varkki/up326/manual/swot.htm.

16.  Altschuld, J. W., & Witkin, B. R. (1999). *From needs assessment to action: Transforming needs into solution strategies.* Thousand Oaks, CA: Sage Publications.

17.  Altschuld, J. W., & Witkin, B. R. (1999). *From needs assessment to action: Transforming needs into solution strategies* (p. 110).

18.  Lewin, K. (1948) *Resolving social conflicts: Selected papers on group dynamics.* In G. W. Lewin (Ed.). New York: Harper & Row.

19.  Mosaic.net International. (n.d.). *What is Mosaic.net International?* Retrieved July 15, 2004, from http://www.mosaic-net-intl.ca/whatis.html.

20.  Yin, R. K. (1994). *Case study research: Design and methods* (2nd ed.). Thousand Oaks, CA: Sage Publications.

21.  Kretzmann, J. P., & McKnight, J. L. (1993). *Building communities from the inside out.*

22.  Ibid.

23.  Chambers, R. (1999). *Whose reality counts?—Putting the first last.* London: Intermediate Technology Publications. Also see Pretty, J. N., & Vodouhê, S. D. (1998). Using rapid or participatory rural appraisal. In B. E. Swanson, R. P. Bentz, & A. J. Sofranko (Eds.). *Improving agricultural extension: A reference manual.* Rome: Food and Agriculture Organization of the United Nations. Retrieved July 15, 2004, from http://www.fao.org/docrep/W5830E/w5830e08.htm#chapter%206%20%20%20using%20rapid%20or%20participatory%20rural%20appraisal

24.  Schumacher, E. F. (1999). *Small is beautiful: Economics as if people mattered* (2nd ed.). Vancouver, B.C.: Hartley & Marks Publishers.

25.   Chambers, R. (2003). *Notes for participants in PRA-PLA familiarisation workshops in 2003.* Participation Group, Institute of Development Studies, University of Sussex. Retrieved July 15, 2004, from http://www.ids. ac.uk/ids/particip/research/pra/pranotes03.pdf

26.   Stoecker, R., & Beckwith, D. (1992). Advancing Toledo's neighborhood movement through participatory action research: Integrating activist and academic approaches. *The Clinical Sociology Review, 10,* 198–213.

27.   Stoecker, R., & Stuber, A. (1999). Building an Information Superhighway of one's own: A comparison of two approaches. *Research in Politics and Society, 7,* 291–309.

28.   Just in case your mother didn't teach you this, it translates as ass-backwards.

# *Five*

# Prescribing

## *Researching Options*

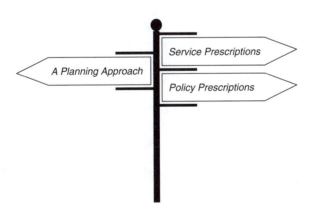

## WHICH WAY SHOULD YOU GO FROM HERE?

For those of you not familiar with the famous story of *Alice in Wonderland*, it is a quite amazing fantasy of a little girl's attempt to find her way home from a very strange place, full of wondrous characters and numerous challenges. At one point in the story Alice happens upon one of my favorite characters, the Cheshire Cat, whom she asks for directions:

> "Would you tell me, please, which way I ought to go from here?"
>
> "That depends a good deal on where you want to get to," said the Cat.

Now you may have even seen those two lines quoted in a number of places. They are used quite often to illustrate the importance of goal-oriented thinking. But you may not have seen the subsequent lines quoted so much:

> "I don't much care where—" said Alice.
>
> "Then it doesn't matter which way you go," said the Cat.
>
> "—so long as I get somewhere," Alice added as an explanation.
>
> "Oh, you're sure to do that," said the Cat, "if you only walk long enough."[1]

In the world of social change programming, whether the goal is individual change through a social service program or global change through a social movement, we often settle for any change at all. We are content to reduce crime, increase home ownership, improve life expectancy, or make some other general change. And we jump on the latest bandwagon, follow the latest fad, or try to find the cheapest alternative because we lack the resources to figure out exactly what is needed. In addition, we are often so busy trying to stop bad things that we don't have time to think about what good things we want to put in their place. Our work, as a consequence, is often terribly inefficient. Yes, we are sure to get somewhere, if only we get enough grants, hire enough consultants, try enough new ideas, and work long enough and hard enough. There are rarely enough resources to work so inefficiently, however. In addition, those people who are suffering from disinvestment and a lack of corrective development and services that can reverse the effects of disinvestment have neither the time nor the patience to wait for us to get it right. It's better to delay starting a project while we do careful research than delay having a real impact because we haven't chosen the most effective and efficient path.

This chapter is about deciding not just where we want to move from but where we want to get to. It is about figuring out the kinds of communities, the kinds of opportunities, the kinds of possibilities, the kind of future, we want to create. We will of course talk about planning interventions to stop the bad things. But we will also spend time talking about plans to create new good things.

The prescription stage of project development is about the plan. Because prescription involves some form of intervention in an existing condition, it is important to have diagnosed the existing condition in as much detail as possible. I worked with a local foundation a few years ago that wanted to start a program to help community development organizations go beyond "bricks and mortar" development activities to also organize their neighborhoods. They attempted to diagnose the readiness of each organization to do community organizing, but since it was a brand new program they were not sure what questions to ask. It was only after we conducted an intensive evaluation (described in Chapter 7) of the program that we were able to develop effective diagnostic questions. So if you skipped the previous chapter, you may want to go back.

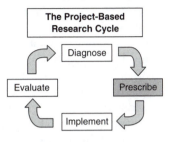

A good diagnosis, then, is the first source of information for developing the prescription. Whether the diagnosis has focused on needs or assets or both, the prescription stage is about figuring out how to fill those needs or deploy those assets.

## INWARD-LOOKING VS. OUTWARD-LOOKING SOCIAL CHANGE: SERVICES AND POLICIES

Researchers who study social change movements have for some time distinguished between those that focus on changing the external world and those that focus on changing their own members.[2] Those externally focused efforts are what we normally see on the news—demonstrations and protests, along with a lot of backstage organizing and lobbying, designed to change some government or corporate policy. The global justice movement, which became famous through massive demonstrations beginning in Seattle in 1999, focuses on trying to change the policies of global organizations like the International Monetary Fund and the World Bank, as well as the global trade policies of individual nations.[3] There are other much more local social change efforts, such as city-level movements for living wage laws so that working parents can earn enough money in entry-level jobs to support a family.

Inward-looking movements are focused on changing their members. Alcoholics Anonymous, whose purpose is to help its members become and stay sober, may be one of the most famous internally focused movements. Groups such as this may occasionally take a stand on social issues, but the main thrust of their work is changing individuals. Other organizations focus not so much on individuals as on their group as a whole. Co-housing communities—experimental forms of community where a group of people live together in a subdivision and cooperate to meet their common needs such as child care, meal preparation, home maintenance, and other tasks—are a form of such an internally focused group.[4] The emphasis here is on providing services, sometimes for individuals and sometimes for groups, toward the goal of helping them sustain or change the community and/or its individuals.

We will not be concentrating so much on the social movement aspects of these and other social change efforts, which is an entire field of study in itself, but on the research methods that support such efforts. For our purposes, the importance of distinguishing between internally focused and externally focused social change efforts is that internally focused efforts often look for service prescriptions, and externally focused efforts often look for policy prescriptions. This isn't a rigid distinction. Sometimes, a service program project will focus on changing policy to allow other service projects to proceed. Often, this involves lobbying for public funds. AIDS advocates engage in a great deal of policy work to obtain funding and research to support the direct services they provide to HIV-positive individuals.[5]

Aside from services being internally focused and policy change efforts being externally focused, there are other differences between these two approaches. It is tempting to think of service programs as simply the internal policies of a group or organization. But they are crucially different. Policies are not concrete how-to guides. Instead, they set the boundaries on what can be done. Programs are actual implementations. For example, as part of a neighborhood improvement program, I have recently been involved in a project trying to measure changes in teen pregnancy in a neighborhood. After discussing the best ways to get the data, we decided that the most accurate information would be county statistics on teen births, which we found out could be sorted by address. But there are strict government policies on disclosing the identities of minors that made the county health officials very concerned about providing the data for us.[6] They were even wary of counting the number of teen births in the neighborhood themselves and just giving us a total number. The

| Service Prescription | Policy Prescription |
|---|---|
| • Inward-focused<br>• Concrete plans<br>• Narrow application<br>• May include policy changes | • Outward-focused<br>• Abstract rules<br>• Wide application |

policy protecting the identities of minors does not say how to run programs for youth. It only specifies the boundaries of collecting and using information about youth and doesn't even do that clearly enough for those county health officials to feel comfortable with providing summary statistics on teen births in a neighborhood.

Another important distinction between services and policies is that services have narrow application to the individuals or community for which they are developed. Yes, it is possible that a community health service program developed in one area might be generally applicable to other places, but it almost always needs to be adapted to the particularities of each context. That is why intensive diagnostic research is so important—to discover the characteristics of the community context that will affect the service program outcomes and make sure that the program is custom-designed to fit those characteristics. Policies, on the other hand, are designed to apply across wide-ranging places and situations. In most cases, policymakers prefer to make as few exceptions as possible.

Even with these differences, however, both the services approach and the policy approach require good diagnostic research. In addition, at the prescription level, they often involve a planning process using an intensive research model. So before we look at the distinctions between the two approaches to prescription, we will look at how a general prescriptive planning process works.

## A PLANNING APPROACH

Whether a group is involved in designing services or changing a policy, at this stage they are engaged in a planning process. There are a number of models a group can use, including strategic planning, visioning, empowerment planning, and other models. All of them use some version of the prescriptive planning process outlined in the chart above and produce a plan based on researching alternatives, developing criteria to evaluate the solutions, and then applying the criteria to the options and choosing the best one. The order of activities is somewhat arbitrary. In some cases it may make sense to develop the criteria before shopping for solutions, especially if the problem or issue is broad and the possible solutions are many. In other cases, especially if the problem is unique and the solutions not readily apparent, it may work better to gather up all the possible solutions and then see what criteria they suggest.

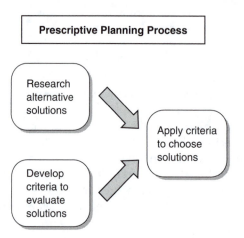

When the city of Toledo, Ohio was considering changing its form of government (we had an appointed city manager rather than an elected mayor, and a city council elected from across the whole city rather than from districts, which many of us thought was rather undemocratic), a group of community activists got together to try and impact the next city government structure. One of the things we did was research city government structures across the country for models that were more representative and democratic. Since there were dozens of options, we established some criteria up front—we would only look at cities of a similar size and that had mechanisms for direct citizen involvement in government. Using those criteria, we ended up with only a half dozen cities, and our research task was much easier. We did our research with zeal, but, as a reminder that the research is only a small part of the project, the organizing necessary to get our ideas into the resultant plan didn't happen, and we ended up with a city government that is only superficially changed from what we had before.

Each of the steps of researching solutions, developing criteria for comparing the alternatives, and then choosing, involves some specific tasks.

## Researching Solutions

How does one research solutions? I have a cool piece of fired pottery on my desk, which my wife found at a rummage sale, with *Alternatives* stamped across the side. I use it as a pencil holder. It's a nice symbolic representation for me since it includes everything from your basic #2 wooden pencil to mechanical pencil to cheapo pen to a fancy, well-balanced, easy-gliding-ink, fine-line writing instrument. When you research solutions, that is what you will often find. There are cheap solutions, which may be practical or just cheap. There are expensive solutions that may be highly advanced or just superficially flashy.

The task of researching alternatives is to fill the alternatives jar, preferably with a variety of possibilities. The process is very much akin to the literature review in traditional research—finding out everything that anyone else had said about this problem or issue. It can be frustrating work for a while. Anyone who has spent hours in the library, pouring over article after article, and book after book, finding nothing until suddenly the one perfect article presents itself, with references to all the information you could ever hope for, knows how challenging this part of the process can be. At least initially, this kind of research is like groping in the dark. And, just like groping in the dark, luck will play some role in whether it takes a long time or a short time to find that one perfect source that leads you to all the other sources.

So don't be tempted to take the easy way out. You may have heard the joke about the guy who lost his car keys. It was late at night, well after darkness had descended. And there under the streetlight he was on hands and knees looking in futility for his keys. A police officer happens upon the scene and asks what he is doing. "I am looking for my keys," the guy responds. "Are you sure this is where you lost them?" the officer responds. "No," says the guy, pointing down the street toward his car, "I lost them over there." "Then why are you looking for them here?" asks the officer. "Because this is where the light is," replies the guy.

We are often tempted to go for the easy way out, to look where the light is rather than where the actual solutions might be. But, of course, such a search often ends in futility. There is often no easy way to fill up your jar of alternatives, and you need to become comfortable groping in the dark. There are some strategies, however, that can make the search more systematic.

Sad but true, sequestering oneself away in a real college or university library with real books and real journal articles for a few days can make a real difference. Your local public library may also be of use, but is unlikely to have a wide range of academic research. You can, of course, do some of the initial searching over the library's Internet site, but eventually you need to go and actually read what you have found. Be forewarned that an increasing number of university libraries are password-restricting their online databases. If you are not on the university payroll or a student, you may have to fight for your right to use their materials.

Another strategy, sometimes a bit more challenging, is to read the insider stories. In most areas of community work there are a number of trade publications— magazine-style periodicals focused on a particular community work niche such as community health, or housing development, or some other area. The nice thing about trade publications is that they concentrate on stories of real projects out there with contact information that you can use to follow up. Once you find the relevant publication, you can get access to a number of alternatives. But many of these publications are rather obscure and may not be available at your local public or university library. An Internet search may help turn them up.

> **Finding Alternatives**
>
> - Use the library
> - Read the trade publications
> - Find and use networks
> - Brainstorm–visioning; charrettes

If you are working on an issue and you don't know anyone else who is, your first task should be to find them. It is nice if you can find other people locally and get together for lunch to trade ideas. But you can also find people on e-mail lists, Web sites, and through library searches and trade publications. You can also sometimes save yourself some time searching through trade publications or libraries if you can find someone who can just tell you where to look. There are even a number of agencies out there that may be good sources of information. If you are working on a public health issue, your local public health department may know where to look for alternatives. You could get transferred a half dozen times before you find the person who can really help, but by that time it will be worth it. Don't be shy about contacting strangers if they are working on something similar. They will probably also appreciate someone to compare notes with.

In situations where there are no recognizable alternatives, the alternatives don't seem to fit, or maximizing participation is paramount, it is desirable to sit down with a group and brainstorm possible strategies. Especially if you have done some research into the possible alternatives and found nothing that fits, you may have learned enough to piece together bits from what you have learned. A typical brainstorming process involves writing down every idea mentioned, regardless of how weird it seems, without people responding. When you have the list of ideas, you then start developing or applying criteria to critique the ideas. Then, when you whittle down your list to the things you really like, you might go back to your network of contacts, especially those who are experts in the area, to get their feedback. The "open space" process has become one of the more popular methods for involving participants in the management of a brainstorming session and producing practical options.[7]

When the focus is broad and long-range, the process is often called *visioning*. In a visioning process, a group of people come together not just to discuss program and project ideas but also to discuss values. In many cases, the community visioning process begins with asking the group what values they can all agree on. This stage can often be the most difficult as conflicting values surface. In community planning, for example, business owners may value population increases, while residents concerned with traffic and other disruptions may value population stability. Finding those core value agreements and disagreements can require expert facilitation.[8]

Visioning processes have often been criticized for producing only lofty, flowery statements, kind of like "The Acme community vision is of a group of neighbors who all hug each other at least once a day and where all the children are happy and smart," which is not helpful at all. Visioning processes that stop at generating core values are worse than useless because they take up people's time and don't generate anything that can be acted upon. Good visioning processes begin with more or less agreed-upon core values and then move on to generating usable ideas. One way to do this is to use an idea board. Participants in the visioning process are instructed to write down ideas on notecards or sticky notes. They then post their ideas on a large board with whatever technology seems safe and convenient. In some cases the board is divided into core values, and participants post their ideas under the heading that fits best. In other cases they just stick them anywhere on the board. Then the fun begins, because the participants next look at the mélange of ideas and attempt to group them for similarity or complementarity or some other criteria. At the end of this step you have a board with groups of ideas.[9]

Another strategy used in architecture but applicable in any setting where pictures are helpful is the charrette. A charrette is a short, intensive planning session, often lasting for one or two days.[10] A charrette usually involves more preparation than a visioning process, however. Visioning sometimes occurs without any diagnostic research at all, while the charrette process involves extensive diagnostic research into existing conditions and available resources. Once that research has been compiled, it is presented to all the participants. In the 1980s the east side of Toledo, which had suffered massive industrial disinvestment, used a charrette process to focus on redeveloping a main industrial transportation corridor in the hopes of bringing industry back to the area. The two-day planning process, including residents and city and corporate officials, focused on issues such as moving heavy truck traffic off residential streets, relocating the area fire station across the railroad tracks to reduce emergency vehicle delays caused by trains, and widening and hardening the road to support the intended industrial traffic. Architects trained in participatory methods projected an outline of the street onto a long sheet of butcher block paper and then literally sketched participants' ideas onto the paper.[11]

The ideas generated from such brainstorming processes or, indeed, from any of the strategies mentioned above, will then need to be winnowed, shaped, and made practical. It's not only okay but preferable not to impose too many restrictions on ideas at the beginning, because it may prevent something new and innovative. In the Cedar-Riverside neighborhood in Minneapolis, for example, one of the ideas that came from their community planning process involved putting new townhouse units in the *middle* of the large square blocks that characterized the neighborhood. And they had to fight hard to gain the right to do that. It was an off-the-wall idea, designed to meet the city's demands for higher-density housing in the neighborhood (which the city was partially funding), that would never have been tried without a very creative, open-ended neighborhood planning process. But then the neighborhood activists had to carefully develop the idea to meet the objections of the fire marshal and city planning officials. So the next step is to develop criteria to evaluate all those wonderful ideas and develop a practical plan.

## Developing Criteria

How does a group choose among the alternatives? Here is where developing criteria is important. Just as a professor develops criteria to distinguish an "A" paper from a "B" paper, or a pipe fitter develops criteria to distinguish a strong pipe weld from a weak one, a group engaging in a community change project needs criteria to distinguish an effective program from an ineffective one. As I mentioned above, you may even want to do this before filling your alternatives jar to make your search more efficient. But the criteria may also emerge as you explore and discuss alternatives. Much of the research you do to find alternatives will also include research on the impacts of those alternatives, complete with the criteria employed.

One source of standards you will often find while researching alternatives in many areas of community work will be called "best practices." *Best practices* is one of those overused insider phrases, and it's unclear what it actually means. At some point in a specific, focused area of community work, such as housing development, an agreement emerges among those working on the issue that certain practices work better than other practices. In housing development, for example, one of the best practices for helping first-time, low-income home buyers is through rent-to-own programs. In community policing there are best practices for reducing crime in a neighborhood through a combination of prevention and enforcement. Studying the best practices will often reveal what problems the best practice was meant to address and will then help you build your criteria. One of the reasons for the rent-to-own option in housing development, for example, is to prevent displacement of existing residents when neighborhood rental housing is redeveloped toward the goal of increasing homeownership, since the existing renters often don't have enough money for a down payment. So you may decide, by studying this practice, that two of your criteria for evaluating various housing development options is that they should support homeownership and not displace existing residents. Funders also often latch onto these best practices and then use them to evaluate other applicants for funds. So it is important to know what the best practices are for your issue because the criteria implied by those best practices will likely be imposed on your grant applications. The problem with best-practices standards, however, is that they often become reified—they thwart the development of other creative solutions. So when you find best practices, don't make those the sole source for your criteria.

> **Criteria for Evaluating Alternatives**
>
> - Apply best-practices standards
> - Derive criteria from existing research
> - Develop standards from theory
> - Include unique community characteristics
> - Derive criteria from project goals
> - Engage stakeholder groups

If there are no best-practices standards, or even if there are, another source of criteria for evaluating alternatives is the academic research. Many projects have been tried in many places, and many of them have been researched. If you are shopping for youth recreation programs in the hopes of reducing juvenile crime, you may be able to find existing studies looking at the impact of youth recreation programs on the juvenile crime rate. Those studies may provide information on the characteristics of such programs that have the most impact. Those characteristics then become part of your criteria. Using such research may also be convenient if you are already searching the academic literature to fill your alternatives jar.

If you can't find any good research showing the effects of an intervention, you may apply a theoretical standard. In other words, can you create a project that draws on theoretical relationships that have been found in academic research? There has been a lot of talk lately about the positive health effects of religious faith, with some research showing a relationship between the two[12] (not necessarily a causal relationship, but at least an association—people who express more religious devotion tend to have better health). You might conclude, based on a thorough reading of that academic literature, that you could develop a communitywide religious recruitment campaign to reduce the incidence of heart disease in a community. Be careful with theoretical relationships, however. It may be that the important health effect of religion comes from creating a sense of community and reducing stress. So it is theoretically possible that any number of stress reduction or community relationship programs could have the same impact.

In addition to any best practices or research-based criteria you develop, you also need to consider the uniqueness of the situation the project is being designed for. Will youth recreation programs developed in poor urban African-American communities work equally well in poor rural white Appalachian communities? If not, how are the communities different and how may those differences impact the program? You may not want to employ these criteria when you search the literature for your alternatives, since that may preclude you from considering alternatives from other places that could actually work. But at some point you will want the unique qualities of your community to inform the criteria you use for choosing an alternative to implement. The question, of course, is what community characteristics to include in your criteria. Some may be highly relevant and others may not be. The research literature will give you some suggestions—various studies may have tested for the relevance of race or age or some other characteristics. If so, you will certainly want to include those criteria. Cultural and ethnic characteristics are also often important, even when they don't appear in the literature. So many projects are conducted in relatively homogeneous settings that it is difficult to test for the effect of ethnicity.

The program or project goals can also be used as criteria for evaluating alternatives. At this stage in project development, however, there may not be goals. In fact, choosing an alternative may inform goal setting, since the diagnostic process may have identified a number of issue areas, but the group or organization may only have the capacity to handle one or a few of those issues. If the group has gone through a visioning process, they will be close to setting goals.

How does a group go about goal setting? Many groups often do not distinguish between goals and strategies. Too often a group or organization will have as a goal "implementing a youth recreation program" rather than "reducing youth crime." In other words, a strategy—the youth recreation program—becomes the goal. Goals should be expressed as outcomes—reducing youth crime—rather than as strategies. The outcome goals can be set on a particular time-line (one year, for example) or for a particular quantity (a 10% change, for example). Goals should be based on what is possible as well as what is desirable, and goals that are set too high may result in no alternative looking acceptable. Here again is where consulting the existing research, or talking to others who have already done similar projects, is helpful.

Be forewarned that choosing criteria can be a political process. One group may be concerned about getting the maximum impact. Another may be concerned about using the fewest resources. One person may advocate for standards that reduce the power of another stakeholder. Situations like this are why Carl Patton and David Sawicki advocate a process for developing criteria that takes into account different groups' interests.[13] A neighborhood group going up against city hall on criteria for funding neighborhood redevelopment plans may not want to use the city's criteria, but they had better know what those criteria are so they can defend against them if need be.

## Choosing an Alternative

Once the criteria for evaluating alternatives are established, it may be obvious which project alternative will work best. But the sit-uation is often more complex than it seems. This step, in fact, can be the most involved of all, since it requires predicting the future, which is one of the most difficult research tasks. Another thing mak-ing this step complicated is the need to weight or rank the criteria you use, accurately measure costs and benefits, and then accurately apply the criteria to the measurements. A lot can go wrong on the way to the final decision with all that measurement.

There are a number of ways to rank criteria. One of the most popular is a ranking method where members each rank the project goals with numbers. The numbers for each goal are then added together and the goal with the highest or lowest score (depending on whether the lowest number or highest number signifies most impor-tance) becomes the most important goal. It is best to not get too rigid with this process, however. It is mostly a heuristic device, designed to help people organize their thinking, not to direct their thinking. Such ranking processes apply quantitative measures to qualitative concepts. If six people rank three goals, with 1 being most important and 3 being least important, and the most important goal gets a total score of 8 while the next gets a score of 11, that means the average scores of the two goals are 2.67 and 3.67. Would you stake the success of your project on a one-point differ-ence? Such a goal-ranking process is mostly a way to get a feeling for how the group is thinking. There are more sophisticated ranking methods, such as Q-sort, paired com-parison, or Delphi survey,[14] but in a planning context they all are aids to decision making rather than methods to determine the best option.

**Choosing an Alternative**

- Rank criteria
- Calculate benefits
- Calculate costs

You can also order criteria using a bottom-line priority. The West Bank Community Development Corporation (CDC) in Minneapolis's Cedar-Riverside neighborhood used the force field analysis results of its previous projects (described in Chapter 4) to choose projects for the next year. Two of the criteria they empha-sized as a result of that analysis were practicality (how easy an option would be) and affordability (how much it would cost). But another criterion they applied was whether an option should be part of the core budget for the CDC. Those activities selected to be part of the core budget would get done first, and the others would get done only if the CDC was able to get grant funds. One of the CDC board's strongest expressed needs focused on economic develop-ment, as they wanted to replace an important historic building in the neighborhood's business strip that had been destroyed by fire. But their force field analysis, looking at the slow economy, the need for city funds, and their oppositional city council member, convinced them that the project wasn't feasible. They also wanted to develop a strong community organizing program. But even though they determined it would not be excessively costly, and would not be terribly difficult, they could not justify giving it core budget status.

Once the criteria are ranked, the next step is to actually apply the criteria. In the Cedar-Riverside example, and in most cases, a group applies the criteria in a two-hour meeting. This is certainly practical for time-stretched groups. But this may not be the best way to approach the task of choosing a project. When time permits, using a *comparative research* process may produce beneficial results.[15] Comparative research is actually an academic research protocol, but it is easily adaptable to practical purposes. In traditional compara-tive research, the researcher chooses a set of theoretical ideas that they believe will explain different outcomes of different cases. Theda

Skocpol (pronounced "thaida skotchpole," in case you were wondering), in a famous study comparing the national revolutions of Russia, France, and China, decided that just a few specific variations in economic and government characteristics would explain most of the differences in those revolutions.[16]

Project-based comparative research is similar except that the criteria—be they best practices or project goals or whatever—replace the theoretical concepts. The primary purpose is not to explain how each option works but to study the extent to which each of the options produces outcomes that best fit the criteria of the group. I have mentioned my work with a program a couple of years ago helping community development corporations engage in community organizing activities. This was quite a change for these organizations, who had been devoting their time to rehabilitating commercial and residential buildings and were now going to organize residents to take control of their neighborhoods. My actual role was to do evaluation research for the project, and you will learn more about that in Chapter 7. But the evaluation research allowed us to also do comparative research between two CDCs. One CDC had an elected board and created a separate community organizing group. The other CDC had an appointed board and tried to organize residents into the CDC itself. The first CDC was much more successful at community organizing. The comparison allowed us to show the kinds of conditions that would help community organizing flourish.[17] Regrettably, it was too late to preserve community organizing in both CDCs, and only one has continued with the program.

To use such a comparative research method before, rather than after a project has begun, can be a bit more challenging and takes some time. Take the example of trying to reduce youth crime. What if one faction of the planning committee thinks that midnight basketball will have the most impact on youth crime, while another faction of the planning committee thinks that after-school peer tutoring will work better? How would you set up a comparative research project to answer that question? Given that there are probably more criteria than just the impact on reductions in youth crime (such as project cost and availability of facilities), you would set up the research to study existing peer tutoring and midnight b-ball. There may be existing projects in your area, and you could study them to see how much they cost, how they obtained facilities, and how much impact they had on crime. Be forewarned, however, that this might be a big research project that could require surveying the youth participating in each of these projects. If there are no projects in your area, the research becomes even more challenging to complete.

As you've probably already suspected, doing such research is often impractical. Not only are there too few resources for such comparative research to choose the best-fitting project alternative, there are also too few resources for doing good research assessing the outcomes of projects. So even when there are other programs out there to compare, we rarely have good outcome data to use in comparing specific projects. That makes a comparative research project into something that often takes a year or more because the outcome data have to be compiled along with the analysis of the project itself.

Most groups, then, choose a project option based on what might be called hypothesized effects. In essence, because they have no research establishing the effectiveness of any single project alternative, they rely on a theoretical prediction that a certain project will produce a set of effects. In the midnight basketball vs. tutoring example above, the group might hypothesize that midnight basketball will involve male youth after dark and thus directly impact the mischief they could otherwise get into, while tutoring would have a more indirect future impact. That may be correct. But it also may not be, making the project itself essentially a quasi-experiment, which we will discuss further in the evaluation chapter.

## THE SPECIAL CASE OF POLICY PRESCRIPTIONS

We have mostly concentrated up to this point on developing prescriptions for projects directly impacting the community. But many communities suffer because of policies that have done harm in the past and continue to do harm, either by allowing bad things to continue or preventing good things from starting. So many groups and organizations find themselves in the position, sooner or later, of bumping up against the rules. One of the most famous community-based policy change efforts came in the 1970s from the nationwide efforts to change a bank lending practice called redlining. Bankers would literally draw a red line around certain central city areas they deemed high risk and would refuse to make home loans in those areas. The Chicago-based National People's Action and other groups undertook a massive amount of research to document the extent and consequences of redlining, diagnosing much of the central city decay of the time as a direct result of this discriminatory banking practice. They then began to develop policy prescriptions to prevent banks from such blatantly discriminatory lending, ultimately resulting in the national Community Reinvestment Act, passed by the federal government in 1977.[18]

**Making Policy Prescriptions**

*Find a Good Issue*

- Keep your eyes and ears wide open.
- Watch the regular sources.
- Keep your eyes and ears open on a specific issue.
- Research a specific issue.

*Find Policy Alternatives*

- Use the methods for developing service alternatives.
- Do a survey of stakeholders.
- Do a survey of experts.
- Imagine the ideal.

*Develop Criteria*

- Develop criteria from the context to determine practical limits.
- Develop criteria from core values to determine acceptable compromise.

*Choose an Alternative*

- Making predictions
- Comparing costs and benefits
- Tracing decision steps

Most community groups and organizations engage in policy prescriptions on a much smaller level, if at all. They are often so caught up in making service prescriptions that they either don't realize how policy helps cause the problems they are treating or they don't have the resources to address the policy issues. Policy work seems like a luxury because it doesn't meet people's immediate needs. But the Community Reinvestment Act provided community groups and poor neighborhoods with millions of dollars in loans and other investments, making it well worth the effort. What follows, then, is a brief outline of how to do small-scale policy prescriptions, following the steps of finding issues, finding alternatives, developing criteria, and choosing alternatives for policy issues.

## Finding Issues

There are policy issues and ideas everywhere. Most people in the field of community work see the problems caused by a lack of decent food, clothing, housing, education, employment, legal protection, and other rights and goods that are unequally distributed. There is no shortage of ideas about policies to address these inequalities. So the challenge is not so much finding policy alternatives as finding winnable policy battles. You will not be able to end capitalism in your city. But you may be able to pass a living wage law requiring employers who receive government funds and contracts to pay their employees a wage that will support a family.[19]

Finding practical policy battles requires an organization to stay in touch with the policy issues making their way through various levels of government. Brian Hogwood and Lewis Gunn[20] draw their strategies for finding juicy policy issues from the management literature. The most general strategy is *undirected viewing*—basically "keeping your eyes open" without any particular purpose to see what the policy issues are that are circulating through government. This is the most challenging strategy in some ways since it involves having someone in your group who is well connected to policymakers and regularly getting fed information on what policy issues are current at different levels of government. This may be impractical for many groups, but a project sponsored through a political science class at Middlesex Community College provides a model for this kind of work. There the students researched the policy issues being debated in the state government, wrote up briefs on those that were relevant to nonprofit organizations, and distributed the packets to area nonprofits. A less labor-intensive strategy for staying current on policy issues is what Hogwood and Gunn call *conditioned viewing*—regularly checking regular sources. Most local and state governments in the United States, as well as the federal government, will provide information on bills under debate from their Web sites. The next more focused strategy is an *informal search*, which involves keeping your eyes and ears open for policy information in a specific issue area. Advocacy organizations will regularly distribute policy alerts in their particular issue area, as will issue-oriented e-mail lists. Finally, the *formal search* is choosing a specific policy issue and conducting intensive research.

Usually, in the project-based research model, a policy issue comes directly from diagnostic research. In the process of diagnosing a community problem, a group or organization will often uncover policy issues that are either causing a problem or preventing a solution. As we discussed in Chapter 3, community workers addressing housing issues recently discovered a new form of redlining called predatory lending. As banking was deregulated and the Community Reinvestment Act weakened, individuals and families in poor communities found it again more difficult to obtain mortgage loans from traditional lenders. But a new form of sub-prime lender, who makes loans that are statistically more risky, has grown to fill the gap. The problem is that the interest on the loan is exorbitantly high, or the loan has fine print that requires a dramatic increase or "balloon" in the monthly payment a few years down the road, and many poor borrowers then default and lose their home to the predatory lender, who then sells the home to the next low-income buyer who can't get a traditional loan. The Association of Community Organizations for Reform Now (ACORN) and other groups have gotten involved in pressing state governments and the federal government to develop policies to better protect low-income borrowers.[21]

## Finding Alternatives

Once the diagnosis is achieved, and it becomes clear that a policy prescription is the best medicine to address the problem, the group or organization begins a search for alternatives. In many ways, the same research methods used for service project prescriptions apply here: Use the library, read the trade publications, find and use networks, and brainstorm. There are also some other strategies, outlined by Patton and Sawicki, that apply specifically to finding policy alternatives. One of those is a survey of the people affected to get their policy opinions. A quick survey of policymakers or experts in the field can also be useful. And a third strategy is to imagine what an ideal circumstance would be—such as low-income lenders being able to get loans that they could actually repay—and then develop a policy alternative to support that ideal.[22]

As with service projects, however, sometimes there are not realistic alternatives. Patton and Sawicki also attempt to develop a systematic method for creating alternatives when there are no ready-made options. The idea is to break a policy issue up into parts.[23] If the problem is youth crime, for example, one aspect of the problem is law enforcement. Another is parental rights and responsibilities. Yet another might be youth employment and recreation opportunities. You may have found policy options in some or all of these categories. Because the problem is broken up into categories, it is possible to creatively combine one policy covering law enforcement with another covering youth employment and recreation.

## Developing Criteria

There are two approaches to developing criteria in policy projects, which are probably best used together. The first is to consider the context. Because the political context is often much more important in policy projects than it is in service projects, understanding that context becomes crucial. The challenge is deciding just what "the context" includes. Ann Majchrzak argues that, once the social problem is selected, the next step is to identify the key policy issues suggested by that problem.[24] Promoting an educational policy that allows for more parent participation in school decision making may involve, for example, thinking about school funding and taxes; union collective bargaining processes; how school board members are elected; how principals are appointed; and numerous other issues. Because how unions, teachers, voters, school board members, and taxpayers will react to a policy initiative is important. Then it is important to conduct historical research on the legislative history of educational reform in general in your area, as well as on the history of the particular reforms you are proposing, to see what has been tried and to understand why some policy efforts succeed and others fail. The group also needs to find or construct organizational charts on the relevant decision-making bodies; in this case probably the school board and administrative bureaucracy. All of this information provides the raw material for a model of the policymaking process—one of those boxes-and-arrows diagrams showing who has what kind of input at what point. If possible, interviewing stakeholders to find out where they stand will allow you to elaborate that policymaking model to see where particular roadblocks may be along the way. By the time you are done with this research project you will be well on your way to a set of criteria showing what kinds of parental participation policies are practical and what interventions are needed to expand the range of practical options.

Some practical criteria that can come out of such a process include effectiveness, efficiency, administrative ease, legality, and political acceptability.[25] A policy has to effectively accomplish the goals for which it is intended. In today's political climate it will also have to achieve its effectiveness with a minimum expenditure of money and other resources. It will have to be easy to administer to avoid getting tied up in red tape and loophole management. A policy of course has to be legal, but here that mostly means that it doesn't create a domino effect of requiring changes in other policies to make it legal. And, finally, it has to be acceptable to the wide range of political players in whatever context the policy is being created.

Relying only on criteria emphasizing what is practical, however, may in the end be impractical. Because maybe what is practical contradicts the group's values. So a second set of evaluative criteria need to come not from the context but from the group or organization itself. This is very similar to the visioning process discussed above for service prescriptions. The focus here is developing and ranking the group's core values. One of the useful things about doing this is that it both helps define criteria for judging policy options and helps the group to look into the consistency of its own value system. A group that realizes it values both better schools and lower taxes may need to decide, when push comes to shove, which it values more highly. The group then uses these values criteria to judge each of the policy alternatives.[26]

And what if the values criteria and the practical criteria produce two different groups of policies? Ah, those situations are where the difficult choices come in and where groups often splinter. The gap between what is valued and what is practical can force a group to choose between defeat with dignity and a meaningless win. You either choose to lose because you realize you can't get an acceptable policy or you take what you can get, even though it seems fatally flawed. In such situations the project may shift from changing a policy to changing the policymakers. In one Tennessee school district, a group concerned about racial equity in the area schools decided that the only way to improve their chances of success in changing the policies of their local school board was to change the composition of the board itself. They were especially frustrated by one longtime school board member who had long opposed their efforts. So they designed and carried out a research project to measure all the candidates against the group's values. They collectively designed questions to measure the school board candidates' views on such issues as affirmative action, racial diversity, and school hiring practices. They mailed the survey to the candidates, and followed up by phone and sometimes in person, and eventually got three quarters of the candidates to respond, including their main target. They graded each candidate on an A to F scale and distributed a booklet describing their questions, research methods, and grades throughout the area. Not only were they able to unseat the worst incumbent (who received an F grade from the group), but all the candidates who were elected had received an A or better. As a consequence, teachers now have access to diversity training, hiring practices have changed to include people of color on hiring committees, and the school district recognizes Martin Luther King Day.[27] Such a method can be enhanced by also researching stakeholders to determine their support or opposition to your group's policy position, the amount of resources they control, their ability to mobilize those resources, and their access to decision makers.[28]

## Choosing an Alternative

The challenge with policy projects is the same as for service projects. How do you actually determine which of the policy options will best achieve the criteria you have set? In contrast to service projects, the field of policy research has developed highly sophisticated research protocols for judging policy options. Since policy prescriptions are necessarily part of a political process, they require supporting research that can convince policymakers that the policy will achieve the predicted effects, not cause overspending and not produce unintended side effects. Three forms of policy research have sprung up to address these three issues.

Predicting outcomes includes a diverse array of research methods.[29] It is beyond our task here to provide a manual on how each of these methods works, especially because some of them involve complex computer analysis. But we will look at what each purports to do. Many of the methods emphasize forecasting. In contrast to traditional social science research, conducted from an extensive research model (see Chapter 1) where prediction involves *ceteris paribus* assumptions that everything but one variable will stay the same, in policy forecasting an intensive research model is used and the assumptions themselves are varied to see what may result. For example, a group trying to develop a policy around access to health insurance may vary their assumptions on the effects of a natural disaster, or another terrorist attack, or an economic slump, or a variety of other factors that could lead to dramatically different forecasts on the cost of health insurance. Such forecasts can also draw on data from past events to *extrapolate* to the future—essentially assuming that economic changes will impact health insurance costs in the future the same way they have in the past. Less sophisticated, but sometimes more effective in a politicized environment, is scenario writing. Scenario writing relies more on telling a story of the future, in contrast to the dry and often numerical presentation of forecasting. Those policy advocates concerned about environmental destruction have done some of the most persuasive scenario writing, perhaps beginning with the famous book *Silent Spring* by Rachel Carson.[30] Finally, computer modeling is the most sophisticated of all the forecasting methods. This is the method used by your increasingly accurate meteorologist. Massive quantities of data on all kinds of variables are fed into a computer, which then makes a prediction on how all of that data will interact. Of course, you may have noticed that even with all of this technological sophistication, your local weather forecaster still is only accurate about four to five days out. We will discuss below the problems of trying to predict policy outcomes four to five *years* out.

Cost-benefit analysis is another way of comparing policy options. This is just your basic process of comparing the expected benefits of a policy option to the costs of implementing it. It is the same thing many people do when choosing a new car. Patton and Sawicki[31] offer a set of formulas for measuring costs and benefits in the present and the future. Such measures are dependent on effective forecasting, however, since both future costs and future benefits can't be calculated without knowing future impacts of a policy alternative. Such analysis is also not just a matter of plugging numbers into a formula. Remember that the practicality criteria may include such things as political acceptability. It may not be politically acceptable to pass a policy requiring private insurers to provide discounted health insurance to low-income workers. But it may help to give those insurers tax breaks if they do so. That strategy will increase the costs of the policy but may also gain it more political support.

Another form of policy outcome evaluation and a cousin of cost-benefit analysis is risk analysis. Again dependent on accurate forecasting, risk analysis is literally an analysis of the risks of a policy alternative to different sectors of the population. This is the kind of research the government engages in to help decide how much air pollution is acceptable or how much automobile safety regulation to impose. The analysis attempts to predict such things as how much death and injury will occur at a given level of air pollution or with a given combination of automobile safety devices such as airbags and strong bumpers.[32]

A final method that attempts to bring together forecasting, cost-benefit analysis, and risk analysis is decision analysis. This method is, in some ways, the most complex of all because it not only includes the complexity of the other methods but then combines them in a step-by-step process. In decision analysis you try to map out the decision steps involved in a policy process, charting the intended and unintended effects and their costs and benefits at each step. However, because this method depends on so much data gathering, all of which can include errors, this is also the method that has the least reliability. It may, ultimately, prove the least useful for groups doing policy lobbying because it is so easy to criticize.[33]

## LOOSE GRAVEL

Perhaps the most dangerous loose gravel in the entire project cycle lies on the path to a good prescription. So much can go wrong. You can make the wrong prescription, based on either the wrong diagnosis or on faulty knowledge of the available alternatives. You can be forced, by either political practicalities or funding practicalities, to compromise the prescription and risk splintering your group. We have dealt with the loose gravel involved in making a good diagnosis in the previous chapter, so here we will focus on challenges involved in making the prescription itself.

### Solutions Looking for Problems

Prescription is the stage of the project cycle requiring the most flexibility. Too often groups at this stage will find themselves becoming attached to a single solution. Someone may have found a funding announcement that gives money for particular types of programming. Recently, I came across an announcement for a funder who will give money to new groups trying to do community organizing. The catch is that groups can only have a budget of $100,000 or less. Well, I know of a community development corporation with a budget far exceeding that, but they have been unable to start up a community organizing project because they can't get funds for it. They did their diagnostic research and came up with a prescription for organizing their community. But now they are faced with trying to redo their prescription for this grant proposal and are scrambling to create some kind of quasi-independent group that can apply for the funds.

Another thing that happens is that some group within the community or organization will have a preferred solution, and they will push their favored solution. The planning process then becomes a referendum on that solution. It is very much the way our form of representative government operates. Instead of beginning with good diagnoses and then moving on to developing custom-made solutions, the bills brought to the legislature propose solutions. Liberals tend to want to subsidize the poor, and conservatives tend to want to subsidize the rich. Look, for example, at welfare reform policies passed during the Clinton administration. The research on the causes of poverty itself was ignored. Instead, the debate was reduced to the question of subsidizing employers to provide low-wage jobs for the poor or subsidizing the poor directly. A good diagnosis of poverty, however, would point in an entirely different direction, requiring prescriptions for much more fundamental change in our economic system.

This also happens, on a smaller scale, in community organizations. I was recently working with a group planning evaluation research. A couple of people in the planning group had become enamored with a particular model of individual skill assessment, while others were much more interested in broader outcome measures such as changes in crime patterns and other social problem indicators.

Also beware of solutions posing as processes. The United Way, the federal Department of Housing and Urban Development, and funders such as the Kellogg Foundation have been pushing something called a "logic model" as the way to both plan and evaluate programs. The usefulness of such a model is that it helps groups focus on what resources they have, what they are going to do with those resources, and what they hope to achieve with those resources. But logic models have gone far beyond simply organizing information to prescribing what information, activities, and outcomes are desirable. They go so far as to designate what units of analysis an organization should use (specifying *outcomes* for individuals and *impacts* for organizations or communities). As with any method that becomes too popular too quickly, logic models are becoming reified. It has become a matter of filling boxes with words, and the process of planning is being neglected.[34]

In cases such as this, working backward really helps. As I mentioned in Chapter 3, when I do planning with groups, we start at the end of the program. What does the group want to achieve? Then we talk about what strategies they are going to use to achieve those goals, which includes a discussion of what resources they need. The research part comes in as we discuss how the group will know whether they have achieved their goals, which gets them thinking about outcome measures, and how they will know whether it is their strategies that are causing the changes, which gets them thinking about process analysis methods. And sure, it is easy to say that is just another form of logic model, but it emphasizes the process of the group constructing their own logic model, not filling in boxes predetermined by a funder. Groups working on community change issues, for example, will often find the distinction between individual outcomes and community impacts to not fit very well at all. It is the planning process that is important to prevent a decision model created for one set of circumstances to be applied in other ill-fitting circumstances.

Another way to avoid getting stuck on a particular solution is to make sure that you have at least three alternatives for people to work with. A couple of decades ago I attended a workshop where the facilitator gave us a controversial issue to discuss and, rather than allowing us to polarize ourselves in the usual pro-con debate, forced us to consider three positions on the issue. It was an interesting experience because it forced us out of dualistic thinking to come up with some creative alternatives. When groups have three options, they can develop their evaluation criteria and assess each alternative, often ending up mixing and matching parts of a number of alternatives.

Ultimately, the best way to prevent solutions taking over the planning process is to stick to the planning process itself. Planning processes can be tedious, and it is often very difficult to get continuous participation, even from the people who have the most to gain or lose. Especially if there are no funds available to implement the plan, making the plan is often considered a waste of effort. The planning processes described in this chapter may also seem as if they will take an enormous amount of time and effort—resources that may not be available to most community groups. It seems impractical to use the few resources available for such research and planning. And yet, if you remember the Cheshire Cat's conclusion to Alice at the beginning of this chapter, just doing anything without having a well-researched path may be the greatest resource waste of all.

## The Problem of Prediction

Whether a group is developing a service project or a policy project, trying to accurately predict the future can feel like a futile exercise in fortune-telling. All of the policy research literature cautions against drawing firm conclusions from even the most sophisticated computer-based modeling. Predicting the future is an extremely difficult task. For one thing, it is difficult to get good data and, as we have seen, you often have to collect your own data. For another thing, there are many unknowns. Planning a program to reduce teen pregnancy is not simply about choosing educational materials. It is also about considering how peer groups may change, how economic changes may lead to changes in family stress levels or availability of other services, how terrorist events may affect self-perceptions, and many other possible variables.

It is easy to throw up one's hands and say it's impossible. Worse yet, you might say, since all of this research won't provide any firm conclusions, and it takes up time and resources that could be used in the projects themselves, let's just skip the research altogether. But the situation isn't quite that bad. The challenge is to not get caught up in the research—something we academics are particularly vulnerable to. Remember, the action is the important part, and you are doing the research only to support the action. You may find that a full-scale, airtight scientific research program with the most sophisticated statistical analysis requiring the most high-end computer will get you no better data than a basic survey of community members.

Also remember that the planning process involving prescriptive research can serve a participatory agenda. The research provides opportunities for community or organization members to get together and discuss what they want to accomplish. A good planning process will help people learn, contribute their own wisdom, and build relationships with each other. Those things are valuable in and of themselves and may be reason enough to do a careful planning process and the supporting prescriptive research.

## We Said, They Said

One of the other reasons to do careful research, particularly with policy projects, is because the opposition is almost certainly going to be doing their research. A small community organization going up against government or corporate bureaucracies with their own research staffs can be quickly scoffed at without their own research. I remember becoming involved in an issue on my own university campus as a young assistant professor. The university was proposing to build a fraternity and sorority house cluster on campus as a strategy to get some disruptive fraternity houses out of nearby residential neighborhoods. A student environmental group on campus was opposing the plan, arguing that the houses would destroy a natural floodplain. The progressive faculty organization—of which I was a member—lent support to the student group. But neither they nor we did careful research to determine how the floodplain would be impacted. We actually got a meeting with the university president, who laughed when we presented the floodplain argument. When we went to actually look at the proposed housing site, we understood why he laughed. The site was perched on top of the bluff above the floodplain, not on the floodplain itself. A simple five-minute walk to do basic observational research would have saved us all a lot of embarrassment.

Remember also that making airtight predictions about the future is extremely difficult. So even when you have done extremely sophisticated research and can establish your expertise, their experts will find every little uncertainty they can to undermine your policy proposal. This is one of those situations where creativity is as important as scientific certainty. For example, as flying has become a more and more popular form of travel, we hear more and more that flying is safer than driving. One of the airlines I fly, as the plane pulls up to the gate, even ends the flight with the announcement "the safest part of your journey just ended." But over a decade ago some General Motors researchers took the airline industry to task for overstating the case for airline safety, arguing that when you looked at the length of the trip and the skill of the driver, shorter trips by skilled drivers were actually safer in a car.[35] The more detailed and nuanced the analysis, showing the specific contexts where the research does and does not apply, the more difficult it will be for the other side to dismiss your claims.

The only thing worse than doing bad research for a policy battle is doing *only* research. Because it is so easy to get caught up in a "we said–they said" debate, you will need more than research on your side. You will also need organized support. This is why it is so important to do research not only on the policy issue itself but on the political context. That research then allows a group or organization to efficiently direct its resources to lobbying and organizing because they know which policymakers and stakeholders are on opposite sides and which are on the fence. Organizing the supporters is often the most crucial test of a policy effort. Remember that an organized coalition of neighborhood groups—because they were organized—passed one of the most sweeping banking reform policies in the history of the country with the Community Reinvestment Act.

## CONCLUSION

This chapter focused on doing research for the prescriptive stage of the project cycle, including:

- Differentiating service prescriptions and policy prescriptions
- How to use a planning approach to develop prescriptions, which includes:
  - Researching alternative solutions
  - Developing criteria to evaluate possible solutions
  - Applying the criteria to the alternatives to choose a solution

We also looked at the special case of making policy prescriptions, including:

- How to find a good issue
- How to find or develop alternative policy prescriptions
- How to develop criteria to evaluate policies
- How to use the criteria to choose a preferred policy

Finally, we discussed the main challenges facing prescriptive research:

- Becoming overly attached to one solution
- Being able to predict outcomes
- Standing up against the other side's research

## RESOURCES

### Brainstorming and Visioning

Owen, H. (1997). *Open space technology: A user's guide* (2nd ed.). San Francisco: Berrett-Koehler.

Humphrey Institute of Public Affairs, Minnesota Extension Service. (2001). *Guide to community visioning.* University of Minnesota, http://www.hhh.umn.edu/centers/rlc/comm/object.htm

Mycoted, http://www.mycoted.com/creativity/techniques/index.php has a large collection of visioning, brainstorming, and planning techniques.

### Charrettes

CharretteCenter.net, http://www.charrettecenter.net/

The National Charrette Institute, http://www.charretteinstitute.org/

Segedy, J. A., & Johnson, B. E. (n.d.). *The neighborhood Charrette handbook.* University of Louisville, http://www.louisville.edu/org/sun/planning/char.html

### Comparative Research

Ragin, C. C. (1987). *The comparative method: Moving beyond qualitative and quantitative strategies.* Berkeley, CA: University of California Press.

### Policy Research Web Sites

The Center of Budget and Policy Priorities, http://www.cbpp.org/

The Electronic Policy Network, http://movingideas.org/

Stateline.org, http://www.stateline.org/, researches policy issues state by state.

Voluntary Sector Public Policy Toolbox, http://www.ginsler.com/html /toolbox.htp, helps nonprofit organizations research and impact public policy in Canada.

## Policy Research Guides

Hogwood, B. W., & Gunn, L. A. (1984). *Policy analysis for the real world.* New York: Oxford University Press.

Majchrzak, A. (1984). *Methods for policy research.* Thousand Oaks, CA: Sage Publications.

Patton, C. V., & Sawicki, D. S. (1993). *Basic methods of policy analysis and planning* (2nd ed.) (p. 57). Englewood Cliffs, NJ: Prentice Hall.

# NOTES

1. Carroll, L. (1994). *Alice's adventures in wonderland.* Chapter 6. The Millennium Fulcrum Edition 3.0. Retrieved July 15, 2004, from http://www-2.cs.cmu.edu/People/rgs/alice-table.html

2. Zald, M. N., & Ash, R. (1966). Social movement organizations: Growth, decay, and change. *Social Forces, 44,* 327–341.

3. Starhawk. (2002). *Webs of power: Notes from the global uprising.* Gabriola Island, B.C., Canada: New Society Publishers.

4. The Cohousing Association of the United States. (2004). Retrieved July 15, 2004, from http://www.cohousing.org/

5. Sawyer, E. (2002). An ACT UP founder "acts up" for Africa's access to AIDS. In B. Shepard and R. Hayduk (Eds.). *From ACT UP to the WTO: Urban protest and community building in the era of globalization* (pp. 88–105). New York: Verso. Cyler, K. (2002). Building a healing community from ACT UP to Housing Works. Benjamin Shepard, interviewer. In B. Shepard and R. Hayduk (Eds.). *From ACT UP to the WTO: Urban protest and community building in the era of globalization* (pp. 351–360). New York: Verso.

6. United States Department of Health and Human Services. (2004). Office for Civil Rights—HIPAA. Retrieved July 15, 2004, from http://www.hhs.gov/ocr/hipaa/

7. Owen, H. (1997). *Open space technology: A user's guide* (2nd ed.). San Francisco: Berrett-Koehler.

8. Humphrey Institute of Public Affairs, Minnesota Extension Service. (2001). *Guide to community visioning: the visioning process.* Minneapolis: University of Minnesota. Retrieved July 15, 2004, from http://www.hhh.umn.edu/centers/rlc/comm/process.htm

9.  North Central Regional Educational Laboratory. (2004). Reach Consensus. Retrieved July 15, 2004, from http://www.ncrel.org/

10.  Dover, V. (n.d.). *Charrettes for new urbanism.* Retrieved July 15, 2004, from http://www.doverkohl.com/writings_images/charrettes_for_NU_in_ FL.htm. See also National Charrette Institute. (2003). *What is a charrette?* Retrieved July 15, 2004, from http://www.charretteinstitute.org/ charrette.html. See also Segedy, J. A., & Johnson, B. E. (n.d.) *The neighborhood charrette handbook.* University of Louisville. Retrieved July 15, 2004, from http://www.louisville.edu/org/sun/planning/char.html

11.  Stoecker, R. (1995). Community organizing and community development in Cedar-Riverside and East Toledo: A comparative study. *Journal of Community Practice, 2,* 1–23.

12.  Koenig, H. G., Idler, E., Kasl, S., Hays, J., George, L. K., Musick, M., Larson, D. B., Collins, T., & Benson, H. (1999). Religion, spirituality, and medicine: A rebuttal to skeptics. *International Journal of Psychiatry in Medicine, 29,* 123–131.

13.  Patton, C. V., & D. S. Sawicki. (1993). *Basic methods of policy analysis and planning* (2nd ed.). (p.57).Englewood Cliffs, NJ: Prentice Hall.

14.  Mycoted. (2003). *Creativity techniques.* Retrieved July 15, 2004, from http://www.mycoted.com/creativity/techniques/index.php

15.  Ragin, C. C. (1987). *The comparative method: Moving beyond qualitative and quantitative strategies.* Berkeley, CA: University of California Press.

16.  Skocpol, T. (1979). *States & social revolutions.* New York: Cambridge University Press.

17.  Stoecker, R. (2003). Understanding the development-organizing dialectic. *Journal of Urban Affairs, 25,* 493–512.

18.  Squires, G. D. (2003). *Organizing access to capital: Advocacy and the democratization of financial institutions.* Philadelphia: Temple University Press.

19.  ACORN. (n.d.) *Living wage resource center.* Retrieved July 15, 2004, from http://www.livingwagecampaign.org/

20.  Hogwood, B. W., & Gunn, L. A. (1984). *Policy analysis for the real world.* (p. 73). New York: Oxford University Press.

21.  Squires, G. D. (2003). *Organizing access to capital.* ACORN. (2003). *Predatory lending: What's happening now.* Retrieved July 15, 2004, from http:// www.acorn.org/

22.  Patton, C. V., & Sawicki, D. S. (1993). *Basic methods of policy analysis and planning* (pp. 233–245).

23.  Ibid. (pp. 245–248).

24.  Majchrzak, A. (1984). *Methods for policy research.* (pp. 33–40).Thousand Oaks, CA: Sage Publications.

25.  Patton, C. V., & Sawicki, D. S. (1993). *Basic methods of policy analysis and planning.* (p. 57).

26.  Hogwood, B. W., & Gunn, L. A. (1984). *Policy analysis for the real world.* (pp. 46–47).

27.  Osborne, G. L. Personal interview. October 22, 2004.

28.  Majchrzak, A. (1984). *Methods for policy research* (pp 77–79). Thousand Oaks, CA: Sage Publications.

29.  Hogwood, B. W., & Gunn, L. A. (1984). *Policy analysis for the real world.* (pp. 129–144).

30.  Carson, R. (2002). *Silent spring* (40th anniversary ed.). Boston: Houghton Mifflin Company.

31.  Patton, C. V., & Sawicki, D. S. (1993). *Basic methods of policy analysis and planning.* (pp. 275–295).

32.  House, P. W., & Shull, R. D. (1991). *The practice of policy analysis: Forty years of art and technology.* (pp. 71–85). Washington D.C.: Compass Press.

33.  House, P. W., & Shull, R. D. (1991). *The practice of policy analysis: Forty years of art and technology* (pp. 85–102).

34.  W. K. Kellogg Foundation. (2001). *W. K. Kellogg Foundation logic model development guide.* Retrieved July 15, 2004, from http://www.wkkf .org/Pubs/Tools/Evaluation/Pub3669.pdf

35.  Evans, L., Frick, M. C., & Schwing, R. C. (1990). Is it safer to fly or drive? *Risk Analysis, 10,* 239–246.

# *Six*

# Implementing

## *When Research Is the Project*

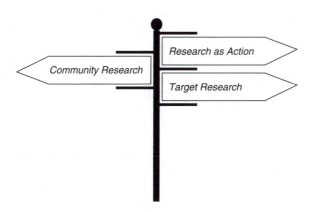

## MAKING WHO-VILLE HEARD

Of all the brilliant children's books written by the great Dr. Seuss, perhaps none is so great as *Horton Hears a Who.* Horton, a kindly elephant, was just hanging out having a good time in the Jungle of Nool when he "heard a small noise." It turns out he happened to hear the shout of a resident of Who-ville—an entire community occupying a small speck of dust. Well, the other animals thought Horton was on the verge of an obsessive-compulsive breakdown, talking to a speck of dust, and they did everything in their power to make him give up this apparent fantasy, even banishing the speck of dust to a clover field (from which Horton miraculously recovered the dust speck). Finally, when the other animals were about to take the speck of dust to which Who-ville clung and boil it in Beezle-Nut oil, Horton pleaded for the residents of Who-ville to make themselves heard. The Who-ville mayor quickly called a town meeting and his people yelled as loud as they could, desperate to make their presence known. Finally, with the addition of little Jo-Jo, who shouted from the top of the Eiffelberg Tower, their voices were heard: "They've proved they ARE persons, no matter how small. And their whole world was saved by the Smallest of All!"[1]

For many poor and underserved communities, simply making their existence known is one of the hardest tasks of all. Research that highlights their community and makes it visible can also help make their members' voices heard. Of course, it takes more than research to accomplish this. But research can be the focal point around which people organize their collective voice.

You might think that once you have done the research for the diagnosis, and then more research for the prescription, you would be done with research. But sometimes the implementation itself is research. To be fair, when research is the project it is usually not because you have done a bunch of diagnostic and prescriptive research that led you to decide that the project should be even more research. Rather, many community projects that center on research are begun without any prior diagnostic or prescriptive research.

It might also seem rather uninspired to think that something as seemingly bland as research could bring people together, energize them, organize them, and amplify their voices. But that is only because we see research in a very narrow light. Our view of how research should be presented is especially problematic. Ever since we wrote that first term paper in college, research has been presented through black letters on white paper. But it's not so with the research that communities do so they can be seen and heard. Their research is presented through photography, quilting, song, theater,

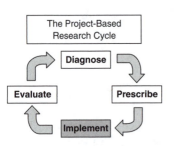

The Project-Based Research Cycle

Diagnose

Prescribe

Implement

Evaluate

painting, Web sites, and a wide variety of other mediums. When the East Toledo Community Organization, a neighborhood-based group on the east side of Toledo, Ohio was trying to get the city government to change its budgeting priorities in exchange for supporting a tax increase, they spent weeks studying the entire city budget. When they finished, and had established their recommendations, just in time for the holidays, they called a press conference and gathered on the steps of city hall. To the tune of "We Wish You a Merry Christmas" they sang:

> We wish you would fix the budget,
>
> We wish you would fix the budget,
>
> We wish you would fix the budget,
>
> And here's our ideas.

The following verses gave their recommendations: a new hotel tax, reallocations, and other ideas all presented in a lively, slightly irreverent, and fun bit of street theater.[2] This particular example of research, as we will see later in this chapter, is part of a target research strategy where the task is to do research showing the weaknesses or problems of some target organization. But many more communities focus their research efforts inwardly, helping to challenge negative stereotypes presented by the mass media, preserve their culture, document their history, and tell their story.

This chapter will cover both of those forms of research as implementation. And it requires expanding on some of the themes introduced in Chapter 2.

## RESEARCH AS ACTION

While we have discussed how community members can participate in research projects, and how such research can produce changes in either the community or its broader social context, here we must explore in more detail just what it means for research to *be* the action. One way that project-based research becomes the action, at any stage in the project-based research cycle, is through changing what John Gaventa called the "relations of knowledge production."[3] Because poor communities are not only on

**Research as Action**

1. A community organizing process

2. Information as an end in itself

the losing end of the market process. They are also on the losing end of the information process. When community members are involved in producing and using knowledge themselves, rather than having others do it for them, they also develop skills to become self-sufficient knowledge producers, which in itself begins to change power relations. When a normal resident can go up against a government or corporate target, armed with good information, they occupy a much different position than a resident armed only with their anger. The former gets heard, the latter gets placated.

What are the components of research as action? First, the research process is a community organizing process. There are many good manuals on community organizing out there,[4] and I couldn't hope to reproduce their many lessons here, but there are some basic points that bear mentioning. A main goal of the process is to produce a larger, stronger, tighter-knit group or organization. When research is used as action it should not only involve community members in the research but, ultimately, bring them into the organization itself. Choosing a research question and process that will inspire enough people's imaginations is the main challenge here. Surveys may not be exciting enough, so many groups turn to community theater or arts projects, such as quilts and photography exhibits. A good community organizing process will also help people build a sense of empowerment by helping them feel successful at doing new things. Someone who learns how to quilt for the first time, or point a camera, or create a Web site, or "speak from the diaphragm" in the community theater production will be forever changed for the better. Finally, a good community organizing process will enhance the public presence of the group—it will be seen as more competent, stable, and influential—which will attract allies and at least give pause to potential adversaries.

Second, when research is the action, information is an end in itself. In other forms of research, the data and often even the research report are relegated to a dusty shelf somewhere at the end of the project. But here the goal is to keep the research as public as possible for as long as possible. If the presentation of the research is a community art project such as a building mural, the research may even outlast the community. Of course, this doesn't mean the research is *only* an end in itself. Especially with target research, where the goal is getting a corporate or government target to change, the research is designed to produce pressure on the target. But this is different from research conducted at the diagnostic or prescriptive stages, where the research is simply preparation for the next project stage. Here the research is not being conducted to support the subsequent evaluation stage but as part of the project implementation itself.

It is because of the need for community involvement that so much research at the implementation stage looks like something other than research. Consequently, it often uses an information process that differs quite a bit from traditional research. It even differs from the participatory and action research models we have discussed earlier because it emphasizes more than those models the importance of having the people at the center of the research process. A professional researcher often does the research work at the diagnosis, prescription, and evaluation stages. But at the implementation stage the people do the research themselves to build the sense of community necessary for carrying out the social change goals developed through those earlier stages. At the implementation stage, then, the research often takes on the character of a popular education process.

When research is the project, people often use a popular education process, which we have discussed briefly already. Popular education has been at the root of so many important social change victories. In the United States, popular education supported the formation of the Congress of Industrial Organizations, which ultimately brought racial integration to the union movement. It supported the implementation of the Brown v. Board of Education school desegregation decision, as well as the 1950s–1960s civil rights movement itself. Around the world, popular education has supported the integration of literacy projects with democratic social movements.

How does popular education work? The crucial difference between popular education and other forms of project-based research is that popular education emphasizes the involvement of community members themselves as sources of information. Much popular education is experience-based. Small groups of 10–30 participants, often sitting in a circle, begin by sharing their experiences on a topic. The famous Highlander Research and Education Center in Tennessee, which has been mentioned a number of times in this book, uses a circle of rocking chairs.[5] Depending on the type of group, the process may involve also drawing or acting out their experiences.[6] As participants share experiences, they are also encouraged to compare experiences. Sometimes this is done casually and sometimes systematically as participants are asked to listen and watch for particular types of themes. The goal here is to help people take control of the knowledge process and begin to see themselves as producers, not just victims, of knowledge. This is also a form of consciousness raising, helping participants to see

---

**Popular Education Process**

- *Research question:* Comes from people's experiences
- *Method:* Process of collecting and analyzing experiences
- *Data collection:* People share experiences and collect further information to better understand those experiences
- *Data analysis:* People reflect on commonalities of experience to develop deeper analysis
- *Reporting:* A plan for change

---

that they are not alone and their experience is not the product of their own failings or weaknesses but is part of something bigger going on.[7]

It is easy to see how that experiential data could be put to use in community research projects that produce art and theater, as participants shape common themes and explore creative ways of presenting those themes. It is more difficult to see how such a process can be used in target research. In target research, popular education helps build the strength of the group to go into battle against a target. But the common experience of oppression or discrimination that popular education uncovers then becomes the basis for a deeper analysis by the group, as they collectively analyze what may be causing that oppression/discrimination. That collective analysis can identify targets, and the group then develops strategies for approaching those targets. We will look at community research first.

## COMMUNITY RESEARCH

Often the impetus for using research as action is the question "Who are we?" For groups and communities used to being defined by outsiders, often negatively, this is one of the most empowering questions anyone can ask. One of the best examples of this comes from the 1960s–1970s women's movement. Concerned that male physicians, and a male-dominated medical system, were fundamentally misunderstanding women's bodies, they began investigating the parts of their own bodies that male physicians never bothered to explain. As the movement grew and women's collective research accumulated, one group of women in Boston undertook the enormous project of compiling this research into the famous book *Our Bodies, Ourselves*.[8] For the first time in the history of modern medicine, there was an integrated study of women's physical and emotional being, written for women by a community of women. And it was not just that they produced a book. This act of research shifted the relations of knowledge production, placing it in the hands of the "patients" and thus transforming them into participants. This was not simply about produc-

> **Community Research**
>
> - Historical recovery
> - Arts documentation
> - Community media
> - Community mapping

ing information but about producing power through both the act of research and the use of the research.

There are many examples less intimate and less personal than this, most focused on understanding communities as collectives, but all with the same fundamental goals. Here we will review some of these projects and the research processes they use.

## Historical Recovery

In my very earliest days as a graduate student in the Cedar-Riverside neighborhood in Minneapolis, after Tim Mungavan confronted me and warned against my becoming just another exploitive researcher, my life was changed forever. I still wrote my Ph.D. dissertation on the neighborhood, and even a book, but I did it very differently than I had planned. Normally, in my field of sociology, the purpose of research is to find and answer profound theoretical questions, so the data itself takes on secondary status. But here I was in Cedar-Riverside promising to give something back. Gradually, I discovered that I had to shift from normal sociology to make good on that pledge. My focus became not deep theoretical questions but the telling of the story. Doing so made for some interesting "pretzeling" of theory into the story for my dissertation, but what the community wanted was for its story to be told.

When I moved to Toledo, Ohio after I graduated with that dissertation on Cedar-Riverside, I wound up collaborating with yet more neighborhood activists. This time it was Dave Beckwith, who had directed the East Toledo Community Organization (ETCO) for a time—the colorful community organizing group across the river on the east side of town that did the city budget action research project described earlier in this chapter. Among the many projects on which Dave and I collaborated was the telling of the story of ETCO. It was in this project, as we carefully traversed the broken floorboards of a condemnable building to rescue old ETCO documents that had been left to rot, that I realized I was engaged in a special form of research. I have been calling it *historical recovery* research. Much of the work in historical recovery research is based in oral history[9] methods, but it also goes well beyond interviewing individuals. In many cases historical recovery research is quite literally a recovery process as communities, their organizations, their documents, and their participants scatter far and wide in a very short period of time. Finding the individuals and the documents can be one of the greatest challenges in such a project. Working with those individuals to put all the pieces together can be the reward of a lifetime.

The work I do with community organizations is little different from the work that so many local history groups do to preserve their community's history. Even the small town I grew up in has a group dedicated to preserving the stories of its history. Their challenges may be greater than the ones I face. Community organizations often leave a clearer trail of documentation than communities. It is easier to get names, as there are often minutes of meetings and individuals who are still in touch with past members. And usually someone has a box in their attic or basement that is chock-full of documents just waiting to be put end to end to tell their tale. But for communities the first challenge is to define what the community is, how far it extends in time and space, and who can be counted as community members. Where does a neighborhood start and end? How long must someone live in that neighborhood to be counted a member of the community?

The answers to these questions may not be best answered by referring to academic standards. Remember that doing historical recovery research as a community-building process requires thinking differently about the research process than if it were a typical academic research process. The hope with such a process is that you will engage community or organization members in the research process itself so that it is truly their research process. They will need to answer those questions for themselves, and I have generally found that the answers are emergent through the research process, as residents produce a "snowball sample" of influential community members and gradually come to agreement on the important community events or turning points. Additionally, many communities and organizations have troubled periods in their histories. I have never encountered a group that didn't want the stories of those periods told, but they wanted them told in a way that made sense to them. Especially when the difficult periods involve faction fights, each side wants its perspective presented, and doing so can sometimes go a long way toward making sense of why the fight took place to begin with.

In those cases where an outside researcher is brought in to manage or do a historical recovery process, dealing with sensitive community information is important. When I do oral histories I typically do not use a tape recorder, as the people I interview sometimes tell me about tactics that could be considered unethical or occasionally perhaps illegal. Instead, I have learned how to take very detailed notes. I then use a two-step process of organizing the information from the interviews. Step one is to return a typed version of the notes to the person I interviewed for them to edit. In traditional ethnographic research this would be a no-no, as it would be seen as making the data impure. But remember back to Chapter 1 where we discussed how social connectedness can often produce more accurate research than social distance. When people see their words in print, they can correct misstatements, overstatements, and other inaccuracies. Yes, they may also decide that some things are better left unsaid, but this is their project, after all. The main difficulty I have run into is that some people do not like to receive exact transcripts that include casual speech like "gonna" instead of "going to" so I now try to reassure people that they can make their language more formal if they wish. Another important consideration is to be sure that the people you give transcripts to have reading literacy. One of my most embarrassing moments came when I gave a transcript to someone who was illiterate, and it was very awkward for both of us. In step two, I insert interview quotes into a report draft without identifying names so individuals can see their words in context. This step often generates some of the most interesting information, as people finally begin to get a sense of what the project is about. It is here that they become engaged and often give me a bunch more information that they originally didn't think was important.

Of course, such projects do not have to result in only a written report. Many communities do cross-generational oral histories,[10] sending community youth out with tape recorders or sometimes even video cameras to interview community elders. Those oral histories are then stored in community archives, the local library, or other places. Cross-generational oral history projects also do much more than produce audio- and videotapes. They build cross-generational relationships and they connect local youth with their place and their culture.

Language and culture preservation projects are another form of historical recovery research. The British-influenced practice of forced assimilation, as children were kidnapped from indigenous communities and imprisoned in assimilation schools in North America, Australia, and other places, nearly wiped out the rich languages, religions, and artistic traditions of those places.[11] Indigenous peoples across the globe are engaging in a great deal of research to preserve their languages and cultures, in some cases writing down the stories of their oral traditions and recording the voices of the last remaining speakers of indigenous languages. The results of such research are used in local history collections but also in survival schools where indigenous youth are taught the language and beliefs of their elders. Sometimes the research is even presented on the World Wide Web when it is culturally appropriate. A digital cultural preservation project of the Bawgutti people of the North Coast of Australia, for example, is available only on CD-ROM.[12]

## Arts Documentation: Quilts, Plays, Photography, etc.

One of the most interesting forms of research as implementation comes from community art. Much more than just aesthetic expressions much community or folk art is also a presentation of people's stories, and consequently their research. Of the many examples out there, perhaps the most dramatic is the example of the *arpillera*. When the brutal dictator Augosto Pinochet came to power in Chile with the help of the United States in 1973, civil rights were squashed and freedom of speech all but disappeared. Those who supported the previous elected government disappeared as well. Their grieving families had no safe way to even express their feelings of loss. As a group of these women came together in the shelter of the church, however, they came on the idea of creating quilts to artistically express their anguish. Using scraps of discarded cloth sewn onto burlap, they told their stories, and the first arpilleras were created. As the method matured, it became more political, telling stories of the oppression wrought by the Pinochet government in their communities. This safe form of political expression even ultimately empowered the women to engage in more public forms of political action, as they organized protests and rallies.[13]

Of course, much community art is not done as code under conditions of brutality. It is, however, often done under conditions of oppression, where other avenues of presenting community information—the schools, news media, and government—are not available to the community. In addition, community members often feel alienated from those staid institutional forms of expression and turn to artistic forms to overcome that sense of alienation. Quilts, baskets, murals, music, poetry, community theater, and many other methods have been used in community after community to express the people's experience.

One of the most dramatic, lasting, and intense forms of community research expressed through artwork is the community mural. The Groundswell Community Mural Project in New York, for example, organizes community mural projects to do much more than create art. Through the process, residents come together to develop artistic skills; research and learn community history; develop collaborative relationships with local and city organizations; and develop a sense of community control over their public respresentation.[14] In another example, students from the Harmar School in Marietta, Ohio created more than 300 drawings that became part of a mural project depicting the history and the future of their community, as well as its important characteristics such as water transportation.[15]

Community sculpture serves a similar purpose, even when it's not supposed to. In the Fremont neighborhood of Seattle, well known for its community art, is a sculpture of a group of people, and a dog, waiting at a bus stop. Look at the sculpture a little closer, and you notice that the face of the dog is human. It takes a little digging to find out how the dog got a human face. That face is that of the city council member who opposed public funding for the sculpture. In my favorite neighborhood, Cedar-Riverside, a unique community sculpture project brought together all the ethnic communities in the neighborhood. The result was a nine-foot-tall pillar covered on all four sides with mosaic squares. If you are not familiar with the mosaic process, it uses pieces of broken ceramic tile, arranged almost puzzle-like, to form images. The project organized each ethnic community in the neighborhood—Somalian, Oromo, Vietnamese, Korean, longtime residents, and other groups—to create a mosaic square symbolizing its community. A plaque included on the pillar helps educate viewers about the symbols and the communities they represent. Also included on the pillar are mosaic squares depicting neighborhood history, adding to the popular education outcomes of the project.

## Community Media

If you have ever walked down the street of a major city and been asked to buy a copy of a *Streetwise,* or *News From Our Shoes,* or *Street Voice,* or a long list of other news magazines produced in coalition

SOURCE: Sarah Penman, West Bank Community Development Corporation.

with homeless people, you have seen a form of community media in action. In many cases the content of those newspapers is produced by people who are homeless, and the end product is sold to you by people who are homeless. The articles range from poetry to hard-hitting policy critique. Some of it is based on good research and some of it is based on bad research. But it is one of the most visible examples of research as action being conducted by the people themselves.

Community media have been around forever and have served every size, shape, and type of community. When I worked with the Cedar-Riverside neighborhood on its historical recovery research, one of the best sources of information was the neighborhood newspaper. *Snoose News,* named for the former Scandinavian residents of the neighborhood, was one of the best sources of urban redevelopment analysis in the city of Minneapolis at the time.

One of the most exciting developments spurring on the growth of community media has been the rise of the Internet. In Sunshine, a working-class suburb of Melbourne, Australia, a small neighborhood service organization called the Duke Street Community House was just getting its first Internet access in the mid-1990s. The people who attended Duke Street for various programs, including literacy training, got excited about this new connection to the world. Duke

Street began to combine computer literacy training with language literacy training. The result was an online 'zine created by the literacy students of Duke Street, at that time with hand-coded html. The 'zine contained personal stories, community stories, and analysis. As with other community media projects, not all of it was solid research (nor was it intended to be), but what some articles lacked in solid research they made up for in artistic quality.[16]

Some communities develop their own Web sites to counter popular media misrepresentations. Poor neighborhoods that are constantly portrayed in the media as only places of guns and drugs have, with the Internet, an opportunity to also present their strengths and spirit. Such has been the case with the Austin Access Model, a community technology project organized by the Austin Learning Academy and the Austin Free-Net. The project is run by the principles of the three Cs—choice, control, and content. The idea is to get community members involved in their community by taking control of technology and using it for the community's benefit rather than being controlled by it. They implement that control through using the technology to produce neighborhood Web pages and other information products. Beginning in the 11th and 12th Street neighborhood in Austin, the project has now expanded to other underserved neighborhood communities.[17]

With the maturing of the Internet, community media have risen to dramatic heights. Perhaps the most developed form of community media on the Internet, using some of the most labor-intensive research, is the community portal. A community portal is basically a one-stop Internet site for all of a community's arts, culture, events, news, shopping, services, and discussion. It is part virtual mall, part town meeting, part community directory. The early pioneers of community portals were the community freenets of the 1980s—no-cost Internet service providers—who made phone calls, held meetings, and knocked on doors to develop Web sites for their communities. The early pioneers of such projects, in Blacksburg, Virginia and Santa Monica, California, set the standard by providing not just community information but also providing online space to discuss community issues.[18] The Seattle Community Network is still one of the best sources of community information in Seattle. SCN not only hosts neighborhood Web sites but provides technical assistance to neighborhoods who want to develop their own sites, an enormous undertaking.[19] All of these examples provide interesting case material of a community research process designed to bring community participants together, even if only virtually.

These are also cases of communities taking information into their own hands. Particularly with community portals, the seemingly simple act of gathering community information becomes a very intense process. Charges of bias take on a unique character in such projects, as groups vie for inclusion in the portal. The pro-choice group and the pro-life group both jockey for space. And with many forms of research as implementation, the presentation of the results often becomes more important than the collection of data. How does one present the collected data of a community on a Web site? If you think back to the first chapter, in many cases the research supporting such community portals takes on the character of an extensive research project, where a little information is collected from a large number of cases. But such portal projects are also supporting intensive research, helping each community organization, neighborhood, or group to present its own information in the form of a Web site linked to that portal. One of the most massive intensive/extensive research projects supporting a community portal is VICNET, Victoria's Network. Victoria is one of the most populous states in Australia, and VICNET was established as the freenet/community portal for the entire state in the 1990s. It was through the work of VICNET that the Duke Street Community House got its own Web site—an intensive research project—as part of VICNET's extensive research project attempting to find and document all of the community activities and projects across the state.

## Community Mapping and Geographic Information Systems

Geographical research used to be one of the least recognized forms of research used in community settings. One of the first examples of geographical research used in the service of community action was presented in *Follow the Drinking Gourd*—a song passed along from plantation to plantation by organizers of the Underground Railroad and an itinerant carpenter named Peg Leg Joe in the pre–Civil War South.[20]

When the Sun comes back

And the first quail calls

Follow the Drinking Gourd.

For the old man is a-waiting for to carry you to freedom

If you follow the Drinking Gourd.

The riverbank makes a very good road.

The dead trees will show you the way.

Left foot, peg foot, traveling on,

Follow the Drinking Gourd.

The river ends between two hills

Follow the Drinking Gourd.

There's another river on the other side

Follow the Drinking Gourd.

When the great big river meets the little river

Follow the Drinking Gourd.

For the old man is a-waiting for to carry you to freedom

If you follow the Drinking Gourd.

Based on research conducted by Underground Railroad organizers,[21] the song charted a path north to freedom, using the stars of the Big Dipper, or "Drinking Gourd" along with other geographic landmarks. Sung on the plantations, with the slave owners and their guards oblivious to its true meaning, it helped countless people of African heritage escape the brutal practice of human slavery.

Today, of course, geographical research is no longer conducted through the on-the-ground, trial-and-error methods of political-economic fugitives. Today we have a form of computer-based mapping called Geographic Information Systems, or GIS. GIS has literally revolutionized community research and information management. Armed with a skilled GIS researcher, any community can carefully track geographical changes in its community. I worked with one community using GIS to look at changes in racial diversity in its neighborhood. In another case we mapped crime locations, particularly corner crimes, which helped identify dangerous street corners. In that same project we also mapped the distribution of owner-occupied and rental housing, comparing two years of data to look for changes. Here we were surprised, however. We expected to find clusters of crimes where there were clusters of rental housing. But we found no significant clusters of rental housing. This was important for targeting community enforcement activity and showed that community policing could not be limited to just a few areas of the neighborhood.

The challenge of GIS, of course, is that it requires a high level of resources. First are the software requirements, which can be extremely expensive unless you are associated with a university or college holding a special license. And old, clunky computers cannot run the software, so a group also needs access to relatively high-powered computer hardware. For a community organization that wants to create wall maps for community residents to work with, an expensive and massive plotter-printer is also a necessity. The hardware is often the big barrier to fully using GIS in a community setting, and to address that gap, communities often turn to their local university or college. Finally, while it is relatively easy to use ready-made databases and make your own maps using free software such as ESRI's ArcExplorer,[22] creating and combining databases (such as crime and housing patterns) can take a fair amount of training. But the basic skills can be taught through informal training. In Trenton, New Jersey, for example, a group of community organizations got together and did peer training on using GIS software.

One might think that, with all this high-powered, high-cost, high-tech mapping stuff, normal community residents would be left on the sidelines. But the truth is actually far different. GIS maps are only as good as the data going into them, and often the most useful data must be collected by hand. Bernie Jones[23] describes a community mapping process that includes documenting the locations of everything from junked cars to community gardens. That is data that exists only if people collect it. And it is also data that can contribute to the community Web sites described earlier. A community that has literally, not just metaphorically, mapped its assets can show those assets to the outside world.

## TARGET RESEARCH

This is a special case of research as action. I remember the first piece of target research I was involved in. But, interestingly, it didn't start that way. A coalition of community organizations and funders, called the Working Group on Neighborhoods, had formed out of our initial needs and resources assessment of Toledo community development corporations (see Chapter 4). As part of the collective cause of getting more resources for community development corporations (CDCs), the coalition decided we needed research on how area funders determined who would and who would not receive money. The original plan was to engage the area funders in a discussion of their priorities in an attempt to leverage some funds for CDCs. We sent letters to the area foundations inviting them to be involved in this process, but only two responded (one of which was already part of the coalition). We quickly realized that the foundations were not interested in having their funding decisions investigated. Even the National Foundation Center, which keeps foundation records, denied us access. So what was planned as a cooperative asset-based project turned into target research. All foundations have to submit paperwork to the Internal Revenue Service every year detailing how they distributed their funds. The forms they complete are publicly available. So we collected the IRS 990 forms for all the area foundations and studied how they distributed their funds, creating a report on foundations' lack of support for community-based development. The public presentation of the report helped bring in over $2 million to support community-based development in Toledo initially and changed the funding priorities of two significant local funders.

Target research such as this is usually not a piece of standalone research but is part of a broader effort to get a corporation or government to either start doing something good or stop doing something bad. But it's also not really diagnostic or prescriptive research, either. The research becomes part of the project itself. A colleague of mine does research with labor unions. She studies the administrative structures and budget of corporations, hoping to find vulnerabilities and internal conflicts within corporations that unions can use to the advantage of their members. The unions she works with have already identified the problem—low wages, poor benefits, lousy working conditions—and they have identified the prescription—a unionization campaign. The target research occurs at the implementation stage, where the union is working toward a favorable vote.

This also applies in the policy arena. In the previous chapter we discussed policy research as a type of prescriptive research. But it can also be action research. When the research focuses on the political issues related to a social problem; the process whereby policy decisions are made; regulatory and control mechanisms; policy implementation processes; stakeholder definitions and values about the social problem; or types of feasible recommendations, the research itself becomes part of the change-making strategy.[24] As with the union example, this is a case where the group has already diagnosed the problem and designed a prescription. The purpose of researching the policy process is to find the best way to get the group's policy prescription turned into actual policy.

As the name implies, target research is not a project conducted among friends. It is often a research strategy of last resort, as a community group or organization has been shut out of all previous efforts to obtain information on a government or corporate entity, and is forced into a strategy of gathering information clandestinely. As such, this is a research process conducted out of a conflict framework and used in a conflict process. It can be likened to the intelligence-gathering process used in any adversarial relationship. And the targets themselves are not above conducting research. The use of surveillance tactics by the police, including *agents provocateurs* and other infiltrators, has been well documented.[25] Targets also gather intelligence on their opposition to use in SLAPP (Strategic Litigation Against Public Participation) suits—basically filing a lawsuit with shaky grounds against a challenging group to make them spend what few resources they have on lawyers, defending themselves.[26] Al Gedicks tells the story of his target research on mining companies in Wisconsin and the target corporation's attempts to get him fired from his professor position.[27]

Because these battles can get so dirty, it is important for community activists to carefully consider the need for airtight research when going into battle. If the research is sound, a target doesn't stand a chance in trying to distract the effort with a lawsuit or derail it with infiltrators. Because the research will stand on its own. This is what the Infant Feeding Action Coalition (INFACT) learned when it went up against the Nestlé Corporation for selling prepackaged infant formula in the Third World. INFACT's research carefully documented the damaging effects of Nestlé's attempts to create a captive market for its infant formula by encouraging women to bottle-feed, causing them to stop producing breast milk and becoming dependent on formula they couldn't afford. Coupling the research with an effective boycott campaign, they motivated the World Health Organization and the United Nations International Children's Emergency Fund (UNICEF) to write an International Code of Infant Formula Marketing, and got Nestlé to follow it. After winning with Nestle, they went on to do battle with General Electric, eventually getting GE to end its involvement in nuclear weapons technology by producing a documentary on the health effects of its nuclear weapons production.[28] INFACT won these battles because of good research *and* good organizing.

As with any good social change project, if it is possible to work directly with the target, rather than antagonistically, this is a path worth pursuing. No sense starting a fight if you don't need to. But often, you will find that the target will cooperate only up to a point and will provide information only up to a point. That point is where you need to engage in a target research strategy.

The actual methods involved in target research can vary considerably depending on whether the target is a corporation or a government or other entity. All organizations are required to make some information public. But those requirements are very different for corporations, nonprofits, and governments. There are even variations among corporations, which can be private (owned privately by individuals or family members) or public (owned through stocks traded on a public stock exchange), and which may have different reporting requirements depending on whether they are engaged in banking, insurance, or pension fund management.

> **Types of Targets**
>
> • Government
> • Public corporation
> • Private corporation
> • Lenders and insurers
> • Nonprofits
> • Foundations

## Researching Government Targets

Governments are required to provide the most information of any target organization, though it is surprising how often people are refused the information or are forced to access the information in tiny bits and pieces in a dark basement storeroom where they are allowed to see only about a half hour's worth of documents at a time. At times, governments even attempt to hold secret meetings, though most meetings of government representatives are subject to the provisions of "sunshine laws" that require both public announcement of meetings and provisions for public observation of those meetings. So here is a situation in which placing research before the action can be an especially bad strategy. An individual or a small group of people, lacking political clout, may find it extremely difficult to get government data in the form they want on the schedule they want. But a well-organized group that is prepared to make a loud public fuss, and can convince the government agency that they can carry out that threat, may likely get much more cooperation in their research efforts.

In other cases of recalcitrant government officials refusing to provide data, it may be necessary to use a legal strategy. The national *Freedom Of Information Act,* whose acronym FOIA is pronounced "foya," provides a legal remedy for citizens seeking information about their government.[29] States and some localities have their own lower-level versions of such rules. Beware, however, that the wheels of information freedom can grind extremely slowly, so plan your research schedule accordingly. A last-minute target research effort may easily fail on the turtle pace of government compliance with its own rules. Especially with new laws such as the Patriot Act, hastily passed in the wake of the September 11, 2001 terrorist attacks, the federal government is much more able to collect information about us while simultaneously making it much more difficult for us to collect information about the government.

In many cases, researching government is a two-step process. If you meet resistance in your attempts to access government information, you may first need to research what information is available and what the rules are regarding its accessibility. Then you can quote those rules to your local government bureaucrats if they resist your information needs. Often a sympathetic city council member, state representative, or congressional representative can help with understanding the rules of access and overcoming interference. Once you know the rules and can use them in an information battle, you are in a much better position to move on to the second step of actually doing your research.

In the worst-case scenario, government lawyers will deny you access to information, and that is when you will have to find your own lawyers. The American Civil Liberties Union, that much-derided defender of the Constitution of the United States, has been in the forefront of challenging the Patriot Act. In addition, the National Lawyers Guild, a progressive alternative to the American Bar Association, takes on many cases of government discrimination and secrecy as well. Both of these organizations will likely have a chapter near you, if you should need them.

Once you achieve access, governments have a wide variety of information available. In some urban areas, you can get an electronic database of all property ownership in a city or county, allowing you to identify absentee landlords, land and housing sale prices, and a variety of other things. City budget information is invaluable—remember how the East Toledo Community Organization used city budget data in its campaign for better services? In those cases where you can't achieve access, or where the government unit doesn't keep usable data on its services, you may have to gather the data yourselves. The Los Angeles Bus Riders Union, for example, has used an action research framework to document inequitable and segregated public transportation services, overcrowded buses, and other public transit issues in its campaigns. By studying the transit budget, they were able to show that L.A. was spending the majority of its budget on a small fraction of its riders—emphasizing light rail over bus service. The result was a $1 billion 1996 federal civil rights consent decree for bus system improvements.[30]

## Researching Public Corporations

Corporations are quite different from government. The first thing you need to find out in doing corporate target research is whether the company is private or public, which can be done through Web sites such as Hoover's Online.[31] If your target is publicly traded, things are much easier. Publicly traded corporations are required to submit documents to the federal Securities and Exchange Commission (SEC). Those documents become government documents, and the rules of access to government documents then apply. Publicly traded corporations also need to supply information to state governments, which is also available according to freedom of information policies.[32] In addition, a number of watchdog groups out there, such as CorpWatch, regularly compile and make available information on morally or legally questionable corporate activity.[33]

There is a wide variety of information that can be pieced together from other sources. You can get information from company Web sites or annual reports.[34] Newspaper searches can yield a wealth of information. For large national and multinational corporations, the *New York Times* and the *Wall Street Journal* both have large indexed databases. For local corporations, consult your local newspaper, which may or may not have an indexed database. Since corporations are so active in politics these days, it is often useful to know the kinds of campaign contributions they are making. The Federal Election Commission maintains such data and makes it available through its Web site. Others have also attempted to make the information they provide more user-friendly.[35] The Environmental Protection Agency maintains publicly accessible information on corporations' compliance with environmental regulations. The U.S. Occupational Safety & Health Administration provides information on corporations' safety track records. The U.S. Equal Employment Opportunity Commission and the National Labor Relations Board maintain information on labor and employment disputes.[36]

All of these data can be used in a wide variety of corporate campaigns, even when the data may be tangential to the actual campaign. When Saul Alinsky, the famous community organizer, helped a coalition of community groups go up against the Kodak Corporation in Rochester, New York, charging that Kodak was engaged in discriminatory hiring practices, they needed to have both their data and their community troops well organized. The story of the long drawn-out struggle to get Kodak to hire local minority residents is one of the more instructive tales of the importance of both getting good information and doing good community organizing.[37]

## Researching Private Corporations

Private companies are the most difficult to get information about because they are not required to report to the SEC. CorpWatch lists some information resources for learning about private corporations, but information will be sketchy at best.[38] In such cases, an oppositional group may need to consider whether to engage in clandestine research through an infiltrator or informants.

There are both practical concerns and ethical concerns in doing such clandestine research. The practical concerns have to do with getting accurate information, particularly from informants, who may have a grudge or complaint of their own and are more concerned with bearing their grudge than providing accurate information. Here it is particularly important to practice the research strategy of *triangulation*,[39] which involves getting information from multiple sources—the more agreement across sources, the more reliable and valid the information.

The ethical concerns of clandestine research have to do with collecting information from an organization without its consent. Consent is a standard requirement in academic research, and it is very difficult to get university approval to do research without the consent of the subjects. Informants also often risk their careers and even prison time if they divulge certain kinds of information to outsiders. Of course, community organizations will experience those ethical dilemmas different than universities will, and may find the ethical problems of not doing everything possible to stop a company from poisoning their water, for example, to be far worse than gathering information about that company without their consent. In cases of community organizations doing battle against predatory developers—those developers who put up the billboards that say "cash for ugly houses" or other such things, buy houses cheap, sell them to people with bad credit using predatory financing schemes that the buyer can't afford, then repossess the house and repeat the process with the next unsuspecting buyer—the company is often private. Community organizations then seek out informants to find out who the company's investors are and organize public demonstrations against those investors in hopes they will withdraw their funds from the company.

## Researching Lenders and Insurers

Two of the most targeted kinds of corporations recently are banks and insurers. And one of the reasons is because of their practice of "redlining" poor neighborhoods and refusing to provide home loans or home insurance in those areas. The Home Mortgage Disclosure Act (HMDA) of 1975, which resulted from community organizations doing local research that showed redlining was occurring, established reporting requirements for lenders. You may recall from the previous chapter how that data made the extent of redlining widely known, and led to the Community Reinvestment Act (CRA) of 1977, which made redlining illegal. These two pieces of legislation have been perhaps more important than any other in the practice of target research.[40] Banks in particular have been vulnerable to target research because of the reporting requirements of the Community Reinvestment Act. Banks wanting to expand or move operations need to have a "satisfactory" or "outstanding" CRA rating. Oppositional groups that can obtain a bank's CRA information can potentially stop that bank from either closing old branches or opening new ones, which has been a common strategy of central city organizations attempting to get banking services for poor neighborhoods. The Federal Financial Institutions Examination Council (FFIEC) maintains an aggregated online HMDA database available to the public, along with contact information for central repositories in metropolitan areas.[41] In addition, the public, if they follow lists of banks undergoing review on regulators' Web sites, may comment on a bank's performance while the review is conducted.[42] Regrettably, however, CRA reporting has changed significantly in the past few years, as both the reporting requirements and penalties were weakened. Smaller banks now have to report their CRA data every four or five years, and there is more paperwork required of community organizations to disclose their relationships with banks.[43]

Insurers have been less vulnerable to such pressures, but in the past several years as the banking industry has been deregulated and insurers are providing more investment-oriented services, they too have become vulnerable to charges of discrimination against poor communities. High-profile lawsuits against Nationwide Insurance, State Farm Insurance, and others established the value of careful research on insurance practices.[44] Along with traditional statistical research on numbers and types of policies provided to different groups in different places, in many of these cases a research method called paired testing is also used to establish discrimination. In paired testing, people of different groups (men and women, Anglo and African-American, young and old) are sent to the target, requesting services. The results are then analyzed to see if there are any consistent differences between the groups.[45]

Be aware that such challenges of discrimination are not cut and dried, which is why the research is so important. The Nationwide insurance case, for example, involved gigabytes of data and testimony from expert witnesses regarding how the data was collected, measured, and analyzed. These are cases where expert assistance can be crucial, as corporate targets have very deep pockets to hire very effective lawyers and powerful research experts.

In this shaky economic era, when corporate and even government pension funds are in danger, many people are engaging in actions to make those funds more accountable as well. One of the most interesting efforts has been the group targeting TIAA-CREF, a teachers' retirement fund. Their research has exposed many problems with the TIAA-CREF investment strategies, and they have been successfully pushing for TIAA-CREF to develop a socially responsible investment portfolio that does not invest in tobacco companies and other corporations with morally questionable products and programs.[46]

## Researching Nonprofits

While it may seem contrary to the spirit of community change, even nonprofits are the subjects of target research. Of course, we are not talking about the corner homeless shelter here. More often we are talking about the mega-nonprofit: hospitals, private colleges and universities, and other such large institutions. Even the United Way, which is part funder and part nonprofit, has been targeted for its refusal to fund social change efforts. The research into United Way funding patterns, as well as its overhead expenses, has resulted in changes in the United Way leadership as well as the establishment of competing funds such as the Community Shares movement.[47]

Nonprofits have to report information on their missions, boards of directors, and finances. In addition, like government, their meetings are often subject to "sunshine laws" that may require prior public announcement of meetings and allowing the public to observe meetings.

## Researching Foundations

Foundations are actually another type of nonprofit organization, though so much attention is directed at them by communities that they deserve their own section. As government has provided less and less funding and service to historically underserved communities, those communities have turned to private sources of money. Philanthropic foundations have been a primary source of such funds. Foundations basically exist as tax shelters for the excess wealth of corporations and individuals. But they are also required to give away a certain proportion of their earnings. (The principle is usually invested, and grants are made from the interest or other earnings.) Some foundations are more responsive to community needs than others. Private foundations are often very closed, giving funds only to select charities. Community foundations are often more open, attempting to find and serve community needs. Most large cities have community foundations. In both cases, however, they are required to comply with government rules disclosing their board of trustees, how much they give away, and whom they fund.

One of the first steps in foundation research, especially if you are interested in overall foundation activity in an area, is finding the universe of foundations. The Foundation Center maintains a database of foundation information[48] though, as I discovered, they only share portions of it. In addition, if you have a local *community foundation*—whose mission is often more oriented to community service—they will often be a good source of information on the overall foundation scene.

The next step is to gather information about those foundations. A main source of information on foundations is their annual IRS 990 tax forms, which are publicly available. You can obtain copies from the IRS, but many urban libraries are designated as cooperating collections of The Foundation Center and maintain microfiche or electronic collections of those completed forms. You can also request annual reports from foundations, which may or may not respond.

## LOOSE GRAVEL

Doing research as a project itself can be very tricky. In some ways, the problem on this stretch of road to social change is not so much loose gravel as it is being stuck between a rock and a hard place, or a number of rocks and hard places. Here we will consider the problems with having this kind of research taken seriously by both the outside world and the community.

### Is This Research?

Some of you reading this chapter may have been thinking to yourselves along the way "is this research?" So much of this seems like art, or information cataloging. It certainly isn't the hardcore, hand-out-a-survey-code-the-responses-run-it-through-the-computer-write-the-report form of research that is so often held up as the standard. And that is part of the problem. Especially in academic circles, our conceptualization of research is so unimaginative that it is difficult to organize people around it, and, consequently, it often has little influence beyond academia. On the other hand, in community settings, when people's hard work of gathering information and presenting it in an engaging way doesn't look like research, it also doesn't get the legitimacy it deserves. Getting legitimacy for this kind of research is challenging.

Whether the project is community research or target research, the final product is often seen as just the community's perception. Especially when the form of presentation is a mural or community theater, it is treated as only art. That is what makes it less risky than explicit political activism in undemocratic settings since it appears much less threatening than a position paper, especially when it is created in a community setting rather than by a famous figure. Even the Czech Republic President Vaclav Havel was imprisoned more for his outspoken political activism than for his politically charged plays, which were prohibited during the era of Soviet occupation of his country.[49]

Convincing the outside world that the project is real research becomes especially important in target research. First, you want the target to think that you really have the goods on them. If a group's research shows things that the target already knows are true, and thought were secrets, the group will already have an important source of leverage. If the group can then get that research publicized through the media, their leverage will increase further. Getting such leverage, however, requires the drudgery of documenting, double-checking, and citing sources. It does require real research. Groups who compile a target research report from IRS forms, SEC reports, and other government information will be able to make a much stronger case than those who base their reports on informant information alone. Comparative research methods also can help in target research. The Farm Labor Organizing Committee has been organizing migrant farm workers for over three decades. When it organized its recent boycott of Mount Olive pickles, FLOC chose Mount Olive based on a careful comparative analysis of pickle growers, looking at the wages, working conditions, and vulnerabilities of each grower. The analysis showed Mount Olive to be the worst offender.[50] Just in time for the final revisions for this book, I received word that the research, and the organizing, paid off. FLOC had won a union contract with one of Mount Olive's largest growers.

Even with relatively innocuous community research, however, getting people to take it seriously is important. Projects like community theater and murals do require funding for a location, supplies, and the services of experts such as visual artists or directors. Funders often have two concerns: (1) will this project actually happen? and (2) will it be controversial? They prefer the first question to be answered "yes" and the second "no." Both of their fears will be allayed if they can be convinced that the project is being carefully researched. In a recent case of community theater that was not well researched, one of the main sponsors pulled out after they decided the play would be too controversial for them. The play made heavy use of "hillbilly" stereotypes, which are as insulting to Appalachian people as racist stereotypical portrayals of Native Americans, African-Americans, and other racial and ethnic groups are to members of those groups.[51] In this case, most of us might feel sympathetic to the sponsor not wanting to be associated with a play promoting stereotypes. But there are other cases where a play might expose corruption among a community's corporate or government leadership, or a discriminatory culture like that portrayed in the community theater described by Mark Lynd in Chapter 1. Careful research can make the difference in getting funding for a potentially controversial project. Had the playwright done better research, he may have ended up with both a better play and better support for its production.

It's not just the legitimacy of the outside world that is important when the project is research, however. Because, ultimately, these projects will succeed based on how much legitimacy they gain inside the community.

## Whose Research Is It?

I have had the honor of working with a wide variety of university-community partnership programs around the United States over the past few years. And of the many stories I have been told, one which stands out is the story of a geography professor. He was deeply concerned about environmental issues and had spent months carefully documenting and researching the pollution of a nearby river, with detailed information on the pollution sources and carefully developed proposals on remedies. He was terribly depressed, however, because he couldn't get anyone in the community or in government to pay any attention to him.

It was one of the most important lessons I have learned in the six years I have been researching and working with such programs. This was a researcher who had chosen the issue, chosen the method, collected the data, analyzed the results, and produced the report, all by himself. And, in the end, all of that work was useless. While it is possible for a professional researcher to do most of the work alone in the other stages of the project cycle, such lone ranger work at the implementation stage rarely works. For success at the implementation stage requires community involvement, whether that means bodies at demonstrations, testimony at hearings, donations of time, or whatever. There is no real community change without community participation. Those who go it alone, regardless of how good their research is and how deep their commitment may be, will be unsuccessful. For social change is a collective effort, particularly when that change requires a redistribution of power or money.

When the research is the project, getting community participation is more important than ever. Because when the research is the project, one of the goals is to build a stronger community, and that can't be accomplished unless the research organizes the community. At Mars Hill College, in the spring of 2000, a class of students worked in collaboration with Helpmate, an area organization serving abused women, to organize a local presentation of The Clothesline Project. The Clothesline Project produces T-shirts hung on a clothesline and decorated by and on behalf of women who are survivors and victims of sexual violence. Community women produced T-shirts, and the students produced statistics and compiled information on sexual assault for an audiotape that was played throughout the presentation. The result brought campus and community together, empowering and educating both.

## CONCLUSION

This chapter focused on doing research as the project itself, using a community organizing process that emphasizes information as an end in itself.

Some implementation research projects focus on the community itself:

- Historical recovery research
- Arts documentation
- Community media
- Community mapping

Other implementation research projects focus on targets the community wants to change, such as:

- Government
- Public corporations
- Private corporations
- Lenders and insurers
- Nonprofits
- Foundations

The two important challenges facing research at the implementation stage are:

- Is it really research?
- Whose research is it?

# RESOURCES

## Historical Recovery

Kieffer, C. M. (1999). *Oral history in your community.* University of Missouri Extension, http://muextension.missouri.edu/xplor/aging/gg0008.htm

Sommer, B. W., & Quinlan, M. K. (2002). *The oral history manual.* Walnut Creek, CA: AltaMira Press.

Institute for Oral History. (n.d.). *Oral history workshop on the Web,* http://www3.baylor.edu/Oral_History/Workshop.htm

## Arts Documentation

Barnett, A. W. (1984). *Community murals: The people's art.* New York: Art Alliance Press.

Groundswell Community Mural Project, http://www.groundswellmural.org/

Randolph, D. (2002). *Creating a community mural.* Daniel Smith, Inc., http://www.danielsmith.net/learn/inksmith/200312/

## Community Media

Community-Media.com. (2003). *Services and resources for community organizations,* http://www.community-media.com/resources.html

Center for Community Journalism. (n.d.). *Tips on doing community journalism.* State University of New York at Oswego, http://www.oswego.edu/ccj/archive.html

## Community Mapping

Almedom, A. M., Blumenthal, U., & Manderson, L. *Hygiene evaluation proce-dures: Approaches and methods for assessing water- and sanitation-related hygiene practices, community mapping,* http://www.unu.edu/unupress/food2/UIN11E/uin11e0c.htm

Rambaldi, G., Fernan, M. L., & Siar, S. V. (1998). *Resource mapping: Participatory methods in community-based coastal resource management* (Vol. 2.). Silang, Cavite, Philippines: International Institute of Rural Reconstruction, http://www.iapad.org/publications/ppgis/resource_mapping.pdf

GIS.com. *Your Internet guide to geographic information systems,* http://www.gis.com/

## Community Planning

Jones, B. (1990). *Neighborhood planning: A guide for citizens and planners.* Chicago: Planners Press, American Planning Association.

Peterman, W. (1999). *Neighborhood planning and community-based development: The potential and limits of grassroots action.* Thousand Oaks, CA: Sage Publications.

## Target Research

Corporate Research Project, http://www.corp-research.org/

Couey, A. (2001). *Hands-on corporate research guide.* CorpWatch. http://corpwatch. radicaldesigns.org/article.php?id=945

Federal Financial Institutions Examination Council (FFIEC), http://www.ffiec.gov

The National Community Reinvestment Coalition, http://www.ncrc.org.

Freedom of Information Center, University of Missouri, http://web.missouri.edu/~foiwww/

## NOTES

1. Dr. Seuss. (1954). *Horton hears a Who!* New York: Random House.
2. Beckwith, D. (1991). Personal interview, March 6.
3. Gaventa, J. (1993). The powerful, the powerless, and the experts: Knowledge struggles in an information age. In P. Park, M. Brydon-Miller, B. Hall, & T. Jackson (Eds.). *Voices of change: Participatory research in the United States and Canada* (pp. 21–40). Westport, CT: Bergin and Garvey.

4. Bobo, K., Kendall, J., & Max, J. (1991). *Organizing for social change: A manual for activists in the 1990s.* Santa Ana, CA: Seven Locks Press. *Training and Technical Assistance.* (2004). COMM-ORG. Retrieved July 15, 2004, from http://comm-org.utoledo.edu/train.htm

5. Highlander Research and Education Center. (2002). Retrieved July 15, 2004, from http://www.highlandercenter.org/

6. Boal, A. (1982). *The theatre of the oppressed.* New York: Routledge.

7. Freire, P. (1972). *Pedagogy of the oppressed.* New York: Continuum.

8. Norsigian, J., Diskin, V., Doress-Worters, P., Pincus, J., Sanford, W., & Swenson, N. (1999). The Boston Women's Health Book Collective and Our Bodies, Ourselves: A brief history and reflection. *Journal of the American Medical Women's Association, 54,* 35–39. Electronic version retrieved July 15, 2004, from http://www.ourbodiesourselves.org/jamwa.htm

9. Sommer, B. W., & Quinlan, M. K. (2002). *The oral history manual.* Walnut Creek, CA.: AltaMira Press.

10. Generations CanConnect. (n.d.). Retrieved July 15, 2004, from http://generations-canconnect.ic.gc.ca/english/program/index.html

11. Canada Broadcasting Corporation. (2004). *A Lost Heritage: Canada's residential schools.* Retrieved July 15, 2004, from http://archives.cbc.ca/IDD-1-70-692/disasters_tragedies/residential_schools/. The national inquiry into the separation of aboriginal and Torres Strait Islander children from their families. (1997). *Bringing them home: Report of the national inquiry into the separation of Aboriginal and Torres Strait Islander children from their families.* Government of Australia, Human Rights and Equal Opportunity Commission. Retrieved July 15, 2004, from http://www.austlii.edu.au/au/special/rsjproject/rsjlibrary/hreoc/stolen/. Smith, Andrea. (n.d.) *Soul wound: The legacy of Native American schools.* Amnesty International. Retrieved July 15, 2004, from http://www.amnestyusa.org/amnestynow/soulwound.html

12. CTC@NSW. (n.d.) *CTCs: A rural IT success story.* Retrieved July 15, 2004, from http://ctc.nsw.gov.au/static/20030719_67.jsp

13. Moya-Raggio, E. (1984). Arpilleras: Chilean culture of resistance. *Feminist Studies, 10,* 277–282. See also Agosín, M. (1996). *Tapestries of hope, threads of love: The Arpillera movement in Chile, 1974–1994.* Albuquerque: University of New Mexico Press.

14. *Groundswell Community Mural Project.* (2000). Retrieved July 15, 2004, from http://www.groundswellmural.org/

15. *The Harmar Murals.* (n.d.) Retrieved July 15, 2004, from http://www.tcom.ohiou.edu/community/murals/harmar.html

16. Pobega, D. (1998). *@lbe Electronic.* Retrieved July 15, 2004, from http://home.vicnet.net.au/~twt/oldfrontpage.html

17. Rhodes, L. (1997). *Building a civic network: The Austin Access model.* Presented at the Community Space & Cyberspace Conference, Seattle,

March 1–2. Retrieved July 15, 2004, from http://www.scn.org/ip/cpsr/diac/lodis.htm

18.  Cohill, A. M., & Kavanaugh, A. L. (Eds.). (2000). *Community networks: Lessons from Blacksburg, Virginia.* Boston: Artech House. O'Sullivan, P. B. (1995). Computer networks and political participation: Santa Monica's teledemocracy project. *Journal of Applied Communication Research, 23,* 93–107.

19.  Seattle Community Network. (2004). Retrieved July 15, 2004, from http://www.scn.org

20.  New Jersey State Museum Planetarium and Raritan Valley Community College Planetarium. (2003). *Educator's guide to . . . "Follow the Drinking Gourd."* Retrieved July 15, 2004, from http://www.madison.k12.wi.us/planetarium/ftdg1.htm

21.  Madison Metropolitan School District Planetarium and Observatory. (1997). Time to . . . follow the drinking gourd. *Madison Skies, 3.* Retrieved July 15, 2004, from http://www.madison.k12.wi.us/planetarium/ms_1297.htm

22.  ESRI. (2004). *ArcExplorer.* Retrieved July 15, 2004, from http://www.esri.com/software/arcexplorer/

23.  Jones, B. (1990). *Neighborhood planning: A guide for citizens and planners.* Bigtown, IL: Planners Press, American Planning Association.

24.  Majchrzak, A. (1984). *Methods for policy research.* (pp. 24–32). Beverly Hills, CA: Sage Publications.

25.  Marx, G. T. (1974). Thoughts on a neglected category of social movement participant: the agent provocateur and the informant. *American Journal of Sociology, 80,* 402–442.

26.  Potter, L. (2004). *Overview.* First Amendment Center. Retrieved July 15, 2004, from http://www.firstamendmentcenter.org/petition/topic.aspx?topic=slapp

27.  Gedicks, A. (1996). Activist sociology: Personal reflections. *Sociological Imagination, 33,* 55–72. Electronic version retrieved July 15, 2004, from http://comm-org.utoledo.edu/si/sihome.htm

28.  *INFACT.* (n.d.). Retrieved July 15, 2004, from http://www.infact.org/aboutinf.html

29.  *Freedom of Information Center.* (2004). University of Missouri. Retrieved July 15, 2004, from http://web.missouri.edu/~foiwww/.

30.  Los Angeles Bus Riders Union. (n.d.). Consent decree compliance: Documents and images. Retrieved July 15, 2004, from http://www.busridersunion.org/Campaigns/consentdecree/consentdecreedocumentsandimages.htm. Motavalli, J. (2001). See also Second-class transit? Los Angeles' Bus Riders Union fights for equal treatment. *emagazine.com, Sept/Oct.* Retrieved July 15, 2004, from http://www.emagazine.com/september-october_2001/0901curr_transit.html

31.  *Hoover's Online.* (2004). Retrieved July 15, 2004, from http://www.hoovers.com/

32. Corporate Research Project. (2003). *How to do basic corporate research on the Internet.* Retrieved July 15, 2004, at http://www.corp-research. org/howto.htm

33. CorpWatch. (n.d.) Retrieved July 15, 2004, from http://www. corpwatch.org/

34. Couey, A. (2001). *Hands-on corporate research guide.* CorpWatch. Retrieved July 15, 2004, from http://www.corpwatch.org/research/PRD.jsp?articleid=945

35. Couey, A. (2001). *Corporations and politics.* CorpWatch. Retrieved July 15, 2004, from http://www.corpwatch.org/research/PRD.jsp?articleid=948

36. Couey, A. (2001). *Hands-on corporate research guide.*

37. Finks, P. D. (1984). *The radical vision of Saul Alinsky.* New York: Paulist Press.

38. Couey, A. (2001). *Hands-on corporate research guide.*

39. Brewer, J., & Hunter, A. (1989). *Multimethod research: A synthesis of styles.* Newbury Park, CA: Sage Publications.

40. Squires, G. D. (2003). *Organizing access to capital: Advocacy and the democratization of financial institutions.* Philadelphia: Temple University Press.

41. Federal Financial Institutions Examination Council. (n.d.). *Community Reinvestment Act public data.* Retrieved July 15, 2004, from http://www.ffiec.gov/cra/publicdata.htm

42. Center For Community Change. (2003). *CRA examinations.* Retrieved July 15, 2004, from http://www.communitychange.org/

43. Center For Community Change. (2003). *CRA and financial modernization.* Retrieved July 15, 2004, from http://www.communitychange.org/

44. Squires, G. D. (Ed.). (1997). *Insurance Redlining: Disinvestment, reinvestment, and the evolving role of financial institutions.* Washington, D.C.: The Urban Institute Press. See also Inner City Press. (2003). *Insurance redlining.* Retrieved July 15, 2004, from http://www. innercitypress.org/insure.html

45. Turner, M. A., Godfrey, E., Ross, S. L., & Smith, R. R. (2003). *Other things being equal: A paired testing study of discrimination in mortgage lending.* University of Connecticut Department of Economics Working Paper Series. Retrieved July 15, 2004, from http://www.econ.uconn.edu/working/2003-09.pdf

46. Wollman, N. J., & Fuller, A. (2003). *Social choice for social change: Campaign for a new TIAA-CREF.* Retrieved July 15, 2004, from http://www.manchester.edu/Academic/Programs/Departments/Peace_Studies/njw/

47. National Committee for Responsive Philanthropy and National Alliance for Choice in Giving. (2003). *Giving at work, 2003.* Retrieved July 15, 2004, from http://www.ncrp.org/PDF/GivingAtWork.pdf

48. The Foundation Center. (2004). Retrieved July 15, 2004, from http://fdncenter.org

49. Keane, J. (1999). *Vaclav Havel: A political tragedy in six acts.* New York: Basic Books.

50. Farm Labor Organizing Committee, AFL-CIO. (n.d.). *Don't buy Mt. Olive pickles.* Retrieved July 15, 2004, from http://www.floc.com/boycott/boycott_menu.html

51. Blake, E. (2003, July 17). Hancock County controversy surprises playwright. *The Blade* (pp. B1–B2).

# *Seven*

## Evaluation

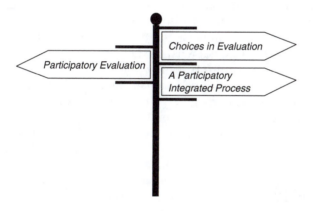

## BACK TO THE FUTURE, OR MESSING WITH THE SPACE-TIME CONTINUUM

*Back to the Future* was one of those shallow, goofy 1980s movies. But it was still fun and for reasons I can't explain has remained stuck in my consciousness. When Marty's friend Doc called and instructed him to meet in a mall parking lot after closing time, little did Marty realize the adventure he was about to begin. Arriving at the appointed time on his skateboard, Marty learned he was about to witness the wizened inventor's first test of his attempt to turn a

DeLorean luxury sports car into a time machine. But terrorists soon arrived, turning the test into a flight for life. As Doc was gunned down in cold blood by the terrorists, Marty jumped into the DeLorean and hit the gas. When he reached the magic 88 mph at which the car would leap across the time-space continuum, there was a brilliant flash, and he was suddenly in the 1950s. Having used up the plutonium that supplied the time machine, and wanting to get back to his own time, he went to find Doc (who was much younger but still wizened in the 1950s). Well, of course, their ingenious plan worked, whisking Marty and the DeLorean back to the future just in time to witness Doc's murder. The pain of watching Doc killed in rerun was doubly painful because Marty tried to warn Doc in a note before coming back to the future. But Doc ripped up the note, lecturing Marty on how dangerous it is to have knowledge of the future. Then, as in all good schmaltzy movies, just as Marty was grieving over his apparently dead friend and mentor, Doc's eyes popped open, he sat up, and revealed the bulletproof vest he had donned. He had taped Marty's note back together and heeded its advice. When Marty asked him "Doc, what about all that stuff about screwing up future events—the space-time continuum," Doc answered "Well, I figured, what the hell."[1]

What the hell, indeed. If only we could travel back in time, knowing how the future had turned out the first time, make the appropriate interventions, and then get a better future. In *Back to the Future*, everyone lived even better than happily ever after, as Marty's escapades in the past altered the future much to his own advantage.

We can't, at least at the time of this writing, travel temporally. But we can draw lessons from this "back to the future" thinking. So much project-based research involves imagining and predicting the future. Evaluation could be an integral part of those community change projects if only we didn't act as if time travel really was possible. Because we typically evaluate our work only when it is finished. At the end of a project we hire a researcher or get some volunteer to collect a bunch of data and tell us how we did. And then we find out what we did right or wrong. (And we hope we did a lot more right than wrong!) It's too late to fix whatever may have gone wrong with the original project. The money is spent and the project is completed. But wouldn't that evaluation data be nice if we could do time travel? Those of you who are students often experience this as well. You often don't even get your first test until a third of the way into the term, and by the time you get a grade for it the term is almost half over. It's not until you get your final grade that you have a good idea of how you are supposed to study for the class. So you, too, must wait until time travel is invented to make full use of the feedback you receive.

To rub salt into the wound, evaluation is so often an imposed process. It's done to us by authority figures or resource providers. We have little say in how the evaluation is designed and little power to hold the evaluator accountable for their work, whether that is the professor giving the test or the funder conducting a site visit. Evaluations consequently feel threatening and arbitrary, increasing our resistance. I remember working with one community project where a potential funder spent two days interviewing a handful of the dozens of people involved in a project, and attended one contentious project meeting, after which they declared the project unfit for funding. It made me livid, as I was the official "evaluator" for that project and had collected and written up nearly two years' worth of field notes, interviews, and survey results that showed the tremendous accomplishments of this particular project. But I was using a very different model of evaluation than the funder, and they trusted their "helicopter" evaluation—hovering above the ground briefly and observing from a distance—more than my "empowerment" evaluation, which involved the people doing the project in the evaluation process.

This chapter is about how to do evaluation in such a way that it can be used without the need for time travel and without the feeling of it being imposed on an organization or community. In many ways, the placement of this chapter so late in the book is wrong because it implies that the time travel model of evaluation is correct—it is something you do at the end of the project. I will ask you to bear with me while I try to convince you that evaluation is actually something that you do at the *beginning* of a project. Think about the convoluted rationalizations that have built the standardized

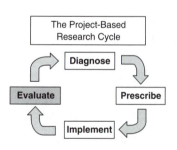

testing fever across the country. Our public schoolchildren are now being subjected to the same reviled method of testing used in law schools—the comprehensive final exam. It seems to me that the average grade-schooler is a little young to take on such an awesome responsibility. Plus, the fact that year after year so many students fail those comprehensive final exams means that the evaluation process is pretty useless. If those tests mattered, we would be seeing a real improvement.

But what if we evaluated students at the beginning of the year rather than the end, frequently rather than just once, and designed the tests to assess changes in learning rather than factoid memorization? What if we set learning goals and assessed the school's ability to meet the learning goals rather than the students' ability to pass the tests? And what if we moved to a coaching and reflection method of teaching rather than the teacher-centered model of education?

All those questions are too big for a humble book on project-based research methods. But they do have implications for doing evaluation research in a community setting that we must explore. Because when you are in an organization and are required to evaluate some aspect of your organization's work, you will have some choices to make.

## CHOICES IN EVALUATION

Of all the stages of project-based research, none has had more written about it than the evaluation stage. Yoland Wadsworth lists 87 different evaluation models.[2] Michael Patton's authoritative text on utilization-focused evaluation has 385 pages of choices.[3] And then there are all the books and articles written about each of those models and choices. There is even a professional association dedicated to the craft of evaluation, the American Evaluation Association, which attempts to create and maintain standards to guide evaluation research.[4]

All this professional concentration on the craft of evaluation has produced some wonderful tools and techniques. But it is unclear whether it has actually improved the craft of evaluation itself or had any meaningful impact on the work being evaluated. It is so easy to get overwhelmed by the possibilities and debates in what is known as the "field" of evaluation that deciding how to design and carry out an evaluation can seem like a crapshoot.

> **Questions to Guide Evaluation in Project-Based Research**
>
> 1. Are you making a difference?
>
> 2. Why or why not?
>
> 3. Who wants to know?

I am convinced that, for community groups and organizations, the relevant models and choices are far fewer than those presented by all the textbooks out there. The two most important questions of evaluation in project-based research are: (1) whether your project is making a difference; and (2) why or why not. A third question is far less important for the evaluation itself but very important for how the evaluation is used. The evaluation can look quite different if the people who want to know are actually doing the project or are outsiders funding or otherwise holding the project accountable. So given these different questions, I see two choices for the evaluation process: external vs. participatory evaluation, and outcome vs. process evaluation.

## External vs. Participatory Evaluation

In most discussions of evaluation, even the good ones, this choice is usually described as a choice of internal or external evaluators. The external evaluator model is the traditional approach, where someone without strong organizational ties conducts the evaluation. Usually the evaluator is familiar with the type of project the organization is doing and has a stock format that they use. The internal evaluator is often found in larger organizations and is the person constantly running around collecting data on what is happening in the organization. They are less likely to be managing full-blown evaluations.[5]

But that is not what we are talking about here. Because in both of those models, the evaluation is typically controlled by someone other than the people actually engaged in the project. Consequently, whether the evaluator is an insider or outsider is not as important as whether control over the evaluation process comes from those involved in the project or external to them. An external evaluation, then, is controlled by someone not directly involved in the project. The purpose of external evaluation is to prevent the evaluation data from being "contaminated" by the wishes of the project participants. In this form of evaluation, the research questions and research methods are determined by external standards; the audiences for the evaluation are external decision makers or funders, and the evaluator plays the role of a disinterested outsider.[6]

A participatory evaluation is controlled by, or at least accountable to, those directly involved in the project. This form of evaluation has grown in popularity since the mid-1990s and now goes by the term empowerment evaluation[7] as well as participatory evaluation. Michael Patton, who proposes a form of participatory evaluation he calls utilization-focused evaluation, developed a set of principles for the practice that includes: (1) involving participants at every stage of the research process; (2) making sure they own the evaluation; (3) focusing the process on the outcomes they think are important; (4) facilitating participants to work collectively;

(5) organizing the evaluation to be understandable and meaningful to all; (6) using the evaluation to support participants' accountability to themselves and their community first, and outsiders second if at all; (7) developing the evaluator role as a facilitator, collaborator, and learning resource; (8) developing participants' roles as decision makers and evaluators; (9) recognizing and valuing participants' expertise and helping them to do the same; and (10) minimizing status differences between the evaluation facilitator and participants.[8]

As you can see, this is just a minor variation on the participatory research model described in Chapter 2. And, to most of you, the participatory model probably sounds much better than the external evaluation model. Indeed, that is the case for me. I have been involved with only one external evaluation when I was the chair of a committee assigned to evaluate a program at my university. Basically, our job was to verify what the program staff had reported in their own internal evaluation. I didn't realize that until I was well into the work, but when I did I quickly became resentful that the university would waste resources duplicating research that had already been done accurately and with integrity. I also felt extremely awkward being part of the culture of distrust that this evaluation was symptomatic of. My fellow committee members felt the same. So we redefined our role as advocates for the program, using our work to amplify the needs expressed in the self-evaluation already done by the program staff.

So if participatory evaluation is so much better than the adversarial external evaluation approach, why is there even a choice between it and external evaluation? There are two conditions that might cause a group to go for an external rather than participatory evaluation. First, there are cases where the group or organization is split either vertically or horizontally. Maybe the director doesn't believe a project is really as successful as the staff asserts and can only be convinced by a rigidly independent evaluation. Or maybe there is dissension among the staff about which way to take the second stage of a project because there is disagreement about what happened in the first stage. In both of these cases an external evaluator can provide information that will be trusted enough for both sides to agree on what to do next. The second reason to do an external evaluation is because you are told to. There are still unenlightened funders out there who think that the only way to get accurate data about a project is for some outside expert to weigh in with their opinion.

The conditions demanding a traditional external evaluation are more and more rare, however. Indeed, in the 1990s, the Kellogg Foundation, realizing the problems with the traditional external evaluation process, decided to not only support but promote

| External Evaluation | Participatory Evaluation |
|---|---|
| • When factional disputes prevent unity<br>• When funders or managers demand it<br>• When time resources are short | • When there is unified purpose and a commitment to open participation<br>• When there is desire for organizational self-reflection and improvement<br>• When there is commitment to the time required to participate |

participatory evaluation.[9] They had watched as their grantees went through the motions of evaluation but didn't use the results to make any changes in their programming. What was needed was an evaluation process that actually engaged organization members in self-reflection and organizational self-improvement. They realized the standards could not be imposed from outside so began developing a model of participatory evaluation.

The potential benefits of participatory evaluation are many. The buy-in from participants means that a lot of good and useful information will be generated, and the process will produce more and stronger relationships. But a true participatory evaluation process also requires a lot from a group or organization. Most important, there needs to be some degree of unity and openness to participation overall. In my city, the school board and teachers union try to pass school taxes without inviting parents to participate in determining local educational priorities. Consequently, the parents regularly vote against school taxes, and our schools are in the dumpster. This is not a good setting for a participatory evaluation. Likewise, social service agencies who don't want their service recipients involved in developing programs are also not likely to want them involved in any evaluation process. This can also be a pretty threatening process, especially if the organization is under the funding gun, so there needs to be some openness to organizational self-reflection and change. I once worked with a community organization receiving city funds that was on a "watch list," which meant they were being scrutinized even more than usual because they had not met city-assigned productivity goals. They had the opportunity to join a new, but somewhat politically risky, program. Somewhat ironically, they chose not to join because the watch list stigma made them less willing to try new things, even if there was a chance they could increase their productivity by doing so. Doing a good participatory evaluation also takes a lot of staff and leadership time. An external evaluator can do a quick-and-dirty helicopter evaluation with a minimal amount of time from the organization itself. But participatory evaluation requires meetings to plan the evaluation, collect the data, analyze the data, and then do planning based on the evaluation results.

Because of the challenges involved in doing "true" participatory evaluation, a number of groups opt for a hybrid model. An increasing number of us academics are practicing various forms of participatory research—including participatory evaluation—that we use with community organizations. We are the external evaluators. But we use participatory processes. In such situations, evaluators make themselves accountable to the group or organization first, and the external authority or funder second. And since some of the biggest barriers to conducting any evaluation, let alone a participatory evaluation, are time resources, the external participatory evaluator is especially good at managing the workload so there are still enough opportunities for participation without overburdening the organization staff and leadership. Often, that means that the external evaluator becomes responsible for collecting the data and providing an initial analysis, with planning meetings on the front and back ends of the process, as we will see below.

## Outcome vs. Process Evaluation

Anyone working in the broad industry of community change has felt the pressure to produce measurable outcomes. Every grant funder wants to see measurable outcomes. And by measurable outcomes they often mean countable outcomes. What the people doing the projects often want to know, however, is *how* to produce those outcomes and how to tell whether any changes they see are a result of what they are doing. Funders are becoming more and more insistent that organizations move beyond simply documenting *output* measures such as how many clients are served or how many houses are built. They want to see data on *outcomes,* such as how many clients stayed off drugs for six months or how many residents of the new homes improved their economic standing. And some even want data on impacts, which makes the research task considerably more abstract and difficult, as it requires theoretically connecting community indicators measures such as crime or building permits or other measures to the project interventions.[10]

This tension between outcome evaluation and process evaluation is often, interestingly, based in the tension between intensive research and extensive research. Recall from Chapter 1 that intensive research studies one or a few cases intensively to trace a causal path, and extensive research studies many cases superficially to map the distribution of their characteristics. Researchers who want to know *how many* people burn their fingers on hot stove tops would likely do a survey—a form of extensive research. Those who want to know *why* people burn their fingers would probably do in-depth interviews with a select few stove-top finger-burning victims—a form of intensive research.

In the evaluation business we talk about this as the difference between outcome evaluation and process evaluation. Outcome evaluation studies what happens at the end of a project. Process evaluation studies what happens during the project. As the field of evaluation grows more convoluted and intertwined, the distinction between these two approaches to evaluation also becomes more difficult to understand. With models like context-based outcome evaluation,[11] which tries to link explanation with outcomes, there is some melding of the two approaches. These integrative attempts, however, do not understand the fundamental distinction between the two, and that is where we can get into trouble.

Funders have been pushing increasingly hard for solid outcome evaluation. They want to know whether crime decreased, whether community health improved, and so on. They want to know that their money made a difference. Those people engaged in such community change efforts also want to know whether they are having an impact. And, on its face, it seems simple. Most of the changes that groups are trying to make seem easily countable. You count the number of pregnant teenagers. You count the number of arrests. You count the number of homeless people. You count the number of people with diabetes. It's easy. Theoretically.

In outcome evaluation the first problem is determining how to count something. Let's say you are running a project to reduce teen pregnancy in a central city neighborhood. You have to know how many teenaged females there are and how many got pregnant. Often, health departments don't keep statistics on teen pregnancy, only on teen births. And with the new federal privacy laws, getting even that data can be challenging. Plus, the government agencies responsible for collecting that data often are so stretched that they collect it only for a wide geographic area—not your neighborhood. You could try to get the population of teen females from school records, but school officials are not likely to let you paw through their records to find out how many students have addresses in your neighborhood. And they are also not likely to do it for you. The alternative is to actually go out and count the number of teen females in the neighborhood. That means going door to door, census style—an enormous undertaking. Then you have to try to get accurate information on how many of them became pregnant. And since the number of pregnant teenagers in a neighborhood is likely to be small (a central city neighborhood of 1100 households that I worked in showed fewer than two dozen), an error of even three or four people can be important.

> **Challenges to Outcome Evaluation**
>
> 1. Finding countable things
>
> 2. Interpreting what you count accurately
>
> 3. Explaining what you interpret accurately

The second issue in outcome evaluation is that you never just count things, even when that is what you are trying to do. Outcome evaluation is really like a quasi-experiment.[12] It is designed to measure the difference between a baseline (data collected before the project begins) and an endpoint, with some form of intervention in between. But we call it a *quasi-experiment* because it often lacks a control group (a group of people who don't receive the intervention that you can compare to), and it does not control for the influence of other variables because, of course, it is operating in the real world rather than in a laboratory. The goal, however, as in an experiment, is to test whether the intervention made a difference. Because this quasi-experiment is operating in the real world, observing a positive change in outcome numbers compared to the baseline numbers doesn't necessarily mean that your project succeeded. Something else could have caused the change. A drop in crime after the introduction of a community policing program may be the result of an improving economy rather than new policing strategies. Likewise, observing a negative change doesn't necessarily mean that your project was a failure. Say, for example, your outcome evaluation shows that crime actually increased in the project area. But what if crime increased only 2% in your area compared to 6% citywide? This is why context is so important. You may not have a control group, but you can find comparison groups—similar neighborhoods or the broader area.

The third issue in outcome evaluation is successfully explaining how the change you observed is due to your project and not to some other change. Maybe the reduction in smoking was due to the local public health campaign. Maybe it was due to the recent cigarette tax increase the governor enacted to balance the budget. Determining that the change was the result of your intervention, and not other factors, can be extremely tricky. Because it is impossible, and possibly even unethical, to use a traditional experiment in which only some people receive the intervention, it is difficult to know what caused the change if you are doing only extensive research measuring the change. You also need to engage in intensive research to learn how the change occurred. And this is where process evaluation shows its strengths.

Many groups avoid outcome evaluation altogether and instead try to redefine parts of their process as outcomes. How many people attended the community block watch meeting is not exactly an outcome measure if the purpose of the project is to reduce crime in the neighborhood. It is, however, data that can be used as part of a process evaluation. Likewise, how many teens got involved in the community mural project measures part of the process, not outcomes. Outcomes measure the goals of the project—reducing crime, increasing community pride. Questions about how many people got involved or what they did measure parts of the process. Funders demanding outcome evaluations will rarely accept such measures as outcomes and may in fact even wonder if you know the difference between outcomes and processes if you try to present them as outcomes.[13]

That doesn't make such measures useless, however. Many groups and organizations, especially at the beginning of a project, want to know whether their project is going according to plan. Are all the parts working the way they expected? Are the resource levels adequate? Are people reacting in the way predicted? The chances of getting good outcomes are limited if the process doesn't work. Process evaluation, then, is particularly helpful in the early stages of a project. When I was hired to facilitate the evaluation for the Toledo Community Organizing Training and Technical Assistance program, one of the things most important to the group was process evaluation. This was a complicated program with a number of projects going on simultaneously—training of neighborhood leadership in community organizing, mentoring of paid community organizers and organization directors, and ongoing technical assistance. In the neighborhood leadership trainings, one of the main questions was whether the trainings were interesting enough for people to return, so we did short questionnaires at the end of each training to inform adjustments for the next training. In the mentoring, one of the concerns was that much of the mentoring was occurring at a distance, since the mentors were all a plane ride away from Toledo. So we did in-depth interviews with the trainers, organizers, and directors to find out how they were reacting to speaker-phone mentoring. We found out early on that the organizers didn't like the speaker-phone debriefings, and that part of the project was quickly changed.[14] Process evaluation avoids the problems of the outcome-oriented final comprehensive exam model. It is more like the tennis coach model, providing early feedback to inform project adjustments before problems show up in poor outcome measures.

Process evaluation is also extremely helpful in the explanation part of outcome evaluation. Finding people who quit smoking and asking them why can help determine whether the public health campaign to reduce smoking mattered more than the cigarette tax increase. And if you use an intensive research design of in-depth interviews with former smokers, you can find out both whether the campaign made a difference and whether it could have made an even greater difference. It can also help you understand what it was about the campaign that was most effective. A couple of years ago my wife, who had recently purchased a Ford Focus (remember we are just a poor-professor family), was invited by the auto manufacturer to a day-long focus group meeting. They paid $100, ensuring a good response rate, and we joked about Tammy attending a "Focus focus group." Essentially, Ford was conducting an evaluation of the car's design. One of the most interesting parts of the process for Tammy came when a researcher joined her as she drove around the area, asking questions about things like where she put her sunglasses, how she dialed the radio, etc., while she was driving. It was the most amazing example of process evaluation occurring right in the midst of the process itself. And it allowed Ford to hear about what people liked and disliked as they demonstrated it, building an explanation for *why* people liked and disliked various aspects of the car.

Outcome measures without this in-depth explanation of how the outcome occurred are not only useless but dangerous. Someone could try to replicate a project in another place, not understanding what it was about the original project that made it a success (and not doing that important prescription research described in Chapter 5), and actually make things worse. Perhaps the most famous example of the problems of outcome evaluation comes from the famous Hawthorne studies, conducted at the Western Electric Hawthorne Works in Chicago in the 1920s and 1930s. The researchers were trying to evaluate whether changes in work design or work conditions would have any impact on productivity. So they changed the lighting, and productivity went up. They changed the rest breaks, and productivity went up. No matter what they did, it seems, productivity went up. Eventually, moving into more of a process evaluation model, they began to understand that it wasn't the particular changes they were making that created the outcome but the fact that they were paying attention to the workers. The workers were responding to the attention being directed to them, not to the specific interventions.[15]

## PARTICIPATORY EVALUATION FROM THE BEGINNING

Because it is so much more user-friendly, and useful to those involved in community change projects, participatory evaluation will be our framework for the bulk of this chapter. I recommend to every group I work with that they use a participatory evaluation method if they want information that is useful during, rather than after, a project. But because a participatory evaluation process, particularly when it involves an outside researcher (which it often does simply because the group lacks the

| Steps in Participatory Evaluation |
| --- |
| • Determining the question |
| • Choosing the methods |
| • Gathering the data |
| • Analyzing the data |
| • Presenting the data |

capacity to do such an involved research process themselves), is so unfamiliar to most of us, this section will use the project-based research model steps to show how it can be done.

### Determining the Questions

Interestingly, the initial stage of participatory evaluation is easily disguised as a project planning process with some measurement thrown in. When I am lucky enough to be involved in an evaluation planning process at the beginning of the project, the first thing I do is facilitate a project planning process. In that early meeting we concentrate on setting project goals and devising strategies for the project. (And remember, the success of setting goals and strategies is based on previous diagnostic and prescriptive research.) The research question, in such circumstances, comes from the project goals: Are we reducing teen pregnancy? Are we controlling crime? Are we reducing the lead poisoning of children? Are we improving student test scores? The emphasis, usually at the insistence of funders, is on outcome goals. They want to see change in some external indicator. Having more kids attend the community center program often isn't good enough. It's reducing juvenile delinquency that matters to them. That is the interest of the community organization as well, but from the community side there are often also process questions. When I facilitated the evaluation of a community organizing training program, the group also wanted to know how effectively they were implementing their actual training strategy. In this case the questions were related to how many people were involved in what kind of training activities and how they evaluated those training activities.

Another important part of this initial stage of planning the evaluation research is to establish some sense among the group that they really do control the research process and that it won't be used against them. As part of the first planning meeting, one of the things I do is have the group develop a list of evaluation "dos and don'ts." For half an hour to an hour, we talk about all the nasty things evaluators have done to people and how to avoid those things in the current project. I record all of their advice on one of those huge pads of paper on an easel and then include it in the draft evaluation plan that I send to them. People sometimes have methodological concerns. In one case of evaluating a social services project, the planning group was adamant that they did not want to see any control group methods that deprived people of access to services. But mostly people's concerns are focused on the accountability of the process. They want confidentiality, they want the opportunity to review report drafts, and they want opportunities to have input along the way. Along with guiding the evaluation, this also sets the tone for the relationship between the researcher who is facilitating the evaluation and the people who are doing the project and helps to build some initial trust.

It is important to not become too attached to the research questions at this early stage, however. I was once part of an evaluation where the grant was written with the evaluation questions already set, without a participatory process. In trying to gather data for the evaluation, we discovered that a number of the questions couldn't be answered at all. A participatory planning process that included evaluation planning would have been able to identify this problem before the grant proposal was submitted, and we could have spent our time focusing on data that we could actually get.

## Choosing the Methods

The next step in the planning process is asking the group to think about how they will answer their research questions. As we work through that question, the group begins to come up with measures for the goals and methods for gathering the necessary data. If the goal is to build a community organization, they may decide, for example, that measuring membership growth over a six-month period will provide good information on their level of success. This is an easily measured outcome. More difficult is deciding how to measure the strategy, and some groups are pretty creative in their suggestions for how to research the strategy, suggesting close participant observation, in-depth interviews, and even detailed record keeping.

If you have a good planning group, they will often also know what information is easy and difficult to get. In other cases, however, even if you have a well-informed planning group, it may be exceedingly difficult to actually collect data that seems relatively easy to measure. I recently facilitated the evaluation of a community development program that included community policing, social service, and community development components. Many of the measures for the community policing components were easy to come up with, as the police involved with the program either knew what data was available or were able to call on the expertise of their crime data department. But coming up with methods for gathering the social service data was much more challenging than it first appeared, even though we had many of the social service providers around the planning table. They warned us about how hard it would be to find good data on alcohol and other drug abuse but had ready referrals for where they believed good data on domestic violence, truancy, teen pregnancy, and other social problem data could be obtained.

## Gathering the Data

Even when you think you can get the data, however, it is easier said than done. Even though we were warned about the difficulty in getting alcohol and drug abuse data in the previous example, we ultimately found it difficult to obtain even the data that we thought *was* readily available. We did not realize that the data we sought for evaluating this program just was not out there. One of the most important problems, which is unique to community projects that have a geographical focus, is that social service data are often not gathered on a geographical basis. Many domestic violence shelters, for example, don't even take a previous address for people seeking shelter from a batterer. Other data is gathered geographically, but the organizations keep their records by hand and don't have the capacity to go through all their files and pull out only the people served from a particular neighborhood. Evaluation is a threatening enough activity, and asking to go through an agency's files is even more threatening. In addition, those agencies have legitimate client confidentiality concerns that restrict who can view what information.

Data-gathering capacity is a problem in all kinds of evaluations. Remember that evaluation research is often a funder requirement, even when those funders don't provide any funds to do the evaluation. In addition, when there are evaluation funds, the money often goes to an outside evaluator. Consequently, not only do the people involved in the project feel resentful that they are being evaluated, but they also have to do extra work without compensation to provide extra data to the evaluator, or put up with an evaluator pawing through their files. Getting already overworked and underpaid community organization staff to change and often increase their own data collection procedures is a challenge indeed. This applies even to those you'd think would be most sympathetic to research. In facilitating the evaluation of a community-higher education partnership program, in which faculty and students provided research support to community projects, getting the faculty to provide data on those projects was exceedingly difficult. They too were severely overworked and had little time to fill out forms on their projects.

## Analyzing the Data

In my approach to evaluation, one of the things I tell a group is that I never give a grade. Since they are the ones coming up with the evaluation questions, my job is only to make sure that they have good information to answer their questions. It is not my job to tell them how good a job they are doing. I rarely have the expertise to judge whether a group could have done better or should have done something different. Instead, I simply provide the data to the group and then facilitate a planning meeting where they review the research results, using a combination of popular education and strategic planning processes that we've already discussed. They conduct the analysis, deciding what the data says about the project. In the recent evaluation of the community development/crime/social service project I have been discussing, one of our findings was a discrepancy between actual crime statistics, which had dropped substantially, and resident perceptions of crime in the community, which made it seem as if crime was the same or even getting worse. The organization doing this project then decided that the reason for this discrepancy was that they had not made a concerted enough effort to educate the community on their accomplishments, and they embarked on a community education campaign to let people know how much crime had decreased.

The closest I ever get to actually grading the work of a group is to add some of my own analysis around what I call *creative tensions.*

In the 1970s and 1980s, Kenneth Benson developed a form of "dialectical methodology" designed specifically to study contradictory tensions within organizations. Benson used the methodology to locate contradictions between the goals of an organization and the practice of those goals that can create contradictions within the organization.[16] This method works particularly well in projects tackling controversial issues. In one case where we facilitated an evaluation of a community-university partnership network, we looked at the tensions between pressures from community organizations for the network to be involved in social change work and pressures from the universities to avoid any direct involvement in advocacy campaigns so as to maintain an appearance of objectivity. Being able to present this situation as a creative tension helped the partner members see it as part of the collision of higher education and community activist structures being combined in a single organization. Accepting it as a reality helped the group to develop strategies for working with the tension and to come up with creative ways to actually put it to work. In this particular case, the group decided to adopt a division of labor that made the most of each group's strengths—the universities provided the research that community activists needed, and the community organizations took responsibility for the actual social change campaigns.

## Presenting the Data

One of my other personal rules for evaluation is that I never report to the funder. I report to the group or organization, and they report to the funder. And I have been surprised at how cooperative the funders have been about that. They, too, understand how threatening evaluation can be and how difficult it is to get good information. One might wonder, of course, whether reporting to the group, particularly when they have the chance to revise drafts, could bias the results. Here, too, I have been pleasantly surprised. There have been occasions when people have questioned the data—in one case we went back and conducted two more sample surveys of a community to make sure we had accurate data—but they have never tried to censor the results. That is partly because the evaluation report doesn't pass judgments on the program.

Instead of using the evaluation report to pass judgment, we wait to write the final draft of the report until after the group has gone through a planning process that uses the evaluation results. Then, instead of a section grading the project, there is a section talking about managing the creative tensions the research identified or changing strategies to improve outcomes. This helps the group show that it is actually thinking strategically about the research and implementing concrete changes based on the results.

The other reason groups don't feel compelled to censor research results in participatory evaluation is because the research gets presented early enough to make those crucial midcourse corrections. When you can report initial evaluation results three to six months into a three-year project, the project participants can use them to improve their outcomes early in the process. By the time you get to the final evaluation cycle, the evaluation has already contributed to enough program improvements that you know the final outcomes will be positive.

## PARTICIPATORY EVALUATION AS AN INTEGRATED PROCESS

My hope in the preceding section was to show that evaluation is not simply a research process. It is in fact a combined participatory research, popular education, community organizing, and participatory planning process.

We have already seen how participatory evaluation is another form of participatory research. But it also involves the related practice of popular education. Particularly in capacity-stressed organizations, participants may not be involved in the actual collection of data, but they are involved in the analysis and interpretation of that data, using it to educate themselves about how their project is actually working. Participatory evaluation is not simply about getting participants to provide data about outcomes but about increasing their *understanding* of the relationships between strategies and outcomes. Why is crime going down? What is leading teens to reduce their sexual activity? Why are people leaving the neighborhood less frequently? "Learning" is consistently mentioned as an important concept in participatory evaluation.[17] In many ways, this involves thinking theoretically about the data by understanding the relationships among organizational roles, community structures, social context, and various other variables appearing or being tested in the data.[18] One of the most interesting perspectives on this approach comes from Laura Vargas, who explicitly combines participatory evaluation and popular education. Evaluation is fundamental to a popular education process, but because popular education is participatory, so must be the evaluation. When the evaluation is participatory, it "is necessarily an educational process, because each step helps to bring more comprehension of what has been done, how and why. All conclusions are obtained from collective reflection which is part of a learning process on reality."[19]

A good participatory evaluation will also use a good community organizing process.[20] This puts us researchers in a very different role than we are used to. We are used to our research being front and center and to our results leading the way. But for those who think in terms of participatory strategies, the research takes on more of a background character. Ernie Stringer describes the "researcher" as a catalyst.[21] In such a role, the researcher's job is to stimulate people's thinking rather than impose prepackaged interpretations on them. Here the emphasis is on the research process more than it is on the final product, using that process to enable people to be involved in the research process even to the point of them doing it themselves. Sometimes this means starting where they are. They may be interested, at the beginning, only in simple outcome measures, but as they are drawn into the process their curiosity takes over. This helps people think more carefully about the relationship between strategy and outcome. As such a research process builds momentum, the researcher shifts into the background. This is so similar to the role of an organizer, whose job is not to lead people but to help them define a problem; develop a strategy to address that problem; build their own leadership in implementing their strategy; and then develop their own judgment about how well they are doing along the way. The organizer's role is not to lead but to facilitate.[22] Likewise, the researcher's role, particularly in evaluation, is not to tell people what they are doing right or wrong but to help them critically analyze what they are doing so they can arrive at their own conclusions and take action on those conclusions.

Finally, participatory evaluation is nothing unless it leads to plans for continuing and perhaps tweaking the project. Consequently, it integrally involves a participatory or empowerment planning process.[23] Most participatory planning has focused on the physical planning of neighborhoods, putting neighborhood residents in charge of deciding what they want, and do not want, in their neighborhood. Even when it emphasizes physical neighborhood planning, however, a participatory planning process is not just about accomplishing measurable goals but also building interpersonal relationships through the process.[24] Though it was not a formal evaluation process, during my early research with the Cedar-Riverside neighborhood in Minneapolis, residents told me about how one of the side effects of their successful housing development was a disruption in relationships within the neighborhood as old residents moved out and new ones moved in. As that situation increased in intensity through the 1990s and into the new millennium, we worked together on a research project to develop strategies for rebuilding neighborhood relationships. Such a planning process, just like participatory research, emphasizes respecting the skills of the people involved in the project, including service recipients. One of the beauties of participatory evaluation is that the research process can recruit service recipients into the process and then move them into actual project planning.

To describe participatory evaluation as an integrated process does not only mean showing how it integrates the practices of participatory research, popular education, community organizing, and participatory planning. It also means showing how evaluation becomes integrated into the ongoing efforts of a group to understand what they are doing and what impact they are having. I always find it interesting to meet a new group for the first time as "the evaluator." The initial vibes I get from the group are the same vibes that I imagine I send out when I go to the dentist—having endured endless torture at the hands of dentists and orthodontists as a child. Evaluation is seen as an "other"—opposed to and separate from an organization. Even when the organization members define it as "good for us," doing the evaluation feels like a disruption of the "real work" of the organization. The act of gathering data needs to be shoehorned into the schedules of already overstretched staff or even volunteers.

The goal of participatory evaluation, ultimately, is to make evaluation something that is seen as a nonthreatening, ongoing activity of the group or organization. Evaluation should not be a separate activity done only at special times under special circumstances. Yoland Wadsworth talks about developing a "culture of evaluation" where the organization is so engaged in thinking about what is and is not working that it becomes a normal part of everyday practice.[25] In many community organizing models, evaluation is conducted after every door-knocking session, every action, and even meetings. Called "debriefings," these semiformal discussions try to better understand what worked, what didn't work, and what to do different the next time. Cheryl Grills and her colleagues developed an interesting model in which they used an organizer and evaluator team to conduct a community organizing needs assessment. They used the evaluation data throughout the organizing process for "identifying issues, clarifying problems, prioritizing agendas for action, developing strategies with policymakers, defining goals, selecting targets for organizing, and critically assessing actions taken."[26] Research, then, became an integrated part of the daily work of the community organizing process.

At a minimum, a group or organization involved in a community change project should be collecting whatever outcome data they can on a regular basis. At some point, a group or organization should sit down and ask themselves the following:

- What are our goals?
- What countable things can we identify to determine how well we are meeting our goals?
- Which of those countable things are already in our own records?
- Which of those countable things could we easily include in our own records?
- Which of those countable things are easily available from other organizations' records?
- Which of those countable things would have to be collected from scratch?
- Which of all the countable things are most important to measuring our goals?
- What uncountable things are also important in determining how well we are meeting our goals?
- How do we collect information on those uncountable things?
- How much effort will it take to collect information on those uncountable things?
- How important are those uncountable things in determining how well we are meeting our goals?

The purpose is not to then go out and spend all your time collecting data. You can set priorities. The data which is most important and most easily obtained is, of course, data that you collect without question. After that, it is a judgment call. It may be that some data comes in a set, such as alcohol abuse and alcohol abuse treatment numbers. It may be easy to get data on how many people receive treatment from various services around town. It may be very difficult to find out the extent of alcohol abuse. But knowing how many people are receiving treatment may not be very useful without also knowing the extent of the problem. It is also possible that, if you discover some of your goals require outcome data that is all but impossible to get, you might even change your goals.

An organization that can achieve this level of integration of evaluation into its daily activities will no longer lack the capacity to do its own evaluations. Such an organization will have developed regular data collection and storage activities that it can draw on with a few clicks of a mouse. It will have a culture rewarding staff and leaders for engaging in self-reflection and developing plans for improvement rather than punishing them for lack of achievement and consequently encouraging them not to collect information that could be used against them. It will also have regular cycles of more focused evaluations as part of its regular annual or semiannual planning process. And, if I am correct, such an organization will be more productive and more successful.

## LOOSE GRAVEL

Of all the stages of the project cycle, the gravel shoulders of the evaluation stage are the loosest and the drop-offs the steepest. Evaluations often determine not just which projects survive but which organizations survive. Consequently, they are political, both inside the project and outside of it. And while the most political part of the evaluation is the report, the concerns about how the report will make the project look infect every stage from the initial generation of the research question all the way through to the report itself. These concerns manifest themselves in three ways: the concern about negative results; the concern about control; and the concern about cost.

- What if the evaluation makes us look bad?
- How do we control it to make sure it doesn't look bad?
- How do we afford an evaluation in the first place?

### The Concern About Negative Results

The big fear on everyone's mind, of course, is that the evaluation will make the project look bad. Used to the external comprehensive final exam model of evaluation, project staff members often see evaluations as something designed to expose weaknesses and failures. Their response, consequently, is to "spin" or even withhold some information to present, perhaps, more success than is justified. This is, however, more a failure of the external outcome evaluation model than of the project staff trying to protect their work. And the way to deal with this challenge is to shift to a participatory process evaluation. The beauty of participatory evaluation is that it is actually a strategy to enhance success rather than to judge success. I have used participatory evaluation with numerous community change efforts. In each case we have been able to identify problems and glitches in a project early on and correct them, so that when it became time to collect outcome data we already knew the data would look good. Early and frequent feedback, along with the adjustments that follow, relax people. They know where they stand right at the beginning and can see their progress. Remember the coaching model—frequent feedback with concrete adjustments. The final report, then, will not just list weaknesses but will also list what steps the group took to overcome those weaknesses and, in the best cases, the outcomes of those new strategies.

It is important to understand, however, that the ability of participatory process evaluation to actually impact the project along the way is what most unnerves those who follow a traditional evaluation model. We social scientists have been taught that there is nothing worse than when our research "affects the system." Evaluators are supposed to be objective. Like journalists in an urban war zone, we are supposed to stand passively by while innocent bystanders are gunned down around us, even though we could have easily saved them by yelling "Duck!" Some funders still believe that an evaluator who becomes invested in helping a project succeed, rather than simply measuring the extent to which it does not succeed, can't possibly be objective. And they are correct. It's not objective. But remember back to Chapter 1, where we found out that there is no necessary relationship between objectivity and accuracy. Our job as evaluators is to convince funders that there are many paths to accuracy and that they should prefer an evaluation method that produces both accurate measurements and increased project success. That job is getting much easier through the leadership of foundations such as the Kellogg Foundation and the acceptance of the method by an increasing number of both government and private funders.

## The Concern About Control

The concern about control is inextricably related to the concern about negative results. Anyone who has been through the traditional school system has been subject to evaluations outside of their control. The seemingly arbitrary and imposed nature of such evaluations, far from encouraging us to seek feedback, encourage us instead to avoid it. Those of us who got our hands slapped for coloring outside of the lines, or not following the assigned color scheme, became especially paranoid about opening our innovations up to scrutiny. And so we have sought ways to control the information flow in any kind of evaluation setting. This is particularly the case in many community projects, which are accountable to not only the target constituency and the funder but probably also to an organization board of some kind. The project director, often caught in the middle, is faced with trying to balance the impractical hopes of the board with the unrealistic expectations of the constituency and the underresourced demands of the funder.

Being caught in the middle means also trying to manage the information flow. The project staff are often in the best position to know what is going on and are regularly trying to communicate information accurately to the other stakeholders. Creating a participatory evaluation process that involves these other groups, especially the constituency, can be quite disruptive. In so many cases projects are planned without the involvement of the constituency, and then it is especially difficult to involve them in the evaluation of something that they didn't have a hand in designing. This creates a no-win situation in which inviting the constituency to influence the evaluation invites critique of the entire project after the fact, when it is too late to make fundamental changes. Many evaluations, in such a situation exclude the constituency from anything but answering survey questions determined without their input to measure the goals and strategies set without their input.

This is a fundamental problem in the design of social services in the United States. Participatory evaluation can be difficult to implement with social service projects because it operates out of a community organizing model rather than a social services model, focusing on empowering the constituency rather than maintaining control by the project staff. That is why it is so important to implement a participatory evaluation at the very beginning of a project, when the constituency can become involved in designing the project. That is also why the core group, which we discussed in Chapter 4, is so important. A well-functioning and representative core group can transform clients into participants and often achieve one of the overarching goals of most community projects—the empowerment of the constituency—through the process of designing the project.

## The Concern About Cost

Regrettably, one of the strongest barriers to carrying out a useful evaluation is cost. Evaluating a project requires real skills and real time. When it is added to the job of an existing staff person, it rarely gets done with any more than superficial analysis of unreliable data. And because funds are short, and the real goal of the project is to accomplish the outcome goals rather than measure whether the goals were accomplished, evaluation becomes a secondary concern. At the same time, however, the lack of good data on project success makes it difficult to achieve project success. It is possible to get lucky and do all the right things in all the right ways. But community change projects are normally messy enough and the social ground on which they operate shifts often enough that success is much more often only tentative and fleeting. Imagine trying to bake a cake without measuring spoons and measuring cups. Imagine trying to build a birdhouse without a ruler. When we do community projects without good evaluation research, that is exactly what we are doing.

How much does an effective participatory evaluation process cost? I have found that it is difficult to do a year-long participatory evaluation with less than $15,000 for a single-site project where the evaluation studies both process and outcomes. And that is the cost for doing it yourself or hiring a moonlighting academic and some qualified students. Hiring a private research firm or working through a high-powered university can produce a bill up to ten times that high. Here again, funders need to be educated that if they expect a careful, useful evaluation, they need to fund it. But the organization or group also needs to be educated to seek funding for the evaluation.

Evaluation costs can be reduced if the organization gets into the habit of collecting data as part of its daily activities, as we have discussed. By integrating data gathering into everyone's work, the burden can be spread throughout the organization. Such data gathering is especially useful for annual strategic planning sessions. And regular strategic planning is especially useful for determining what data to gather on a regular basis. There still needs to be someone in the organization whose job description involves making sure that the data is gathered and stored in an efficiently usable form such as an electronic database, but the actual collection can be integrated into regular staff reporting activities. One complaint of organization staff focuses on the amount of reporting they do that never seems to matter. Using strategic planning to set goals, and then to decide how to measure goal achievement, leads to reporting that does matter, because all that reporting gets used throughout the project to adjust strategy and implementation and then gets reused in the next year's strategic planning process.

## CONCLUSION

This chapter focused on doing evaluation research, emphasizing the importance of beginning evaluation at the beginning of a project rather than at the end.

We explored two important choices in designing an evaluation:

- External vs. participatory evaluation
- Outcome vs. process evaluation

We looked at how to do evaluations in relation to the steps in project-based research:

- Choosing the question
- Designing the methods
- Collecting the data
- Analyzing the data
- Reporting the results

We discussed evaluation research as an integrated process integrating:

- Participatory research
- Popular education
- Community organizing
- Empowerment planning

Some of the challenges facing evaluation research include:

- Concerns about negative results
- Issues of control over the evaluation
- Worries about cost

# RESOURCES

## General Evaluation

American Evaluation Association, http://www.eval.org/

## Participatory and Utilization-Focused Evaluation

Estrella, M., with Blauert, J., Campilan, D., Gaventa, J., Gonsalves, J., Guijt, I., Johnson, D., & Roger Ricafort (Eds.). (2000). *Learning from change: Issues and experiences in participatory monitoring and evaluation*. London: Intermediate Technology Publications.

Fetterman, D. M., Kaftarian, S. J., & Wandersman, A. (Eds.). (1996). *Empowerment evaluation: Knowledge and tools for self-assessment and accountability.* Thousand Oaks, CA: Sage Publications.

Patton, M. Q. (1997). Utilization-focused evaluation: The new century text (3rd ed.). Thousand Oaks, CA: Sage Publications.

## Outcome Evaluation

Outcome Measurement Resource Network. United Way of America, http://national.unitedway.org/outcomes/

Durrance, J. C., & Fisher, K. E. (2002). The outcomes toolkit 2.0. Ann Arbor, MI and Seattle, WA: University of Michigan and University of Washington, http://ibec.ischool.washington.edu/ibecCat.aspx?sub Cat=Outcome%20Toolkit&cat=Tools%20and%20Resources

# NOTES

1. *Back to the future.* (1985). Directed by R. Zemeckis. Universal Studios.

2. Wadsworth, Y. (1991). *Everyday evaluation on the run.* Melbourne, Australia: Action Research Issues Association.

3. Patton, M. Q. (1997). *Utilization-focused evaluation: The new century text* (3rd ed.). Thousand Oaks, CA: Sage Publications.

4. AEA Task Force on Guiding Principles for Evaluators. (1994). *Guiding principles for evaluators.* American Evaluation Association. Retrieved July 15, 2004, from http://www.eval.org/

5. Patton, M. Q. (1997). *Utilization-focused evaluation.*

6. Ibid. (pp. 138–139).

7. Fetterman, D. M., Kaftarian, S. J., & Wandersman, A. (Eds.). (1996). *Empowerment evaluation: Knowledge and tools for self-assessment and accountability.* Thousand Oaks, CA: Sage Publications. See also Fetterman, D. M. (2002). *Collaborative, participatory, and empowerment evaluation.* Retrieved July 15, 2004, from http://www.stanford.edu/~davidf/empowermentevalua tion.html

8. Patton, M. Q. (1997). *Utilization-focused evaluation.*

9. Millett, R. A. (1996). Empowerment evaluation and the W. K. Kellogg Foundation. In D. M. Fetterman, S. J. Kaftarian, & A. Wandersman (Eds.). *Empowerment evaluation: Knowledge and tools for self-assessment and accountability* (pp. 65–76). Thousand Oaks, CA: Sage Publications.

10. *W. K. Kellogg Foundation logic model development guide.* (2001). Retrieved July 15, 2004, from http://www.wkkf.org/Pubs/Tools/ Evaluation/Pub3669.pdf

11.   Durrance, J. C., & Fisher, K. E. (2002). *The outcomes toolkit 2.0.* Ann Arbor, MI and Seattle, WA: University of Michigan and University of Washington. Retrieved July 15, 2004, from http://ibec.ischool.washington.edu/ibecCat.aspx?subCat=Outcome%20Toolkit&cat=Tools%20and%20Resources

12.   Cook, T. D., & Campbell, D. T. (1979). *Quasi-experimentation: Design & analysis issues for field settings.* Boston: Houghton Mifflin Co.

13.   United Way of America. (2002). *Outcome measurement: What and why.* Retrieved July 15, 2004, from http://national.unitedway.org/outcomes/files/TPsOMWhatandWhy.pdf

14.   Stoecker, R. (2003). Understanding the development-organizing dialectic. *Journal of Urban Affairs, 25 (4),* 493–512.

15.   Roethlisberger, F. J., & Dickson, W. J. (1939). *Management and the worker.* Cambridge, MA: Harvard University Press. Mayo, E. (1933). *The human problems of an industrial civilization.* New York: MacMillan.

16.   Benson, K. (1983). A dialectical method for the study of organizations. In Gareth Morgan (Ed.). Beyond method: Strategies for social research. Beverly Hills, CA: Sage Publications. Benson, K. (1977). Organizations, a dialectical view. *Administrative Science Quarterly, 22,* 1–21.

17.   Estrella, M., with Blauert, J., Campilan, D., Gaventa, J., Gonsalves, J., Guijt, I., Johnson, D., & Ricafort, R. (Eds.). (2000). *Learning from change: Issues and experiences in participatory monitoring and evaluation.* London: Intermediate Technology Publications. Estrella, M., & Gaventa, J. (1998). *Who counts reality? Participatory monitoring and evaluation: A literature review.* IDS Working Paper 70. Brighton, UK: Institute for Development Studies. Retrieved July 15, 2004, from http://www.ids.ac.uk/ids/bookshop/wp/wp70.pdf

18.   Fetterman, D. M. (1996). Empowerment evaluation: An introduction to theory and practice. In D. M. Fetterman, S. J. Kaftarian, & A. Wandersman (Eds.). *Empowerment evaluation: Knowledge and tools for self-assessment and accountability* (pp. 3–46). Thousand Oaks, CA: Sage Publications.

19.   Vargas, L. (1991). Reflections on methodology of evaluation. *Community Development Journal, 26,* 266–270.

20.   Stoecker, R. (1999). Making connections: Community organizing, empowerment planning, and participatory research in participatory evaluation. *Sociological Practice, 1,* 209–232.

21.   Stringer, E. T. (1999). *Action research: A handbook for practitioners* (2nd ed.). Thousand Oaks, CA: Sage Publications.

22.   Bobo, K., Kendall, J., & Max, J. (1991). *Organizing for social change: A manual for activists in the 1990s.* Santa Ana, CA: Seven Locks Press.

23.   Reardon, K. M. (1999). Promoting community development through empowerment planning: The East St. Louis action research project. In D. Keating & N. Krumholz (Eds.). *America's poorest urban neighborhoods:*

*Urban policy, redevelopment and planners* (pp. 124–139). Thousand Oaks, CA: Sage Publications. Stoecker, R. (1999). Making connections: Community organizing, empowerment planning, and participatory research in participatory evaluation. *Sociological Practice, 1,* 209–232. Butterfoss, F. D., Goodman, R. M., Wandersman, A., Valois, R. F., & Chinman, M. J. (1996). The plan quality index: An empowerment evaluation tool for measuring and improving the quality of plans. In D. M. Fetterman, S. J. Kaftarian, & A. Wandersman (Eds.). *Empowerment evaluation: Knowledge and tools for self-assessment and accountability* (pp. 304–331). Thousand Oaks, CA: Sage Publications.

24. Cassidy, R. (1980). *Livable cities: A grass-roots guide to rebuilding urban America.* New York: Holt, Rinehart, and Winston. Friedman, E. (1978). *Crest Street: A family/community impact statement.* Policy Paper #2 of the Center for the Study of the Family and the State. Institute of Policy Sciences and Public Affairs, Duke University. Jones, B. (1990). *Neighborhood planning: A guide for citizens and planners.* Bigtown, IL: Planners Press, American Planning Association. Pyatok, M., & Weber, H. (1978). Participation in residential design: A method for generating choice and its ideological consequences. In H. Sanoff (Ed.). *Designing with community participation* (pp. 173–204). Stroudsburg, PA: Dowden, Hutchinson, & Ross, Inc.

25. Wadsworth, Y. (1991). *Everyday evaluation on the run.* Melbourne, Australia: Action Research Issues Association.

26. Grills, C. N., Bass, K., Brown, D. L, & Akers, A. (1996). Empowerment evaluation: Building upon a tradition of activism in the African-American community. In D. M. Fetterman, S. J. Kaftarian, & A. Wandersman (Eds.). *Empowerment evaluation: Knowledge and tools for self-assessment and accountability* (pp. 123–140). Thousand Oaks, CA: Sage Publications.

# *Eight*

# Beyond Information

*Research as an
Organizational Lifestyle*

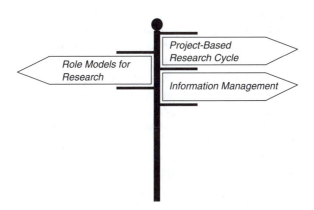

## THE MONTESSORI, GOOSE APPROACH, POPULAR EDUCATION, TENNIS COACH MODEL OF PROJECT-BASED RESEARCH

As a parent, I feel increasingly humbled and awed by my daughter. As much as she is her own person, she is also the product of an educational model called the Montessori method. Founded by the early 20th century Italian educator Maria Montessori, the method emphasizes not the memorization of facts but the process of learning how to learn.[1] My daughter has been a Montessori student since preschool and has been writing research papers (with references!) since 4th grade. In the Montessori method, the child, not the teacher, is at the center of the process. Children are even encouraged to teach each other, which is why Montessori schools group children into three year cohorts. As of this writing my daughter just finished the third year of the 4th, 5th, and 6th grade group and has been helping the 4th and 5th graders learn, just as she was helped when she was younger. She is learning the Goose Approach to research and education (remember Chapters 1 and 2?) at an age where it can take hold with much less struggle than we adults have to endure.

One of my fondest memories of her in those early Montessori days was when I caught her with our standard poodle—one of those *big* poodles so maligned for their often silly-looking haircuts. We chose the breed for its hypoallergenic qualities—they don't shed. But because they don't shed, their hair creates all manner of complications, particular in the ears, which have to be plucked regularly. My daughter, having witnessed those many ear-plucking sessions, became curiouser and curiouser. So one day I found her with our extremely cooperative standard poodle, the dog's ear flopped back, flashlight and magnifying glass in hand, peering down its ear canal, studying. Now she is 12 and is already putting to shame my own adolescent-era fight for independence. The other day we were having one of those parent vs. preteen struggles—she wanted to plaster the sandpaper-coated deck of her skateboard with paint and stickers, thus turning the surface designed to keep her from slipping off and breaking her neck into a skating rink and, of course, giving my imagination visions of an emergency room visit. In the midst of our argument, I explained to her that, if she followed her plan, she wouldn't be able to get any *traction*. She looked momentarily puzzled, but recovered in a nanosecond, exclaiming "I would too!" Well, I knew I had her, and played my parental trump card: "You don't even know what traction means!" She stomped away, only to return a few moments later, and shot back: "I would too be able to get friction." She had, of course, gone and researched the concept of traction.

For my daughter, research is part of her lifestyle. And it can be part of yours, if it's not already. The popular education model, which we have discussed on and off throughout this book, is part of that lifestyle shift. In stark contrast to school learning, where what is learned is determined by politicians or academics, in popular education the topics of learning are set by people's needs. And the answers are at least partly informed by people's experiences. If we all lived according to a popular education model, we would be integrated into a vast knowledge network that would not only include experts but also those of us with common experiences and the knowledge that comes from those experiences. When we had a question, we would readily be able to call upon that network for information.

Such a knowledge network already exists in many places. Founded in the Netherlands but now expanded across the globe, the science shop model—small, locally based research centers— provides information to community residents concerned with all kinds of issues.[2] The Internet has exploded with newsgroups, chat rooms, and other forms of community-based information trading. Challenged by the stranger-to-stranger form of communication, it is difficult to trust the Internet for crucial information, but various groups are overcoming that hurdle, as we will see. Then there are those informal community networks. My parents, retired and lacking adequate prescription drug coverage like so many retired citizens, started researching the Canadian mail-order prescription business that so many senior citizens are using to save thousands of dollars a year on medicine. They read the magazine articles and researched the Internet, but mostly they talked to their friends who are facing similar challenges in affording prescription medicines. They gave my parents leads on companies to check out, companies to watch out for, and questions to ask. And this is the essence of popular education—people pooling knowledge from their own experience and their own research.

Perhaps the most important aspect to making research a central feature of one's lifestyle involves seeking feedback. I am still regularly surprised by how resistant we are to getting feedback. I am fresh out of a meeting in our department about assessment—doing research to find out how well we are serving our students. There is still a surprising amount of resistance to the idea of assessment, though it shouldn't surprise me, given how often evaluation is used against people rather than for them. But if we shift to the tennis coach model, so that we get early and frequent feedback while we still have a chance to adjust what we are doing, then the feedback is both less scary and more useful. People with diabetes, for whom frequent feedback in the form of blood tests is a part of their lifestyle, have already learned this lesson. At the community level, I am working with a community-based alternative to the United Way, called Community Shares, which seeks funds through donations from employees at various workplaces. As this group organized itself, they sought out the assistance of a staff person from the National Committee for Responsive Philanthropy, who visited monthly for a while, giving the group feedback on its attempts to build its membership and get permission from workplaces to solicit employees. Coupled with a popular education method that creates knowledge-sharing networks, we could find someone who could give us regular feedback on everything from home plumbing repair to community crime prevention programs.

Perhaps the most dramatic shift required of us in making research part of our lifestyle is also bringing back a do-it-yourself attitude. Because research is pretty useless unless we are engaged in actually using it. Think of how we manage our daily lives. So many of us take our computer to the computer repair worker to get upgrades, hire a plumber to repair our leaky faucets, hire painters to paint our homes, hire accountants to do our taxes, etc. Back in the "good ol' days" however, people did these things themselves, or did them with the assistance of their neighbors, using skills passed down from generation to generation and across from neighbor to neighbor. I have been fortunate in having parents who are highly skilled do-it-yourselfers and who raised me to be the same. It's not that I magically know how to do things like install windows (our current home remodeling project) but that I know how to find out how to do those things, try it, and then seek feedback. I have even been able to apply the principle to do my own computer repair and software customization. My parents knew nothing of computers—I didn't even see a desktop computer until I was in graduate school. But the do-it-yourself attitude allowed me to transfer the learning process from plumbing to programming and even to giving our standard poodle haircuts (though not the silly-looking kind).

The responsibilities inherent in such a shift are pretty dramatic. At the community organization level, it requires a different kind of reliance on consultants. Today, community organizations hire consultants to do all kinds of work *for* them—from doing the research to developing a strategic plan. In the Montessori, goose approach, popular education, tennis coach model of project-based research, the consultants became educators and trainers, not replacement managers. That may be more expensive in the short run, since it adds an educational component to the process, requiring community organization staff and often leaders to learn how to do things rather than just have those things done for them. Over the long haul, however, this is the kind of knowledge an organization can pass from staff member to staff member, reducing the need for consultants.

Why is do-it-yourself research so important and why should I be asking community organizations to put even more resources into it? If the goal of our community work is empowered communities, then the foundation for that empowerment is interdependent self-sufficiency rather than isolated dependency. A famous, or some would say infamous, social critic of the 19th century charged that the development of capitalism brought with it the problem of alienation—that people began buying things that they used to make for themselves, and they took jobs that required less and less skill.[3] As they lost the skills, or became *alienated* from the process that allowed them to grow their own food, sew their own clothes, and build their own furniture, they became *dependent* on capitalists for those things. The most extreme results of that alienation are the deteriorated central city neighborhoods we see today, which were left high and dry when the jobs moved out of town and the people possessed neither the skills to self-sufficiently meet their own needs nor the interdependent knowledge networks to relearn those skills. Both the people of those communities and the organizations that work with them need to redevelop those missing skills and rebuild those missing networks. In the long run, such a practice will reduce both risks and costs.

The project-based research model provides a framework to begin rebuilding a practice of interdependent, self-sufficient communities.

## THE PROJECT-BASED RESEARCH CYCLE REVISITED

What would community work look like if research were a daily part of it? Think of the project-based research cycle. Rather than community work being driven by funders, or even by staff preconceptions, it would be driven by an information process.

At the diagnostic stage, groups would determine the problems and opportunities in their communities based on a regular research process. This could even be an annual event. The big annual meeting that so many community organizations have, instead of just a celebration

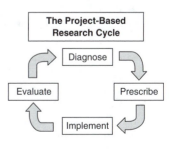

of past successes and a listing of future goals, could be an information-gathering process that seeks the knowledge of community members and uses the annual meeting as an information analysis event. Such a process should not be seen as an added burden but in fact as an important recruitment tool. Organizing residents to knock on their neighbors' doors, call them on the phone, or hold house meetings doesn't just gather data. It educates people about community issues, recruits them to community activities, and builds community relationships. Data is often a useful fringe benefit of such a process, and the small extra effort required to gather information while also accomplishing those other goals makes it easily doable.

And just because data gathering may be a secondary concern doesn't mean it should be hidden. Because we need to change the culture of community work to become more information-driven and less funder- and staff-driven, we need to build the legitimacy of gathering data. When research is seen as a separate activity, disconnected from the action, getting participation in the research is like pulling teeth. We just got done with a third round of community surveys in one neighborhood to inform the work of a community development effort. Even with a group of students going door to door, we only netted a 17% response rate, so wary are residents of those seeking information. If we had residents involved in the surveying, and made the survey a community event, our response rate may have become much closer to that achieved in the community described in Chapter 4.

One of the responses to my plea for research at the diagnostic stage of a community change project is that everyone already knows what the problems are, so all that research really isn't necessary. And that can be true, though if a group is trying to recruit residents to the cause anyway, they might as well also collect some needs and assets data along the way. At the prescription stage, however, the choices are so muddled by the whims of funders and the pressures of often arbitrarily determined best practices that careful research becomes crucial. I have watched so many community change projects fail because they were demanded by funders or transplanted from other, and significantly different, places. Resources are wasted, hopes are dashed, and cynicism is increased when projects fail, making it all the more difficult to try the next project.

Creating the most effective prescription poses the most difficult set of research challenges of any stage of the project-based research cycle. Determining just what the options are can be an extremely time-consuming task, requiring organization leaders or staff to build networks in order to even find other groups trying different things. The lack of research in the area of community change, except in a few areas such as youth programming and public health, often requires original data collection. In addition, it requires a nose for comparative case study research, determining what the most relevant characteristics of each community are, how community change projects interact with those characteristics, and developing an informed prediction of how each project option will then impact your community. It is often like predicting the weather, as there are far more variables than cases, making a statistical analysis impossible and long-range forecasting iffy. And discouraging as that may be when a group is facing the prospect of gathering a lot of data that may or may not assure success, the alternative is winging it. With good research, if a project fails, at least we have good information to help us understand why. And even if a project is preordained by a funder or other authority, good research can help shape the project in such a way as to increase its likelihood of success.

At the implementation stage, the pressures surrounding research are more easily transformed into positive energies. Whether it is doing historical recovery, community murals, neighborhood mapping, or any of the myriad of implementation research projects, having fun is a much easier goal to achieve. Research at the implementation stage is more likely to be used in creating a description of the community than to trace a causal path. It is also more likely to produce a concrete public product (sometimes literally concrete) that people can point to and say "I did that." Even in the case of target research, where the group is going after a bad guy, the research is filled with energy because it is directed toward a specific objective.

It is at the implementation stage that we also see the most innovations in what constitutes research and find it most integrated into community change projects as a normal and natural component. Community Web sites, theater, art, photography, songs, quilts, and a wide variety of activities often seem much more like presentation than research. And that is as it should be. The fun part is in the presentation, and the main challenge is making sure that people are doing the careful research needed for their presentation to withstand the challenges of those opposing or victimizing the community. There is a tension here between trying to make the research part of the project explicit enough so that people do it carefully, and letting it become embedded in the project in such a way that people no longer think of research as something separate. When it can become both explicit and embedded, community members can develop confidence in their research abilities and can say "I am a researcher too." There are lessons here for the other stages in the project-based research cycle in how to make research fun and how to make its results noticeable.

Finally, the most threatening research is at the evaluation stage, as we have already seen. Our approach to evaluation is so convoluted and distorted by the demands of funders and the culture of punishment that have historically surrounded evaluation that it is almost inherently distrusted. It is also at the evaluation stage that the community is most likely to define the research as separate from the community life and from daily practice. And it may be that the most effective way to reduce the sense of threat surrounding evaluation is to integrate it as much as possible into the daily practice of community work. The old cynical Chicago political campaign slogan "vote early and often" works even better for evaluation. The more evaluation becomes a practice done early in the life course of a project, and often throughout that life course, the more effect it can have on assuring project success rather than on grading project shortcomings. It is much easier to do evaluation if it will help your project succeed than if it will threaten its continuation.

Doing evaluation early and often also requires the most change in how we operate community organizations and how we manage community projects. Good evaluation requires good ongoing data collection and information management. Consequently, it requires organization members becoming diligent in regular (sometimes daily) data collection, proficient in database development and management, and flexible in program implementation. That is often a difficult shift to make because it does require extra time, particularly in terms of start-up costs. To the extent that groups and organizations lack the capacity to make these shifts, this is the stage of the project-based research cycle that may still require the most outside assistance, either in terms of doing the data collection and analysis or in training organization members in doing it. But groups should be forewarned that even when they get an outside researcher they will still be required to give up time, providing that researcher with regular and frequent access to information, collecting information themselves from constituency members to whom they provide direct services, and participating in regular reflection sessions to make program changes based on evaluation outcomes. Too many organizations see the "outside evaluator" as not only a threat but also as a way to relieve themselves of the burden of evaluation. But evaluation is only useful when the organization takes on the burden of using the research, which requires a real time commitment.

Most groups and organizations will only use research in the project cycle as it serves their ends. But there are organizations out there who have so effectively integrated research into their work that the research and action become almost indistinguishable.

# ROLE MODELS FOR RESEARCH AS A DAILY PRACTICE

Perhaps three of the most famous organizations that have made research part of their daily work are the Applied Research Center, Project South, and the Highlander Research and Education Center. These are more than community-based think tanks producing policy briefs. They also do a wide variety of technical assistance and social change work on the ground. But research is both infused and explicit in everything they do.

## Highlander Research and Education Center

Highlander is the grandparent of those community organiza-tions searching for ways to bring research and action together. Founded in the 1930s by Myles Horton and Don West as a commu-nity-run education and organizing center,[4] Highlander was modeled partly after Jane Addams's famous Hull House in Chicago,[5] partly after a cooperative of homeless residents in the old Soviet Union, and partly after the Danish folk schools of the time.

Highlander's early years focused on Appalachian economic and political issues, including a great deal of direct action on labor and community development issues. But by the middle 1940s its mission had expanded to become a school for CIO-affiliated labor union activities across the South. Highlander was also there for the first steps of the civil rights movement in the 1950s, holding research and education workshops on how citizens could implement the famous Brown v. Board school desegregation decision. Rosa Parks attended one of those workshops, and she cites her experience at Highlander as one of the important experiences that gave her the will to keep her seat on that bus in Montgomery, Alabama shortly thereafter.[6]

In 1960 the school was shut down by a court order for, among other things, practicing racial integration in its classrooms. The school struggled to survive and regain its footing during the 1960s, but eventually was able to reestablish itself less than a mile from the original site, when John Gaventa and Juliet Merrifield took over its leadership and focused its work on participatory research. Among their accomplishments was an enormous study of land ownership patterns in Appalachia that showed the negative impacts of coal companies on health, education, welfare, and the environment throughout the region. Highlander continues to adapt to changing times and changing issues, conducting research and education campaigns that assisted the rise of the environmental justice movement, the global economic justice movement, youth organizing, and others. But always at the center of its work have been the methods of popular education and participatory research, bringing activists and community members from around the country to its education and research workshops.[7]

## The Applied Research Center

The Applied Research Center, headquartered in Oakland, California, was founded in the early 1980s. The early years of ARC were focused on researching and improving the practice of community organizing. By collaborating with the nearby Center for Third World Organizing, they were able to implement the results of their research, creating the Community Strategy and Training Initiative as a model used in multiple locations. ARC was also one of the earliest organizations to recognize the potential of bringing together academics and activists to build an effective formula of integrating research and action.

In the 1990s, ARC expanded its activities in direct technical assistance and research for a variety of organizing campaigns in California and elsewhere. And as they developed their general research prowess, they increasingly shifted into policy research on both local and national issues, particularly those involving race, education, and welfare. Far from morphing into a progressive think tank, however, ARC also embarked on a mission to bring together the methods of popular education and community organizing, thus helping a wide variety of community organizations learn how to use research and education in their organizing campaigns.[8]

## Project South

Project South: Institute for the Elimination of Poverty & Genocide may be the organization that has most integrated research and action within a single organization. Since its founding in 1991, Project South has emphasized the use of popular education and participatory action research as part of direct action campaigns. They emphasize that historical, political, and economic education is crucial to understanding the forces of oppression. With offices in both Washington, D.C. and Atlanta, Project South takes on issues both local and multi-local, ranging from protesting the destruction of affordable housing in Atlanta for the 1996 Olympics, to a research and action campaign on gentrification in a Washington, D.C. neighborhood, to a project focused on the role of money in politics.[9]

Project South also provides technical assistance for a wide variety of community groups and organizations large and small, helping them to develop their own participatory research and popular education skills and integrate them into their campaigns.[10]

## BEHIND THE FUN: INFORMATION MANAGEMENT AND INFORMATION TECHNOLOGY

Behind the inspiring models of groups like Highlander, ARC, and Project South are some less exciting but crucially important lessons of the nitty-gritty of information management. Those groups and organizations willing to make research part of their daily lives will also need to develop their information collecting, managing, storing, and distributing capacity. Working with nonprofit organizations over the past 15 years, I have been continually distressed at how difficult it is for them to obtain, manage, and report on very basic information, such as how many people they serve with what demographic characteristics (race, sex, age, etc.) from what parts of town. And there is nothing incompetent about the groups and organizations I am working with. But there is a capacity problem. Part of the capacity problem is the lack of time available for already overstretched staff and volunteer board members to engage in careful strategic planning. But even when organizations do find the time for the strategic planning, much of it is based on anecdotal records or community opinion. Very little of it is based on good information, which requires even more time and resources to obtain.

> **Developing a Community Organization Information Infrastructure**
>
> 1. An information-based strategic planning process
>
> 2. An information collecting plan
>
> 3. An information management plan

What is required to develop an effective community organization information infrastructure? The three components are information,

# The Project Cycle Decision Chart

> **What activities are we engaged in?**
> In other words, what is the key research question
> that leads to relevant information?

> What information do we have or that is already generated?

> What information is needed? Or, what is the other information
> we do not yet have?

> **What kind of information
> do we need for engaging in
> our activities?**

**HAVE:**
Data already available
in a usable format.

**DO NOT HAVE:**
This includes data
requiring analysis to be
made usable.

| **What kind of information are easiest to get (in terms of skill, time, and money)?** | **What kind of information will provide the greatest immediate benefit to the project?** | **What kind of information is the group or organization in the best position to use?** |
|---|---|---|

SOURCE: Chart courtesy of Kelly Spivey. Reprinted with permission.

technology, and people, in a complex interaction. The flow chart describes how to bring these things together.[11]

## Developing an Information-Based Strategic Planning Process

It is difficult for many groups and organizations to know what information to collect, how to collect it, and what to do with it. Depending on what stage of the project cycle a group is at, they will need to collect different kinds of information. At the diagnostic stage, the concerns are what important issues to focus programming on and what the cause-and-effect sequences are for those issues. Chapter 4 outlines the processes for developing research questions around those concerns. At the prescription stage the questions center on what to do about the chosen issue and how to decide what to do. Chapter 5 presents various research outlines for meeting those tasks. The implementation stage is very diverse, since research *is* the project at this stage, as Chapter 6 describes. Consequently, planning the research occurs in much the same way as any other type of program planning at the implementation stage. Finally, no matter where one is in the project cycle, but especially at the implementation stage, planning should necessarily involve thinking about evaluation. As Chapter 7 discussed, all projects should begin, not end, with evaluation. So, as the group sits down to plan a project, they will also need to spend some time developing project goals and objectives, determining how to measure those objectives, and developing a research plan serving the project.

Information-based strategic planning, then, emphasizes the importance of good research informing a group's or organization's project choices. "Which issue should we tackle?" "What intervention should we choose?" and "How will we know what impact we are having?" cannot be answered without also asking "What information do we need to answer that question?" Answering this last question doesn't require a year-long, grant-funded research project. There are times, in fact, when the information required to make effective choices exists around the table. But there are also times when it does not. Really knowing what the important issues are in a community may require conducting a survey of that community. Really knowing what the intervention options are may require searching the literature or the professional networks to find out the array of possible interventions and evaluating them using a comparative research methodology. And really knowing what impact you are having will almost certainly require carefully collecting information on processes and outcomes. So no strategic planning process is complete without the group asking "What information do we need to decide?"

## Developing an Information-Collecting Plan

Once a group has asked the question of what information they need, it is time to go get it. This can be more challenging than it first appears. Information-collecting can take time as well as specialized skill, especially when it comes to such things as water, soil, or air testing. So the group may need to spend some time doing research about research: What are the standards for good research in answering our questions? What are the best techniques for collecting information answering our question? What skills are needed for using those techniques? Often these questions can be answered with a phone call to your local professor or national organization that specializes in the issue you are tackling. But you need to know who the relevant professors and national organizations are to accomplish your objectives in just one phone call.

Once a group knows how big the research task is, they can begin to develop a plan for collecting the information. Many organizations develop a research plan for information that students can collect in conjunction with a local professor. We discussed in Chapter 2 some of the challenges and opportunities of such community-higher education relationships. Other groups use the information-gathering process as an excuse to recruit their constituency, especially when the research doesn't require extensive training, because it helps constituency members get involved and educate themselves. Regardless of who is involved in creating and implementing the plan, it needs to specify what the research questions are (see Chapter 1), what the methods are for collecting the information, who will collect the information, and what the deadline is for having the information in a usable form. Often, the information-collecting plan will specify a fair amount of information that should be collected on a daily basis as the organization does its business. Organizations working with individuals will probably want to collect information on the contacts they have with those individuals, determining what information to collect based on their own information needs (usually for evaluation research).

## Developing an Information Management Plan

Once an organization has made a commitment to collecting information, there needs to be a plan for storing, manipulating, and retrieving it. Many organizations still collect information in paper form, partly because the start-up costs for fancy computer-based information management systems—both in terms of money and training—can be expensive. The problem with paper records, however, is that they may be initially easy to use for collecting data, but require enormous amounts of time when you want to retrieve the data and analyze, since all that data needs to either be counted by hand or entered into a computer database by hand. It's a lot easier to spend 30 seconds entering data when you first establish a record than to spend 30 hours later trying to do an analysis by hand. Nothing beats the computer for efficient information management.

As I was facilitating the evaluation of the community-based crime prevention and community development project described in the previous chapter, our evaluation planning group expected to get data on a wide array of community outcomes, including domestic violence, teen and adult alcohol and drug abuse, teen pregnancy, and other things. But we ran into numerous obstacles. The county health department kept records on teen pregnancy but didn't have the software or the training to efficiently retrieve records for small geographic areas. Most of the domestic violence shelters didn't keep records of residents' previous addresses, and those that did kept them on paper forms, making it too time-consuming to sort through them for small geographic areas. We ran into roadblock after roadblock because neither nonprofit nor government organizations had efficient information management systems. So numerous were the problems that we are now embarking on a project with the area nonprofits to determine their information needs in hopes of developing training programs and databases to make such research easier in the future.

What would an efficient information management system look like? The foundation for such a system is electronic database software on a computer with regular backups. Some organizations choose to house those facilities in-house on someone's desktop computer. The advantage of keeping it in-house is that you aren't dependent on someone else to responsibly maintain your data. Of course, if you are managing data in-house you need to have at least two people who are well versed in the software you are using and a reliable computer that is backed up as often as data is entered (and that means daily if data is entered daily). Those people should also be well versed in basic computer hardware and software troubleshooting to make sure that a reliable computer remains reliable through the numerous operating system patches, antivirus updates, and software upgrades that are necessary these days to keep computers safe from the viruses, worms, and other cyber-dangers lurking out there. You also need to consider backing up your records off-site, just in case the unthinkable (fire, flood, etc.) happens. Developing such a system may seem daunting, but there are many sources of help out there for community organizations, such as TechSoup, NPower, and Making the Net Work.[12]

Because of the training and technology demands of maintaining data on-site, however, some organizations choose to submit their data over the Internet to a secure, Internet-based database managed by their Internet service provider. Online databases have come of age in the past few years, and they are often easier to use than desktop software. As long as you have a stable Internet connection, you should have no fears about getting information. Small and medium-size organizations can usually download basic databases to their own computers as well, just in case. The costs for hiring a service provider to maintain a small database can be comparable to buying your own software, getting the training to run it, and calling technical support when it doesn't work. The main thing to make sure of is that your service provider does regular backups and also has off-site storage for disaster security.

Regardless of whether you choose to maintain your records yourself or hire a service provider, the important part of the information management plan is determining what information you want to store and how you may want to retrieve it. If you work backward from your research plan to an information plan, you will know how you may want to retrieve information in the future. It may be important, for example, to retrieve information by date, or by geographic area, or to compare different groups, or to look for trends. Most groups and organizations will not need to conduct high-powered statistical analyses, but many will want to have basic spreadsheet statistics for measures such as means, ranges, frequencies, and basic statistical tests to compare differences in groups. Your software needs to accommodate those requirements with as little work on your part as possible. If much of the information you are collecting is in words rather than numbers, you need to have software that can accommodate "qualitative" information. Some databases, for example, have low limits on the size of each text field that allow only a few words per case. Others allow for paragraphs. There is even analysis software out there, such as the bizarrely named NUDIST, that can help you sift and sort those paragraphs according to the occurrence of certain words or phrases.

## LOOSE GRAVEL: INFORMATION MYTHS AND MONSTERS

Well, we are almost through eight long chapters of my attempt to convince you of the importance of research in accomplishing project goals. My main concern now is that I may have convinced you. If I have, then this final patch of loose gravel on the road to successful project-based research is for you. For I don't want you to be *too* convinced. Remember, the focus here is on the action, not the research. The research is a member of the supporting cast, not the lead player. The goal is to solve community problems, improve community life, and support community members. Research is a *necessary* but not *sufficient* condition to achieving those goals. In other words, good research is necessary but needs to be coupled with other necessary conditions such as adequate funding, solid planning, and effective social change strategy. Don't spin out on the oily-patch myth that *information is power* or the low shoulder of *analysis paralysis*.

### Information Is Not Power

Remember that slogan "information is power"? One of the products of the computer revolution, this slogan has supported those who promote reading, computing, schooling, and a host of other related strategies as the means to a bright and prosperous future. This slogan has also justified stopping at the promotion of reading, computing, and schooling as the be-all and end-all of individual success. If information is power, then all you need is information and you will be powerful.

But we know that is not the case. The same amount of education does not translate into as much power for women as for men, for African-Americans as for European Americans, or for people with disabilities as for people without. Doug Schuler[13] quotes University of Washington professor Philip Bereano as saying: "Only the naive or the scurrilous believe the Third Wave claim that 'information is power.' Power is power, and information is particularly useful to those who are already powerful." Doug Schuler himself goes on to say: "Information is actually quite plentiful: we are already on the receiving end of a firehose of information with neither the tools nor the time we need to give it adequate consideration. If all this information were power then surely there would be enough power for everybody! We find that the opposite is closer to the truth: The asymmetry of power is becoming greater every day, and computer networks are probably contributing to the problem."

What Schuler says is important. We must not get caught up in thinking about information access alone as somehow solving ultimate problems of inequality. Yes, poor communities will always have information needs, but those of you who work with poor folks know that they often know *what* is wrong, they know *why* it is wrong, and they know what could make it better. They don't need more information. They need *the means* to gather their information and make it legitimate in the eyes of funders, policymakers, and the public.[14]

For information to become power, or at least to become part of the process of building power in underserved and excluded communities, it needs to be part of a total strategy that includes much more than information. In some cases there is even a tradeoff between information and power. Power operates on deadlines. The grant proposal has to be in by a certain deadline, the city council hearing can't be postponed, the program start date is set. You get whatever information you can, at the best quality you can, within those calendar limits. You may not be able to verify every fact and double-check every statistic. You may need to rely on anecdotes more than you would like. You may have data gaps. Strategically, you will have to decide whether the information that you don't have is more important than the deadline you are facing. If you go forward with too little good information, you may be wasting valuable time and energy on a project destined to fail. If you forgo an opportunity in order to get more information, you risk the possibility that what you already have is enough for success.

There are no hard and fast rules for judging the adequacy of your information. If you can work far enough ahead, however, one of the best ways to learn the powerfulness of your information is to find others to evaluate it. If community members, credentialed experts, current or former decision makers, and others can evaluate your information and agree it is enough, then you can feel more confident in it. Likewise, if they agree it is not enough, then it is time to do more research. This is a difficult process for many of us to submit to. Those of us used to writing that report, or that proposal, the night before it is due risk both embarrassment and dismissal. I have seen more than one project lose its participatory underpinnings because an overstressed staff person was writing a grant proposal the night before it was due and had no time to get input from anyone involved with the project.

Balancing information quantity and quality with calendar timelines can be difficult in different ways for those academically trained in research compared to those trained in project management. Because deadlines in the academic world are so flexible, the emphasis can be on information quantity and quality. I have watched colleagues collect "more data" for months and sometimes years before they feel comfortable concluding something about it. On the other hand, I sometimes get a call from a community worker needing, for example, homeownership and poverty stats for a neighborhood in a week. To some extent, it is easier to help community workers build a research timeline just by helping them understand how long things take. Those academically trained in doing it perfectly, especially if they have only read about it in the textbooks and they want to do it perfectly, can be more challenging because the textbooks make it seem as if every academic researcher develops a perfectly researchable question, a solid methodology, the exact amount of data, and an airtight interpretation. The community worker faced with conducting their first project-based research can sometimes feel caught between getting the work done on time and making sure the research produces an airtight case.

## Action Without Reflection or Analysis Paralysis: Balancing Research and Action

One of the gulfs separating academics and community workers is the weight given to reflective thinking. I have facilitated a few workshops that included both academics and community workers. Typically, in such a workshop, we put the academics in one room and the community workers in another room and assign them a planning or problem-solving task. The community workers, used to managing frequent crises that need immediate action, get right to work, and in short order they have chosen a facilitator, drawn up a task outline, and produced a plan. The academics, used to long, ponderous debates, at the end of 45 minutes are usually still just talking—no leadership structure, no task outline, and no plan, but lots of new and interesting ideas.

Community workers would love the luxury of pondering the issues they face. Those community workers who have been part of study groups created in Texas[15] by the Industrial Areas Foundation, a national community organizing network, or in Washington, D.C. by a Georgetown University campus-community partnership[16] dearly appreciate such opportunities to take a breath and reflect on their practice. But in their daily lives such opportunities are few and far between. The different rhythms, cultures, and processes of research and action make them very difficult to combine. When people's housing, health, safety, and sustenance are at stake, pondering the broader issues is neither practical nor desirable. The important thing is to fix the problem with whatever is available. Consequently, action still takes precedence over research in most community work. So community projects continue to be driven by the foibles of government and corporations, and the whims of funders. The result is action without reflection.

On the academic side, the privilege of pondering, particularly in the liberal arts, can overshadow the importance of the work. There are even times when it provides shelter from the risk of testing ideas in the real world. One of the problems of pondering is that it very effectively trains one to be able to see a problem, and the possible solutions, from multiple perspectives. And while that can lead to a lot of creative ideas, it also reinforces the worry that all of the ideas are uncertain and tentative. The result can be analysis paralysis—the ability to make any thought seem reasonable, and thus to prevent confident prescription. Professional academic programs such as public health or social work, and the increasing numbers of applied programs in a wide variety of liberal arts disciplines, are less prone to analysis paralysis because they are training students to engage in the day-to-day work of social intervention. But even in those fields and programs it is possible to pull out a dozen journal articles on an issue that take half a dozen different perspectives. And the audience for academics is often composed of critical colleagues who have honed their critical thinking skills specifically to introduce doubts in all who question them, rather than community members demanding solutions to immediate problems.

The other challenge leading to analysis paralysis is the demand for perfection in research. Those of you whose research has been subject to academic critique know that there are never enough references, the sample is always too small, the correlation is never high enough, the field evidence is never strong enough. It is interesting, however, that on the couple of occasions where people have been able to compare strictly controlled academic research with the casual community organizer door-knocking surveys, the results are quite consistent. There are going to be times, of course, when strictly controlled methods are necessary to support a legal case or gain access to resources. But there are going to be other times when the choice will be whether to do a quick-and-dirty piece of research or none at all. With adequate training and a cautious enough interpretation, the quick-and-dirty research can also yield useful information. We academics, much as we malign the quick-and-dirty researchers like journalists, may be able to learn something from them.

One of the reasons so many of us have emphasized collaboration between academics and community workers, whether the field is public health, social work, community activism, community development, or others, is to build on the complementary strengths and overcome the distinct weaknesses of each side. Such collaborations offer community workers the chance to reflect on their work with someone. They offer academics the opportunity to overcome their sense of trepidation at actually putting their thoughts into practice with a skilled practitioner who knows how to do it. To the extent that either the practitioner or the academic is able to cross over to the other side, the collaboration is less necessary. But if there is a risk of either action without reflection or analysis paralysis, one of the best preventatives, or treatments, is academic-community collaboration.

## IN CONCLUSION

Well, it's been a long journey from page 1 to the end of Chapter 8. In some ways it's been longer for me than for you. After all, I had to write all of this, worrying all the way whether it said anything to anyone but me. I worry in particular that there are a number of you out there, having read all this, who are now asking "So how do I actually *do* a needs assessment?" I realize I have not offered specific recipes to use. That is because research isn't like that. Of course, neither are community projects. Those who copy and paste community projects from situation A to situation B are as likely to fail as those who copy and paste research protocols from situation A to situation B. Research design is as creative as project development, requiring mixing and matching, shaping and switching, morphing and moving. There are resources listed at the end of each chapter to get specific options on needs assessments, target research, evaluations, etc. My purpose has been to offer a process for determining where you are in the project cycle, looking at the possible models for doing research at different points in that cycle, and then creating your own research process.

This is definitely not a book to read for *the* answer. One of my all-time favorite books, given to me when I was an undergrad by a friend who knew I needed it, is *Illusions* by Richard Bach.[17] *Illusions* is a story about Richard, a rootless wanderer whose income came from selling rides in his old biplane. It is also about Don, a reluctant messiah, seemingly the possessor of magical healing powers and whatnot, trying to escape the necessary attention that comes from having and using such skills. Don brought with him a Messiah's Handbook, which would always open to just the page that was needed, and Richard's consciousness grew mightily as he pondered the lessons presented in each of its magical pages and began to learn for himself some of Don's own talents, like vaporizing clouds. As their friendship grew, however, so did their notoriety and the number of their admirers and detractors. Eventually one of them, and it's unclear whether it was an admirer or detractor, murders Don in cold blood. In the midst of Richard's horror at learning that Don either wouldn't or couldn't heal himself, the Messiah's Handbook falls to the ground and opens to a page that reads: *Everything in this book may be wrong.*

Now, that can be taken in a number of different ways, and we don't get many clues about which one is correct. You'll have to read the book to decide for yourself. For me, the most useful interpretation is that someone's words are neither right nor wrong. They present a way of thinking that illuminates some things and obscures others. My hope is that this book helps illuminate some ways of thinking about how to integrate research into community work. I realize, however, that it likely obscures other ways of thinking about it. It is my attempt to strike a balance between analysis paralysis and action without reflection. Hopefully, if I have achieved the balance, by reading this book you have developed some sense of the process for determining how useful it is for you. If, by reading it, you have developed a way of determining its usefulness, then it has already become useful for you. Even if you decide that everything in it is wrong.

## NOTES

1. Montessori, M. (1912). The Montessori method: Scientific pedagogy as applied to child education. In A. E. George (Trans.). *The children's houses* (2nd ed.). New York: Frederick A. Stokes Company. Retrieved July 15, 2004, from http://digital.library.upenn.edu/women/montessori/method/method. html. See also Wentworth, R. A. L. (1999). *Montessori for the new millennium: Practical guidance on the teaching and education of children of all ages, based on a rediscovery of the true principles and vision of Maria Montessori.* Mahwah, NJ: L. Erlbaum Associates.

2. Mulder, H., Ree, K., de Groot, I., & Schaafsma, E. (Eds.). (1996). *Proceedings. Dutch Science Shops National Day, 9 May 1996: "Knowledge influences/influenced."* The Netherlands. University of Groningen. Retrieved July 15, 2004, from http://www.loka.org/pubs/scishop.txt

3. Marx, K. (2000 [1932]). Economic & Philosophical Manuscripts of 1844. In Martin Mulligan (Trans.) *Karl Marx Internet archive.* Retrieved

July 15, 2004, from http://www.marxists.org/archive/marx/works/1844/manuscripts/preface.htm

4. Highlander Research and Education Center. (n.d.). *History— 1930–1953: Beginnings & the labor years.* Retrieved July 15, 2004, from http://www.highlandercenter.org/

5. Addams, J. (1910). *Twenty years at Hull House.* New York: MacMillan. Retrieved July 15, 2004, from http://digital.library.upenn.edu/women/addams/hullhouse/hullhouse.html

6. Glen, J. M. (1988). *Highlander: No ordinary school.* Lexington, KY: University Press of Kentucky.

7. Adams, F. (1975). *Unearthing seeds of fire: The idea of Highlander.* Winston-Salem, NC: John F. Blair. Glen, J. M. (1988). *Highlander: No ordinary school.* University Press of Kentucky. Horton, A. I. (1989). *The Highlander Folk School: A history of its major programs, 1932–1961.* Brooklyn, NY: Carlson Publishing. Horton, B.D. (1993). The Appalachian land ownership study: Research and citizen action in Appalachia. In P. Park, M. Brydon-Miller, B.L. Hall, & T. Jackson (Eds.). *Voices of change: Participatory research in the U.S. and Canada* (pp. 85–102). Westport, CT: Bergin and Garvey. See also Highlander Research and Education Center, http://www.highlandercenter.org/

8. Applied Research Center. (2004). About ARC. Retrieved July 15, 2004, from http://www.arc.org/Pages/ArcInfo.html

9. Project South. (n.d.). *The Olympic Games & our struggles for justice: A people's story.* Atlanta: Project South.

10. Project South. (n.d.). What is Project South? Retrieved July 15, 2004, from http://www.projectsouth.org/about/index.html

11. Diagram courtesy of Kelly Spivey. Reprinted with permission.

12. TechSoup, http://www.techsoup.org/ NPower, http://www.npower.org/ Making The NetWork, http://www.makingthenetwork.org/

13. Schuler, D. (1996). How to kill community networks. Hint: we may have already started . . . *The Network Observer, 3, January.* Retrieved July 15, 2004, from http://polaris.gseis.ucla.edu/pagre/tno/january-1996.html#schuler

14. Gaventa, J. (1993). The powerful, the powerless, and the experts: Knowledge struggles in an information age. In P. Park, M. Brydon-Miller, B.L. Hall, & T. Jackson (Eds.). *Voices of change: Participatory research in the U.S. and Canada* (pp. 21–40). Westport, CT: Bergin and Garvey.

15. Warren, M. R. (2001). *Dry bones rattling: Community building to revitalize American democracy.* Princeton, NJ: Princeton University Press.

16. Strand, K., Marullo, S., Cutforth, N., Stoecker, R., & Donohue, P. (2003). *Community-based research and higher education: principles and practices* (p. 49). San Francisco: Jossey-Bass.

17. Bach, R. (1977). *Illusions: The adventures of a reluctant messiah.* New York: Dell Publishing Co.

# Appendix A

## *Strategic Planning*

The concept of strategic planning has come up time and time again in this book. One of the reasons for this is that so much project-based research is both guided by and guides strategic planning. In many ways the two are inseparable. A good plan can't exist without good information, and knowing which information is most useful can only be determined through the lens of a good plan.

## WHAT IS STRATEGIC PLANNING?

First and foremost, strategic planning is the knowledge of the relationships among an organization or group's *goals, internal resources,* and *external context.*[1] If you think about the relationship as a sort of Venn diagram, you can see that there are some combinations of goals, resources, and context that fit together better than others. That doesn't mean that a group can only do those things in the center of the diagram. Strategic planning is about identifying what gaps there may be in a group's ability to implement a given set of goals and whether certain combinations of resources and context presents opportunities to pursue new goals. The result of this planning process is a strategy of accessing resources and making the most of the contextual opportunities to achieve the organizational goals.

Most strategic planning guides make a point of distinguishing strategic planning from long-range planning. The main difference is that long-range planning assumes a stable and predictable environment, while strategic planning does not. But any plan must assume a certain amount of stability and predictability in the environment, so it is more accurate to say that strategic planning assumes a shorter time frame, often a year or even less in cases of short-term projects.

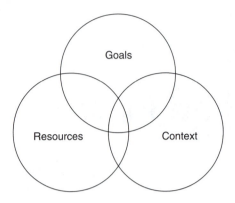

## WHAT RESOURCES ARE REQUIRED FOR STRATEGIC PLANNING?

The actual process of strategic planning can vary enormously, from a long afternoon session to multiple meetings over a period of months. The costs can range from nothing to six figures. And the information-gathering aspect of the process can range from the opinions of those involved in the planning to extensive surveys, outcome data collection, and in-depth analysis of the context.[2] For the small to medium-size nonprofit, however, a series of meetings over no more than three months is probably most beneficial. The most important consideration is to choose a level of strategic planning that the organization can actually sustain. If you can't get organization members to go on a three-day strategic planning retreat, don't try it. And the more hard data, the better. The organization that has made research part of their daily work can bring a lot of information to bear on a strategic planning process.

Effective strategic planning also requires some personnel resources. A successful strategic planning effort requires that someone fulfill the roles of leader, facilitator, and writer. It is possible that one person may be able to fulfill all three roles, but more likely the responsibilities will be spread out or even hired out. The leader is responsible for making sure the strategic planning happens on schedule and that a plan actually gets written. The facilitator is responsible for managing the planning meetings in a way that makes all the participants feel involved and productive. The writer is responsible for taking the content of those meetings and translating them into words on paper.[3]

## WHO SHOULD BE INVOLVED IN STRATEGIC PLANNING?

Certainly the organization's main decision makers need to be involved. In addition, those staff who will be most responsible for implementing a strategic plan should participate. For an organization that serves a group or community, and where that group or community is not represented in the organization's decision making, strategic planning may provide the opportunity to begin supporting "clients" to become participants.[4] This doesn't mean that all of these people should be involved in every meeting and every decision. A good strategic planning team will probably be only about half a dozen people. But others can become involved through special information-gathering sessions or by reviewing draft documents at various stages of the process. And the larger the organization, the more difficult the decisions of who to include.

## WHAT ARE THE STEPS OF STRATEGIC PLANNING?

Many different authors have provided a set of cookbook steps in strategic planning. In general, however, they all use some version of the following steps:

1. Preparation—planning to plan

2. Reviewing past missions and accomplishments

3. Analyzing the current and near future possibilities and challenges

4. Writing a plan

What is involved in each of these steps?

The preparation phase of strategic planning involves making decisions about who to include in the effort and how to organize the process. Will it be a series of two-hour meetings or a single two-day retreat? When does the plan need to be in place? Who will the planning team include? Who will occupy the roles of leader, facilitator, and writer? Who else will be included and in what ways? What resources are needed? What level of commitment is there to writing *and* implementing a plan? What level of trust and unity is there in the organization that might indicate the ability to manage the process internally or the need to hire a consultant?[5]

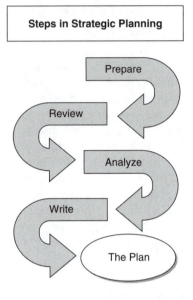

**Steps in Strategic Planning**

Prepare

Review

Analyze

Write

The Plan

Once these questions have been answered, and the answers put into motion, the next step is to review what the organization has accomplished since the last strategic planning, or in the last year or so if there has been no previous plan. This involves reviewing the organization's mission statement, looking at data on program and project outcomes, reviewing the budget, and other information relevant to understanding the organization's recent history. Out of this process may come a set of questions or issues facing the organization. A grant cycle may be ending, a staff member may have left, or a project may have concluded. At this stage the members focus on what has changed in the past year.

The next step is analysis. Sometimes it is difficult or even undesirable to separate the review and the analysis. Generally, however, it is useful for the strategic planning team to have a holistic sense of what the organization says about itself and what it actually does before trying to understand why some things happened and other things did not. Once the team has that sense of the whole organization or program, it is easier to move on to analysis. That analysis often includes a SWOT analysis or a force field analysis (see Chapter 4), looking at the interrelationship between the organization/program and the broader environment. This allows the strategic planning team to evaluate whether the past successes were due to unique environmental conditions that may no longer exist, whether past failures were due to internal weaknesses that can be fixed, and so on.

Finally, there is the step of writing an actual plan. This may begin with revisiting the organization's mission statement if the group determines that the old mission is no longer possible or relevant. It also involves setting goals for the next year and strategies for achieving those goals. In some cases those strategies may simply involve beginning new projects. In other cases they may require organizational restructuring, and these things should be written into the plan. Ideally, this should not be done in isolation, especially if the people who will need to implement the plan, or cooperate with it, are not at the planning table. Testing ideas, offering short drafts for review, and engaging individuals from outside the planning team in working on specific sections of the plan are all ways to prevent the plan from being seen as imposed will.

## HOW DOES RESEARCH FIT IN WITH STRATEGIC PLANNING?

As you have probably already decided, research is essential for effective strategic planning. Even in the preparation phase, good research understanding the organization's internal political dynamics is necessary to inform the structuring of the planning team and overall process. The need for research becomes even more intense at the review phase, which may require gathering outcome data, conducting organization or community surveys, recovering information on the organization's history, and other information-gathering tasks necessary to accurately understand how the organization works and what its accomplishments are. The analysis phase extends the research process to the environment. It may be necessary to collect information on local government budgeting trends, foundation trends, political shifts, changes in the community organization landscape (to see if any competing or collaborating organizations have come or gone in the past year), and other conditions to inform the SWOT or force field processes.

It is easy to get overwhelmed by all the possible research that could be done to help understand the organization and its environment. As with the entire strategic planning process, the need for information has to be tempered by the capacity to actually get the information in a timely manner. Most strategic planning in small to medium-size organizations is done with little to no research. That isn't to say that it should be done that way, as those organizations are often reduced to making strategic decisions based on the limited knowledge of the planning team members. But in general it is better to have a strategic plan based on weak research than no plan at all.

The important thing is to be very clear that the plan is based on shaky information and consequently may provide less direction than it otherwise would.

## RESOURCES AND HANDBOOKS FOR STRATEGIC PLANNING

John Bryson and Farnum Alston. (1995). *Creating and Implementing Your Strategic Plan.* A workbook with creative exercises and worksheets to help your organization achieve lasting strategic change. San Francisco: Jossey-Bass.

John Bryson. (1995). *Strategic Planning for Public and Nonprofit Organizations.* Practical help for looking ahead to achieve your goals. San Francisco: Jossey-Bass.

Jan W. Lyddon. (1999). *Strategic Planning In Smaller Nonprofit Organizations: A Practical Guide for the Process.* Focused on smaller organizations, with a variety of concrete activities. Western Michigan University, 1999 http://www.wmich.edu/nonprofit/Guide/guide7.htm

Michael Allison and Jude Kaye. (1997). *Strategic Planning for Nonprofit Organizations.* New York: John Wiley & Sons. Another of the big book guides.

*Strategic Planning Guidelines.* (1998). Published by the State of California Department of Finance. Appropriate for larger nonprofits. Available on the Web at http://www.dof.ca.gov/FISA/OSAE/SPguide.pdf

Frank Martinelli. (1999). *Strategic Planning Manual.* With good examples and clear processes. The Center for Public Skills Training. Available on the Web at http://www.uwex.edu/li/learner/spmanual.pdf

## NOTES

1. Alliance for Nonprofit Management. (n.d.). *Frequently asked questions: What is strategic planning?* Retrieved July 15, 2004, from http://www.allianceonline.org/FAQ/strategic_planning/what_is_strategic_planning.faq

2. Allison, M., & Kaye, J. (1997). *Strategic planning for nonprofit organizations.* New York: John Wiley & Sons.

3. Lyddon, J. W. (1999). *Strategic planning in smaller nonprofit organizations: A practical guide for the process.* Retrieved July 15, 2004, from http://www.wmich.edu/nonprofit/Guide/guide7.htm

4. Lyddon, J. W. (1999). *Strategic planning in smaller nonprofit organizations.*

5. Lyddon, J. W. (1999). *Strategic planning in smaller nonprofit organizations.* See also Alliance for Nonprofit Management. (n.d.) *Frequently asked questions: What are the basic steps in a strategic planning process?* http://www.allianceonline.org/FAQ/strategic_planning/what_are_basic_steps.faq

# Appendix B

## *Research Ethics*

R esearch ethics look quite different in project-based research compared to professional academic research. Those of you trained in traditional academic research should know the ethical standards of your discipline. Some disciplines' ethical standards emphasize practice and some research. There are very few that attempt to combine the two. Probably the best attempt is at the University of Tennessee at Knoxville, which has developed a specific set of principles for participatory research.[1]

In academic research, ethical standards focus mostly on the protection of the *research subjects.* But academic research has historically assumed that the researcher and those being researched are kept separate and distinct. Researchers are treated as active participants and subjects as passive recipients of the research. In project-based research, because of its association with participatory research, the ideal is that everyone becomes an active participant in the research. This makes the ethical standards governing such research different, and some would even say higher, than for traditional research.

## MAJOR ETHICAL PRINCIPLES

What are the major ethical principles of traditional academic research and how do they differ for project-based research?

*Voluntary Participation.* Research subjects are expected to be volunteers, freely choosing to participate or not participate in the research. In traditional academic research this rule gets bent a bit when *incentives* are used—when subjects are paid for their time. It is unclear, when incentives are used with impoverished populations, whether the subjects would choose to participate if they didn't need the money. In project-based research the appeal to potential research participants is to assist a community project or cause. In many cases the appeal is not just to participate in research but also to volunteer in other aspects of the community project. Recruitment is not sponsored by the researcher but often by the community organization.

*Informed Consent.* Part of the process of recruiting research volunteers is to inform them of what will be done to them, and then gaining their consent to do that. Often, in traditional academic research, this even involves getting the subject's signature on legal paperwork listing the risks associated with the research and absolving the researcher from liability. In project-based research, particularly if it involves treatment procedures, the requirements are often the same. There is increasing concern, however, about the untreated control group model used in research evaluating treatment effects—where one group is given the treatment and another group is not or is given a placebo. The ethics of treating some and not others are often questionable, particularly when there are other research methods that can establish whether the treatment has an impact. There are other situations, however, where capacity rather than research design limits the number of people who can receive the treatment. All research, whether academic or project-based, with children or those legally deemed mentally incompetent will also need to seek informed consent from a parent or legal guardian.

*Confidentiality and Anonymity.* One of the standard practices in traditional academic research is to maintain the privacy of individuals' records (confidentiality) and to report research results in ways that do not identify individuals (anonymity). In project-based research, however, the research often involves community members working with each other as they conduct and participate in the research together. In such cases, maintaining confidentiality and anonymity can be challenging and even undesirable. It isn't necessarily unethical to reveal people's identities and what they say, so long as the research participants are aware of that. There are still cases, however, particularly when working with minors and controlled populations (people who are institutionalized or incarcerated), where confidentiality and/or anonymity may be required not just by ethical standards but by law.

*Using Research Results.* In academic research, most informed-consent statements explicitly state how the research will be used and what will be done with individual records. Project-based research goes beyond these requirements to also establish ownership of the research. Particularly in cases where an outside researcher is partnering with a community or organization, one of the emerging ethical standards is that the research belongs to the community or organization, not to the researcher. In such cases, a researcher wanting to publish the information must seek specific permission from the community or organization and often submit their work to a community review process before they submit it to an academic peer-review process.

One of the main challenges in applying these standards in project-based research is that there are often no review boards to make sure the research is being held accountable. In colleges and universities, human-subjects review boards go over every research proposal to make sure it is following ethical guidelines and legal requirements. In community settings, however, there is only the community decision-making process to hold the research accountable, and often the community is not well educated in the standards for ethical research. It is helpful, in those cases, for the community to have access to an academically trained researcher to help them develop their own standards and accountability process. This is particularly true in the case of research involving children or controlled populations, such as people who are institutionalized or are controlled through the penal system where legal requirements protecting human subjects are much more important.

## THE ETHICAL EXCEPTION: TARGET RESEARCH

While there are many shades of gray in observing the principles above, there is one form of project-based research where nearly all of the principles are violated. That form of research involves investigating targets. Target research is the clearest case of research done in a conflict situation. It is even possible to draw comparisons to war situations, in which good intelligence on the enemy makes the difference between winning and losing.

In such situations, a strict interpretation of the principles of ethical research is not always possible. Target research is often done without the target's voluntary participation or their informed consent. This is not necessarily an ethical violation, as long as the information is gained through publicly available documents. In those cases targets have already agreed to have those documents used by researchers. Other cases, such as soil, water, and air sampling near an active industrial site, become a bit more tricky, though are still within bounds as long as the researcher seeks permission from the owner of the space being sampled. But there are other cases in which information is collected clandestinely, through misinforming an employee of the purpose and use of interview information or obtaining nonpublic documents, where some would say an ethical violation has occurred.

In the most extreme cases, target research can easily violate all of the principles, by collecting data on the target without their voluntary consent, and by presenting that data publicly for the purpose of exposing the misdeeds of the target. If the underlying ethical standard is to do no harm, target research could be interpreted as having the exact opposite goal—to do significant harm to the target. Trying to stop a corporation from dumping toxins into the land, air, and water; trying to expose a corrupt public official; trying to redress a history of unequal treatment under the law; and a host of other problems often require doing economic or political damage to the target before they will either change their ways or be prevented from doing further harm themselves. The problem with applying a strict interpretation of ethical research standards out of context, then, is that not doing the target research may be subjecting others to much greater harm. The people of Yellow Creek, discussed in Chapter 1, did not practice strict research ethics while investigating the upstream tannery. But it seems strange indeed to worry about a corporation's privacy when you, your family members, and your agricultural livelihood are being threatened by a carcinogenic stew seeping into your groundwater.

When we look at the question of research ethics, then, we cannot separate ourselves from social justice ethics. This is where the integration of research and social change becomes most apparent. In project-based research, remember, the research is only a small part of a larger project. The ethics of a piece of research need to be judged in the context of the ethics of the broader social change project. And in those cases one needs to refer more to the ethics of one's faith, one's ideology, and one's cultural context to decide what is ethical and unethical. Such deep philosophical discussions are beyond the scope of our work here and require exploration of the writings of Dr. Martin Luther King, Jr., Mohandas Gandhi, and others who understood the relationship between direct action and life ethics.[2]

## BEYOND RESEARCH ETHICS: COMMUNITY PRACTICE ETHICS

Another set of ethical concerns arise when you are working within a community. Whenever one is doing research about a community that will be used by that community, the potential exists that the information you are uncovering can also uncover old wounds and conflicts. Even doing a simple community historical recovery project may open conflicts over who is recognized and who is not. Especially in communities with a history of internal disputes over development, racial/ethnic change, and other issues, simply trying to tell their story as an objective observer is extremely difficult. The ethics of such situations can be extremely complex. Some of the deeper ethical issues in such research include:

1. *Identification of Individuals.* When individuals will be identified in community research, it may be necessary to go well beyond basic informed consent. It is often not enough to inform individuals of the risks involved in such projects, as it is usually not until they see their words in print that they become aware of the potential consequences. If the researcher presents people's words in natural language, including "gonna," "ain't," and other such commonly used words, it can make someone feel insulted and embarrassed. Likewise, putting stories of people's misdeeds into print can put their community status at risk and, in extreme cases, even invite legal trouble. I handle such situations through a two-step process. First, I send transcripts of the interview back to the individual to review and even revise, acting on the presumption that the words belong to the individual until they tell me otherwise. Second, when the story is fraught with conflict, I put individuals' words into a report but with coded citations so that each individual can identify their own quotes but not others. I then invite further reactions and revisions. Such a process adds about a month to the research process, but it is worth it.

2. *Managing Factions.* Telling the story of a community in struggle with itself is also fraught with ethical dilemmas. It is possible to get strategic information from each faction that they expect to be safeguarded. They may even say "now, don't write this part down." Especially if the researcher feels more allegiance to one faction than the other, this can be quite a dilemma. It is possible, of course, to treat one faction as a target. I find that uncomfortable in community settings, however. A good target, to me, has an excess of power, so I justify engaging in clandestine research as a way to counter that excess power. In community settings, separate factions often have roughly similar power bases, and treating one as a target often creates rather than resolves a power inequality. There are a number of alternative strategies to build a community history that includes different factions' perspectives. One is to use the double review process outlined above, though being careful to keep strategic information

out altogether without explicit permission. Another is to find factional representatives who are willing to sit down together in a joint focus group and tell each other their stories, making sure that both stories become part of the community history. A third way is to tell only one faction's story, making clear that you are only working with that faction. This is the most problematic, as it can still introduce power inequalities into the community that did not previously exist and make the conflict worse rather than better. If the goal is to create positive change, leaving a community more disorganized than you found it is not achieving that goal.

3. *Making the Research Useful.* It is quite possible to do community research in a way that makes it no more useful than the average academic paper that ends up on a shelf and is never read by more than a few people. One of the emerging ethical standards is to make sure a process is in place to make use of the research—a community popular education process, a community theater or art production, or some other form. Participatory research processes are not just good things to do in such situations, they are ethical things to do.

It is also important to remember that community practice ethics go beyond the research itself. It is beyond the scope of this book to cover all of the practice ethics in the fields of social work, public health, and other professional fields. But the Principles of Good Practice of the Community Development Society, which cover all forms of community practice, are of particular note because they come from a participatory framework that is quite consistent with a project-based research model. Those principles are:

- Promote active and representative participation toward enabling all community members to meaningfully influence the decisions that affect their lives.
- Engage community members in learning about and understanding community issues and the economic, social, environmental, political, psychological, and other impacts associated with alternative courses of action.
- Incorporate the diverse interests and cultures of the community in the community development process; and disengage from support of any effort that is likely to adversely affect the disadvantaged members of a community.
- Work actively to enhance the leadership capacity of community members, leaders, and groups within the community.
- Be open to using the full range of action strategies to work toward the long-term sustainability and well being of the community.[3]

For those used to engaging with communities as service providers, these principles promote a shift in thinking that emphasizes the use of participatory practices such as popular education to develop both the community itself and its individual members. The principles are consistent with the practice ethics of the various professional fields, but they also go beyond them, looking for more than individual therapeutic relationships or professional consulting.

## RESOURCES ON COMMUNITY RESEARCH ETHICS

*IPEN Body Burden Community Monitoring Handbook.* (2004). Community monitoring research ethics, http://www.oztoxics.org/cmwg/community/research%20ethics.html

World Health Organization. (2004). *Indigenous peoples & participatory health research,* http://www.who.int/ethics/indigenous_peoples/en/index.html

Steve Wing. (n.d.). Social responsibility and research ethics in community-driven studies of industrialized hog production, http://www.researchethics.org/uploads/pdf/social_%20responsibility.pdf

North American Primary Care Research Group. (1998). *Responsible Research with Communities: Participatory Research in Primary Care,* http://napcrg.org/exec.html

Center for Family, Work, and Community, University of Massachusetts-Lowell. (2004). *Welcome to the Research Ethics Tip Guide!* http://www.uml.edu/centers/CFWC/programs/researchethics/research_ethics1.htm

## NOTES

1. The University of Tennessee, Office of Research, Research Compliance Service. (2002). Participatory Action Research. Retrieved July 15, 2004, from http://research.utk.edu/ora/sections/compliances/humsub/partic.html

2. King, M. L., Jr. (1964). *Why We Can't Wait.* New York: Harper & Row. Gandhi, M. (2002). *Mohandas Gandhi: Essential Writings.* Maryknoll, NY: Orbis Books.

3. Community Development Society. *Principles of Good Practice.* Retrieved July 15, 2004, from http://codewriters.com/asites/page.cfm?usr=commdev&pageid=1694

# Appendix C

## *Writing Proposals*

Those of you working with nonprofit organizations probably already know about the specter of the grant proposal. Grants are the lifeblood of the nonprofit organization. Without them, your projects don't get done and you don't get paid. The grant proposal game is a racket unlike none other. And to understand how it is played, we need to spend some time talking about the players.

## THE WHO'S WHO OF FUNDER TYPES

### Government

Government is still one of the biggest funders out there, whether it is funding research proposals through such organizations as the National Science Foundation or funding projects through block grant formulas and other special grants. Just learning where the money is can be a full-time job. The first challenge is that there are multiple levels of government with multiple forms of grant making. At the entry level is the city council person, who may have their own pot of money for supporting projects in their district. It may only be a few thousand dollars, but that sometimes can make the difference between an underfunded failure and a fully funded success. City governments may have special competitive grant programs, or they may make annual dispersals from their Community Development Block Grant (CDBG) funds—those are monies given to cities each year by the federal government. CDBG fund proposals often require extensive documentation on both the community needs and the organization's past activities and accomplishments. An organization

---

**Types of Funders**

- Government
- Philanthropic foundations
- Charitable campaigns
- Private donations

that does not know how to mine census data and has not kept careful track of its outputs, its outcomes, and its impacts will generally fare poorly in the CDBG competition. Many state governments also have special initiative funds, depending on what has garnered the most favor with the current legislature. My state is currently pushing high-tech research and development projects, for example. Finally, the federal government is a maze of programs and funding pots. Just as with city councils, your congressional representative may have access to a pool of money or may be able to direct you to the funding program that fits your work the best. Then there is the alphabet soup of agencies and offices that fund everything from small demonstration projects to massive research efforts. One of the better sources of information on federal funds is the Catalog of Federal Domestic Assistance.[1]

## Philanthropic Foundations

The other large source of funding is the philanthropic foundation. These are organizations whose main purpose is often to serve as a tax shelter for wealthy individuals and families. By creating a foundation for their wealth, they reduce their tax burden and only have to give away a proportion of the interest on the funds to maintain their tax exemption. There is an enormous variety of such foundations, ranging from tiny family foundations that may give only a few thousand dollars a year to the famous foundations—like the Ford Foundation—who give away millions. The challenge is finding the foundation that may fund your work. Some foundations, particularly *operating foundations* that spend their money on doing their own projects rather than funding other projects, don't even accept applications. Many foundations have geographic restrictions, only giving money in certain places. This is particularly true of local community foundations. Many foundations also fund only certain kinds of projects. Even the community foundations, who are supposed to exist to serve the public needs of the local community, often restrict their funds to special efforts. So it is very important to know where you are sending your proposal in order to reduce the chances that you are just wasting your time. The Foundation Center[2] is one good place to start researching foundations. Some city libraries are also designated local Foundation Center repositories and may have a grants specialist on staff who can help find just the right foundation to apply to.

## Charitable Campaigns

Sadly, what most groups most need, and what government and philanthropic foundations are least likely to fund, is *operating support*. Operating support is the money needed to pay the bills to keep the lights on and the paychecks coming. Government and foundations like to fund projects, not operations. It may be difficult to understand how in the world an organization can do projects if it doesn't have stable operating funds, but that is the grim reality. So organizations often need to resort to other strategies for funding their day-to-day operations. One of those sources is the charitable campaign. You probably know of the United Way, which may have solicited you through your place of work or your university. You give some amount of money out of your paycheck, or as an independent donation, to United Way (or United Way organizations that you select from a list) and they redistribute it to a select group of organizations. Because of restrictions United Way has placed on the kinds of organizations it will fund (which often exclude groups such as Planned Parenthood, which are seen as "controversial") and various scandals in the organization, a number of alternative charitable campaigns have sprung up, including the *Community Shares* movement. The concept is the same. Community Shares negotiates to gain access to your workplace and solicit employees for donations. The main differences are that the list of organizations supported through Community Shares is more likely to include social action groups, and a Community Shares group is governed by the member organizations rather than by a group of elites. Organizations apply to one of these campaigns to become a member organization. If there is space available, and they meet the criteria, they are eligible for funds. It is unlikely that charitable campaign funds will meet an organization's entire operating needs, but it may provide a good start.

## Private Donations

While government, philanthropic foundations, and charitable campaigns all exist as official sources of funds, private donations are quite different. This is a do-it-yourself fund-raising method. Many groups go to local corporations, businesses, and even individuals to raise funds for their work. Door-to-door solicitation is still a big part of the fund-raising for groups like Citizen Action and ACORN. This is very hard work, however, and the results are less than certain for new groups trying to break into the local scene. Especially at the corporate fund-raising level, making the personal connections necessary to gain access to the decision maker who disburses corporate donations can take a lot of time and effort. Some groups even use a form of target research, described in Chapter 6, to learn as much as they can about local corporations in order to target their appeals most efficiently. This is especially true for getting Community Reinvestment Act (CRA) funds from financial institutions, using a method also described in Chapter 6. In addition, these donations are also small and project-oriented, making it difficult to rely on them for daily operating expenses.

## FUNDING STRATEGIES

Given how difficult it is to raise operating funds (not to mention how difficult it is to raise funds in general), most community and nonprofit organizations have an amazingly diverse funding portfolio. A budget spreadsheet for even a small nonprofit with only a few staff can easily show funds from a dozen different sources, all on different fiscal cycles and with different reporting requirements. Private sector employers actually look favorably on prospective employee applicants coming from a nonprofit background because, once you master the complexity of nonprofit budgeting, corporate budgets are easy.

All of these different sources are typically combined through the mixture of operating funds and project funds. And portions of all those project funds are used for operating support. Grant budgets are constructed by estimating the amount of staff time required to run a particular project and then requesting funds for that percentage. Then there is the supply section for things such as paper, phone usage, and even electricity. Those project grants then get legally laundered to pay the operating expenses that allow the project to exist.

All of this leads to a set of principles for raising funds in this extremely complicated environment:

1. *Apply Early and Often.* If your grant funds are going to run out in August, don't wait until July to apply for new funds elsewhere. In fact, start looking the previous August, as some foundation funding cycles can put six months between the deadline for you

submitting the proposal and the time they decide and disburse the funds. And don't expect to score on your first grant proposal, or your second, or even your ninth. The organizations I work with say that even one out of ten is a high batting average. Be careful, here, to not submit the same bad proposal every year or to every funder. Try to get feedback on failure so that you can actually improve.

2. *Gather Intelligence.* Find out what you can about the funder from others. Who are the relevant staff? What are their biases? What or who have they funded in the past? How can you get noticed?

3. *Build Relationships With Funders.* The more you know about how they make decisions, the easier it will be for you to write a proposal they want to fund. In addition, the more they know about you (as long as you are doing good work, of course), the more likely you will get noticed in the stacks of proposals they get every funding cycle. Of course, you have to balance this against the risk of being seen as a pest.

4. *Follow Directions When Submitting Proposals.* Make sure you give the funder exactly what they want and nothing extra. I sit on a foundation board and just finished reviewing 83 concept papers— two-page pre-proposals out of which we will invite a select number of full proposals. Some of those groups sent a four-page proposal with another six pages of attachments. They didn't even make it onto my long list, let alone my short list. When we say two pages, we mean two pages. Other foundations use a common proposal form, thankfully, so you can send the same proposal to a bunch of funders. But even when using the common proposal form, you may want to emphasize different aspects of a project to different funders.

5. *Research is Essential.* A good proposal will result from good strategic planning based on good information. Knowing what is possible, why you have chosen a particular project, and the expected measurable outcomes will help convince a funder that this project is going somewhere. Having a solid budget based in solid research is also important, both for this grant and for the future beyond the grant.

## PROJECT VS. RESEARCH FUNDING

Those of you looking for funds to do project-based research may find yourselves in the most challenging position. The expectations for research proposals are somewhat different from the expectations for project proposals, and in some cases you may find yourself actually writing two different proposals for one project. There are only a few foundations that recognize the connection between research and action. One of them is the foundation whose board I belong to, the Sociological Initiatives Foundation.[3] This may be the only foundation in the country that explicitly invites proposals integrating research and action. Other foundations accept such proposals, though they often emphasize either the project side or the research side. There are also some United States federal programs that provide infrastructure support for project-based research centers or programs, such as the federal Community Outreach Partnership Center or the Corporation for National and Community Service. COPC puts its money into universities, however, rather than into community-controlled projects.[4] CNCS also prefers a higher education component in projects.[5]

What are the main differences between research proposals and project proposals? Most proposals begin with a statement of the problem and then a discussion of the methods that will be used to address that problem. Establishing that something is a problem will look different in a research proposal than in a project proposal. A research proposal will cite a gap or dispute in the literature around some academic question. A project proposal will often cite statistics for a particular community or area to show the extent of the problem. Generally, research proposals are reviewed with an eye to the author's knowledge of the field in which s/he is researching. That means referencing the existing literature. Those reviewing project proposals are less likely to expect a review of the literature. Instead, the reviewers may be looking for other kinds of evidence that the group can carry out the project, such as their successes in past projects. For a research proposal, the bottom-line analysis usually asks "is this research that will produce valid knowledge that will influence the field?" For a project proposal, the bottom-line analysis usually asks "is this a realistic project that will make a difference?"

So what do you do if you are doing both? It is increasingly possible to get funding for the combination, but you have to know your audience. If you are pitching a proposal to a research funder, the important thing will be to emphasize your knowledge of the field and research skills. Showing that real social change will be an outcome of the research will be a nice fringe benefit but will not be the most important thing to the average research funder. Conversely, if you are pitching the proposal to a project funder, you will want to show how the research improves the chances of project success.

# RESOURCES ON GRANT PROPOSAL WRITING AND FUNDRAISING

Beverly A. Browning. (2001). *Grant Writing for Dummies*. New York: For Dummies.

Catalog of Federal Domestic Assistance. (n.d.). *Developing and Writing Grant Proposals*, http://www.cfda.gov/

The Foundation Center. (2004). *Proposal Writing Short Course*, http://fdncen ter.org/learn/shortcourse/prop1.html

*Grassroots Fundraising Journal*, http://www.grassrootsfundraising.org/

The Internet Nonprofit Center. (2003). *Grantwriting*, http://www.nonprof its.org/

Minnesota Council on Foundations. (2001). *Writing a Successful Grant Proposal*, http://www.mcf.org/mcf/grant/writing.htm

S. Joseph Levine. (2004). *Guide for Writing a Funding Proposal*. Michigan State University, http://www.learnerassociates.net/proposal/

# NOTES

1. Catalog of Federal Domestic Assistance. Retrieved July 15, 2004, from http://www.cfda.gov/

2. Foundation Center. Retrieved July 15, 2004, from http://fdncenter. org/

3. Sociological Initiatives Foundation. Retrieved July 15, 2004, from http://www.grantsmanagement.com/sifguide.html

4. Community Outreach Partnership Centers program. Retrieved July 15, 2004, from http://www.oup.org/about/copc.html

5. Corporation for National and Community Service. Retrieved July 15, 2004, from http://www.nationalservice.org/

# Appendix D

## *Data Resources*

One of the things that many groups need, and don't have, is ready-to-use data. On the front end of the project cycle, establishing the need often involves citing demographic data for your neighborhood or area. Community-indicators data, housing data, environmental data, crime data, etc., are sometimes available in already compiled form. The list below will lead you to at least some of those data sources.

## DATABASES

- The Community Resource Guide, by the University Neighborhood Housing Program, has a collection of links to New York City local data sources and U.S. national data sources; http://www.unhp.org/crg.html
- The Contact Center Network has an interactive database where non-profit and community organizations from around the world can tell about their activities and find each other; http://www.contact.org
- Info Resources West Philadelphia, serving the data needs of the West Philadelphia community; http://westphillydata.library.upenn.edu/
- National Fair Housing Advocate Online maintains a database of housing cases; http://www.fairhousing.com/index.cfm?method=page.display&pagename=legal_research_index
- The National Low Income Housing Coalition has developed housing maps and summary data files on the distribution of housing types, down to the state and county level in some cases; http://www.nlihc.org/research/lalihd/

- Neighborhood Change Database provides tract-level information from the 1970–2000 census data. It must be purchased and is quite expensive; http://www.urban.org/nnip/ncua/ncdb.html
- RTK NET, The Right to Know Network, provides databases on environmental and other issues, along with free maps; http://www.rtknet.org
- United States Counties database, by the National Association of Counties, provides basic demographic and political data at the county level; http://www.naco.org/counties/counties/index.cfm
- United States Bureau of the Census provides detailed census numbers and some mapping capability; http://www.census.gov/
- GeoCommunity's GIS Data Depot offers a wide variety of Geographic Information Systems data; http://data.geocomm.com/
- Fundrace collects data on campaign fund-raising by party down to the street address level; http://www.fundrace.org/

# DATA MANAGEMENT RESOURCES

- Database Resource Page of the LINC Project is designed for community organizers who want to learn how to effectively integrate a database into their work; http://www.lincproject.org/toolkit/db/dbresource.htm
- The National Neighborhood Indicators Partnership is a collaborative effort by the Urban Institute and local partners to further the development and use of neighborhood-level information systems in local policymaking and community-building. They have manuals on how to develop neighborhood-level information systems as well as links to those doing it; http://www.urban.org/nnip/
- The Organizers' Collaborative provides access to free database software and training on how to integrate a data strategy into community work; http://www.organizenow.net

# Index

# About the Author

**Randy Stoecker** is a Professor of Sociology at the University of Toledo and is the moderator/editor of *COMM-ORG: The On-Line Conference on Community Organizing and Development* (http://comm-org.utoledo.edu). His areas of expertise include community organizing and development, participatory research/evaluation, and community information technology. He has been involved in a wide variety of community-based participatory research projects and participatory evaluations with community development corporations, community organizing groups, and community information technology programs across North America and Australia. He also helped build and evaluate university-community collaborations through the Corella and Bertram F. Bonner Foundation's Learn and Serve America Community Research Project. Randy speaks and writes extensively on community organizing and development, community-based participatory research, and community information technology. He is author of *Defending Community* (1994) and co-author of *Community-Based Research and Higher Education* (2003). You can find his complete curriculum vitae at http://sasweb.utoledo.edu/vita/stoeckvita.htm. He resides in Toledo, Ohio with his wife, daughter, and 50-pound standard poodle, but prefers Australia, where the road signs say "keep left."